NORTHERN E

MW00490425

Geirangerfjord

NORTHERN EUROPE
By Cruise Ship

THE COMPLETE GUIDE TO CRUISING NORTHERN EUROPE

ANNE VIPOND

Second Edition

YOUR PORTHOLE
COMPANION

OCEAN CRUISE GUIDES

Guidebooks to the world of cruising

Vancouver, Canada   Pt. Roberts, USA

Published by: Ocean Cruise Guides Ltd.
Canada   USA
325 English Bluff Road   PO Box 2041
Delta, BC V4M 2M9   Pt. Roberts, WA 98281-2041
Phone: (604) 948-0594   Email: info@oceancruiseguides.com

Second Edition

Visit our website: www.oceancruiseguides.com

Editors: Mel-Lynda Andersen, Steve Blake
Contributing editors: Stephen York, Michael DeFreitas, William Kelly
Cover artwork by Alan H. Nakano.
Cover design by Ocean Cruise Guides.
Cartography: Reid Jopson, Cartesia – USA, OCG.
Design: Ocean Cruise Guides Ltd
Publisher: William Kelly

Printed in China.

Library and Archives Canada Cataloguing in Publication

Vipond, Anne, 1957-
 Northern Europe by cruise ship : the complete guide
to cruising the Northern Europe / Anne Vipond.

Includes index.
ISBN 978-19277471-0-0

 1. Cruise ships--Europe, Northern--Guidebooks.
2. Europe, Northern--Guidebooks. I. Title.

D965.V56 2015   914.804'7   C2015-902106-1

(Opposite) St. Isaac's
IV   *Cathedral, St. Petersburg*

Contents

Part One

General Information

Stockholm

PART TWO

THE VOYAGE & THE PORTS

Helsinki

Northern Europe is both foreign and familiar. It encompasses the British Isles, Scandinavia and, for the purposes of this book, the countries bordering the Baltic Sea, North Sea and English Channel. These nations each sustain their own culture and centuries-old history, as evidenced by winding medieval streets and hilltop castles. Kings and queens still reign here, royal guards still parade in palace forecourts, and loyal subjects are still knighted by their sovereign.

The famous capitals of Northern Europe – London, Paris, Amsterdam, Stockholm, Copenhagen, Oslo, Helsinki and St. Petersburg – could be described as vibrant, open-air museums with their Gothic cathedrals, baroque palaces and cobblestone streets that have clamoured with activity since the Middle Ages.

One of the best ways to visit these diverse countries is by cruise ship. A European cruise is a cost-effective way to sample multiple destinations without the hassle of daily packing and unpacking. Your nightly accommodation and all meals are part of your cruise fare, and while you're enjoying a sound night's sleep at the end of each sightseeing-filled day, your ship is taking you to the next port of call.

This book is designed to help you get the most out of your European cruise and, like a faithful friend, is meant to share with you the pleasures and the wonder of travelling to this beautiful and fascinating destination.

Bon Voyage!

Anne Vipond

PART I

General Information

Choosing Your Cruise

A European cruise is a relaxing and cost-effective way to visit numerous countries in a single trip. Early-booking discounts and the all-inclusive nature of cruising enhance the good value this mode of travel represents, which is also an efficient use of time. A cruise is an effortless way to travel between cities and countries, sampling the highlights of each destination, then enjoying a good night's sleep while your ship takes you to the next port of call.

Northern Europe cruises vary in length with the majority of itineraries ranging from seven to 14 days. The most popular are cruises of the Baltic Sea, which is bordered by Denmark, Sweden, Finland, Russia, Estonia, Latvia, Lithuania, Poland and Germany.

Copenhagen and Stockholm are major base ports for Baltic cruises, as are Amsterdam and the British ports of Dover, Harwich and Southampton. Popular Baltic ports of call include Helsinki, Tallinn and Warnemünde (for Berlin). St. Petersburg is the premier port of call on a Baltic itinerary, with most ships docking here overnight so their passengers can spend two full days exploring this beautiful and historic city.

The Norwegian capital of Oslo is frequently included in Baltic itineraries, and is sometimes a port of call on cruises of the Norwegian Fjords and/ or British Isles. The main base ports for British Isles itineraries are Southampton, Dover and Harwich. These itineraries often include a port call at Le Havre (for Paris) or Cherbourg (for the D-Day beaches), as well as one or two Norwegian fjords. Iceland and Greenland are usually included in transatlantic voyages that end or originate in New York or Fort Lauderdale.

The Northern Europe cruise season begins in May as ships leave the Caribbean and head across the Atlantic. June and July are the most popular cruising months in Northern Europe, due in large part to Scandinavia's long hours of daylight at the height of summer. By late August or early September most ships are leaving northern waters, many of them heading to the Mediterranean or back across the Atlantic. Spring and fall repo-

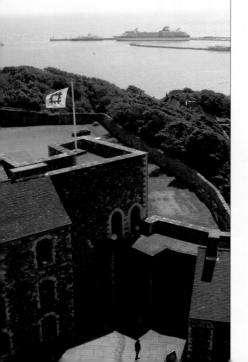

Dover is a major base port for Northern Europe cruises.

sitioning cruises between North America and Northern Europe, or between Northern Europe and the Mediterranean, often feature less-visited ports, such as those in Iceland and Greenland, or those along the west coast of France.

The array of ships servicing Northern Europe includes modern megaships, mid-sized premium ships and small luxury ships which can dock at the smaller ports of call. The Glossary of Cruise Lines at the back of this book provides a summary of the cruise lines deploying ships to Northern Europe.

When choosing a cruise, you're well advised to visit a travel agent who specializes in cruises. Look for an agency displaying the CLIA logo, indicating its agents have received training from Cruise Lines International Association. The cruise lines strongly encourage their clients to book through a travel agent with CLIA accreditation, and these qualified agents are a good source of information, with personal knowledge of many ships. They are able to provide pertinent detail regarding onboard atmosphere, cabin selection and pricing. Supplied with the relevant information, i.e. which countries or specific destinations

A small luxury ship approaches Douglas Bay on the Isle of Man.

you would like to visit, the length of cruise you wish to take, and the type of onboard atmosphere you are seeking, a cruise agent can recommend suitable itineraries and ships. They are also kept up-to-date by the cruise lines regarding special pricing.

It's best to book early for the discounts, selection and chance to upgrade your cabin category as the ship fills up. It's tempting to wait for last-minute deals, but the money you save could be negated by the higher price of your airline ticket.

Booking your flights through the cruise line will save you the time-consuming process of monitoring airfares. These air/sea packages vary with each cruise line and don't necessarily save you any money, but unexpected expenses due to flight delays and missed travel connections are covered by the cruise line. Hotel packages are also available through the cruise lines, enabling passengers to spend an extra day or two in port before boarding their ship or after disembarking at the end of a cruise.

Shore Excursions

How best to spend your time ashore is a big issue for most cruisers. There is no single answer, but plenty of options. One approach is to study your ship's itinerary and decide, port by port, what your priorities are in terms of what you want to see. Then read the 'Getting Around' information near the front of each chapter in this book to get a fix on how easy (or challenging) it is to explore a specific port on your own and decide whether you want to do some independent sightseeing or book a guided tour.

The cruise lines offer organized shore excursions for the convenience of their passengers, and these are described on their websites, in a leaflet enclosed with

your cruise documentation, and at on-board presentations given by the ship's shore excursion manager. Shore excursions can be pre-booked online or after you have boarded the ship, with cancellations allowed up to the day prior to your tour. The prices for shore excursions vary, depending on their length (half day / full day) and the activities involved. Most shore excursions are fairly priced and the local tour operators used are reliable and monitored by the cruise companies, with the added advantage that the ship will wait for any of its overdue excursions.

Full-day shore excursions offered by the cruise lines are usually a combination of driving tour, guided walking tour and lunch at a local restaurant, with an interlude for shopping. The tour guides are local residents providing narration of the sights and answering any questions you might have. When joining a ship-organized excursion, the decision to tip your guide or driver is personal and if you like the service, a small tip is appreciated.

Customized shore excursions can be arranged by travel agents who belong to a consortium. There is no cost saving, but the advantage is that you will be with a smaller group and see exactly what you want. Some cruise lines will arrange a driver/guide and private vehicle for passengers preferring a customized shore excursion.

Tour boats are a popular sight-seeing option in European ports.

Independent-minded passengers need not feel that pre-booked shore excursions are their only option when exploring various ports of call. If the ship docks right beside a town or city centre, you can simply set off on foot to do some sightseeing and shopping. Hop-on/hop-off sightseeing buses are a good way to get around and see some of the attractions.

If the town centre is a few miles from the port, the cruise lines usually offer a shuttle service for a small charge. In instances where the city is several hours away from its seaport, such as Paris and Berlin, one option is to take a ship-organized excursion that provides transportation to and from the city centre but leaves you to see the sights on your own before reboarding the coach at a pre-appointed time for the ride back to the ship. This is a good option for passengers who like the idea of exploring these cities on their own but wish to avoid any anxiety about getting back to the ship on time. A tour guide on board the coach will provide an overview of the city and sightseeing tips during the drive in, as well as answer any questions.

Another option for independent sightseeing is the train. Train travel in Europe is very efficient and is a convenient way to see a port's nearby attractions. The ship's shore excursion manager will likely have a current schedule, which is also posted at the local train station. Double-check the schedule at the other end before leaving the station to take in the local sights. Although the trains generally run on schedule, it's best not to plan your return train ride too close to the ship's time of departure, just in case there's an unforeseen delay. Local currency is sometimes needed to purchase a ticket although most ticket vending machines accept credit cards. (A rail pass is another option for passengers planning an extended stay in Europe before or after their cruise.)

The local buses and tram cars are often a good way to cover short distances, but are not recommended for longer trips, as they make frequent stops and are not always as reliable as trains for keeping to their schedules. Taxis may seem expensive, but if you're splitting the fare with a few others it can be more economical than a ship-organized excursion. Renting a car or motor scooter is often a good way to explore a rural destination, but it's not recommended when visiting large cities where traffic can be extremely congested and fast paced.

Rostock's main train station

The car-free cobblestone streets of Copenhagen (above) and Tallinn (below) invite walking and cycling.

Bicycling is a common mode of transport throughout Europe, and this is another option for tourists. However, walking is often the simplest and best way to view the local attractions. If this becomes tiring, hop-on/hop-off buses operate in most tourist-oriented cities, and public transit (i.e. underground rail, buses and trolley cars), are usually an efficient option. Please refer to the 'Getting Around' section in each chapter for detail on specific ports.

Popular attractions in Europe's major cities attract long line-ups at the height of the summer season. To avoid waiting in line to purchase entrance tickets, there are several options. These include buying beforehand a city tourist card that provides fast-track entry into the popular attractions (as well as unlimited travel on public transit). These can be purchased online, as can individual tickets to specific attractions. Another option is to book an organized tour. Also, keep in mind that museums are generally closed one day a week (usually Monday or Tuesday) as well as national holidays so visit their respective websites beforehand to determine access on the date you will be there. Places of worship are often closed to tourists on Sundays,

Even when taking a guided tour, there is often a fair amount of walking involved, so be sure to wear comfortable, rubber-soled shoes. In medieval towns and historic city quarters, where shopping streets are often designated pedestrian zones, on foot is frequently the only way to explore the winding cobblestone streets and squares.

Pre- and Post-Cruise Stays

If time allows, fly to your port of embarkation at least a day before the cruise begins, thus avoiding the stress of making same-day travel connections. Better yet, stay two or three nights at your embarkation port to recover from jet lag, relax and have time to enjoy the local sights.

Copenhagen, Stockholm and Amsterdam are all base ports for Northern European cruises, as are the British ports of Southampton, Dover and Harwich, which are less than two hours by road or rail to London. Thus, you could, for example, fly to London and spend a few days in this famous city before embarking on your cruise, and spend a few more days at the end of your cruise touring the English countryside before flying home from London.

Most cruise lines offer an air/ hotel package that can be booked in conjunction with your cruise (check with your travel agent).

The hotel packages offered by the cruise lines usually utilize four- and five-star hotels, thus ensuring their clients a consistent level of comfort and service, and transfers between hotel and pier are included. If you're booking a hotel independently, reservations are critical in the major cities. Hotel recommendations are included in this book's chapters covering London, Stockholm, Amsterdam and Copenhagen.

Once you have checked into your hotel, remember that the concierge and front desk staff offer a wealth of information for foreign visitors. They can direct you to the best shops and restaurants, and will usually provide miscellaneous services upon request, such as obtaining information on local tours or calling a taxi and confirming the destination and fare with your driver.

The five-star Hotel Angleterre in the heart of Copenhagen.

If you're part of an organized cruise-tour, an experienced guide employed by the cruise line will be available to answer any questions (see next section).

Land Tours

A cruise is a perfect opportunity to combine a vacation at sea with a land-based holiday, and a fully escorted **cruisetour** is an ideal way to see more of a European country. The tours offered by the cruise lines are a seamless form of travel, for the cruise companies maintain the same level of service on land as at sea, with well-planned itineraries, first-class hotel accommodations and professional tour direction. Hotels are centrally located, within walking distance of major attractions and shopping streets, and several hosted meals are often part of the package, while plenty of free time allows clients to do a bit of independent sightseeing, leisurely shopping or lingering in a sidewalk café. The group travels by comfortable motor coach or high-speed train, and the tour guides employed by the cruise companies are well-educated and highly qualified to introduce visitors to the history, culture and cuisine of the country they are visiting. All tours must be booked at the same time as the cruise, as part of a cruisetour package. Cruisetour itineraries vary with each cruise line. See the Cruise Lines Glossary at the back of this book for specific tours each cruise line offers.

With a rental car you can explore country roads and stop at places along the way, such as Arundel in the south of England.

On Your Own

If you plan to embark on an independent tour outside the major cities, your options include **renting a car** or purchasing a rail pass. If you cherish total independence and the freedom to meander along country roads, stopping on a whim to admire a valley view or visit a picturesque village, then consider renting a car. Obtain an International Driver's Permit before leaving home if you'll be travelling in areas where you are not fluent in the language.

When reserving a car, confirm a number of details, such as whether the 'all-inclusive' rate includes taxes, drop-off charges and unlimited kilometres. European cars are generally smaller than North American models, with a 'compact' comfortably holding two people and two pieces of luggage; the next size up is usually worth the extra cost. Standard-shift transmissions are popular in Europe, but automatics are available in larger cars at higher rates. In Britain, where driving is on the left-hand side of the road, the steering wheel is on the right side of the car. If you plan to use a credit card for insurance, ask for a copy of the policy's coverage; theft protection insurance is also required in some countries. (Visit autoeurope.com or autoeurope.ca for more information on car rental.)

Rail travel is another option for independent travel in Europe. It is efficient and comfortable, and is a relaxing way to see the countryside as you settle into your window seat and watch the scenery slide by (or whiz by on a high-speed train). An extensive rail system connects countries, cities, towns and villages, and most train stations are centrally located – whether in a resort town or a large city – so your hotel will likely be just a short taxi ride away.

In 1958, Western Europe's railroads developed the idea of an easy-to-use, multi-country, prepaid ticket for unlimited mileage use, and that concept evolved into the popular Eurailpass, which now comes in a variety of forms. The range of passes offered by Rail Europe is exhaustive, including the EurailDrive Pass with which a person can combine four days of unlimited train travel with two days of car rental through Avis or Hertz. The flexible Eurorail Select pass provides

A high-speed TGV train is planned for Paris-LeHavre in the future.

The Eurostar departs from London's St. Pancras International Terminal.

unlimited first-class train travel within a two-month period for lengths of five, six, eight and 10 days, and is valid in four bordering countries.

To obtain more information about Rail Europe's selection of passes and point-to-point tickets, visit the company's website at raileurope.com. Rail passes must be purchased before you leave for Europe, and reservations are required for some trains. Porters and luggage carts are not always available, so you must be prepared to handle your own bag-

gage if travelling by train.

Rail travel between London, Paris and Brussels was revolutionized in 1994 with the opening of the Channel Tunnel. Originally high-speed trains would depart London's Waterloo Station on existing rail track, then switch to a high-speed track just outside London for the remainder of the journey through England to the southeast coast and under the English Channel to France and Belgium. Upon the opening of central London's St. Pancras International Terminal in 2007,

Hotel accommodations in rural England include original coaching inns, such as The Bear in Woodstock (above).

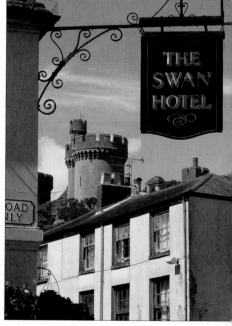

the Eurostar now travels on high-speed track the entire way. This has shaved an average of 20 minutes from the trip, with the Eurostar arriving in Paris two hours and 15 minutes after departing London. The London-to-Brussels train ride is an hour and 51 minutes. (For more information, visit www.eurostar.com.)

In addition to city hotels, another type of accommodation to consider in Europe is a hostel. These used to be large dormitories with communal bathrooms but many of today's hostels feature family rooms with private bath that can accommodate four or more guests. Visit www.hostelseurope.com for more information. If you're planning to spend a week in Paris before or after your cruise, renting a fully furnished apartment is a popular option (visit www.parisattitude.com). In Britain, rural accommodations include modified castles, manor houses and original coaching inns replete with oak beams and stone fireplaces (for more information, see www.visitbritain.com).

Documentation

Several weeks before your departure date, you will receive (or be able to print out) all pertinent documentation for your trip, including your cruise ticket, airline ticket and a mandatory pre-registration form that can be completed online, or faxed or mailed to the cruise line. Before your departure, leave a detailed travel itinerary with a family member or friend, in case someone needs to contact you while you're away. Include the name of your ship, its phone number and the applicable ocean code, as well as your stateroom number – all of which will be included in your cruise documents. With this information, a person can call the international telephone operator and place a satellite call to your ship in an emergency.

A valid passport is required for travel to all countries visited on a Northern Europe cruise. As a precaution, you should photocopy the identification page of your passport, along with your driver's licence and any credit cards you will be taking on your trip. Keep one copy of this photocopied information with you either in paper form or on a flash drive, separate from your passport and wallet, and leave another copy at home.

Travel insurance is recommended. A comprehensive policy will cover trip cancellation, delayed departure, medical expenses, personal accident and liability, lost baggage and money, and legal expenses. You may already have supplementary health insurance through a credit card, automobile club policy or employment health plan, but you should check these carefully. Carry details of your policy with you and documentation of your health plan.

Currency

When travelling abroad, it's best to take various forms of currency – cash, credit cards and bank cards. If you're staying in a foreign city for a few days before or after your cruise, obtain some petty cash in that country's currency to cover incidentals. US currency is not widely accepted in Great Britain, Scandinavia or Western Europe. Major credit cards are accepted by most hotels and restaurants, and ATM machines are widespread.

Once you're aboard your ship, travellers cheques can be cashed at the purser's office and it's sometimes possible to obtain cash advances from credit cards. Most ships also have a currency exchange facility on board, offering a competitive rate on foreign currencies, so that passengers needn't spend time at each port of call exchanging funds into local currency. The rates offered by local currency exchange offices can vary and some will charge a higher commission on Sundays. The euro is the official currency in 18 of the 28 member states of the European Union, including Belgium, Estonia, Finland, France, Germany, Ireland, Latvia and the Netherlands. One euro is divided into 100 centimes. The approximate rate of exchange:

$1 (USD) = .88 euro; £1 (GBP) = 1.35 euro. Other Northern European countries that are members of the EU but use their own currency are Denmark, Lithuania, Sweden and the United Kingdom. Norway and Russia are not members of the EU and have their own currencies.

For major purchases or expenses, a credit card is recommended (rather than carrying large amounts of cash) and although a currency conversion fee is charged (usually 2 or 3%), the difference in service charges between using a credit card or withdrawing cash in the local currency from an ATM is not substantial. It's best to carry several credit cards, and married couples should arrange for at least one set of separate cards (without joint signing privileges) in case one spouse loses his or her wallet and all of the couple's joint cards have to be cancelled. It's also wise to take along a handful of small US bills and euros to cover tips for guides and other sundries when ashore.

Health Precautions

Most countries in a Northern Europe itinerary present no health concerns with the exception of Russia, where only bottled water should be drunk. Check with your doctor that your inoculations are up to date (you may need a booster for diphtheria, which is prevalent in parts of Russia). All ships have a fully equipped medical centre with a doctor and nurses. Passengers needing medical attention are billed at private rates which are added to their shipboard account. This invoice can be submitted to your insurance company upon your return home. You may already have supplementary health insurance through a credit card, automobile club policy or employment health plan, but you should check these carefully. Whatever policy you choose for your trip, carry details of it with you and documents showing that you are covered by a plan.

The overall standards of cleanliness on board cruise ships are extremely high, yet contagious viruses that are spread by person-to-person contact (such as the Norovirus, which is a brief but severe gastrointestinal illness) do occasionally plague a small percentage of passengers. To avoid contracting such a virus, practise frequent, thorough handwashing with warm, soapy water.

Motion sickness is not a widespread or prolonged problem for most passengers, but for those who are susceptible, a number of remedies are available. One is a special wrist band, the balls of which rest on an acupressure point. These 'sea bands' are available at most drug stores. Another option is to chew meclizine tablets (usually available at the ship's infirmary) or take Dramamine, an over-the-counter antihistamine. It's best to take these pills ahead of time, before you feel too nauseous, and they may make you drowsy. Fresh air is one of the best antidotes, so stepping out on deck is often all that's needed to counter any queasiness.

What to Pack

Pack casual attire for daytime wear – both aboard the ship and in port. The weather can range from sunny and warm (occasionally hot) to cool, cloudy and rainy, so pack clothes that can be layered and include a water-proof jacket and a hat that will keep the rain (or the sun) off your face. A comfortable pair of rubber-soled shoes is essential for walking along cobblestone streets.

Your evening wear should include something suitable for formal nights held on board most ships. Women wear gowns or cocktail dresses, and men favour dark suits or tuxedos. For smart casual evenings, women wear dresses, skirts, pantsuits or slacks and blouses, and the men wear dress slacks with a shirt and jacket or a golf shirt.

Check with your travel agent regarding on-board facilities; for instance, most cabins will have a built-in hair dryer. Some ships have coin-operated laundrettes with ironing boards; those that don't provide laundry service at an extra charge. Steam pressing and dry cleaning are available (for a charge) on most ships, and it's easy to do hand washing in your cabin. Poolside towels are provided, as are beach towels – upon request – for taking ashore.

To save room in your suitcase, pack sample sizes of toothpaste and other toiletries, which can also be purchased on board the ship. If you wear prescription eyeglasses, consider packing a spare pair. Keep prescribed medication in original, labelled containers and carry a doctor's prescription for any controlled drug. Other items you may want to bring along are a small pair of binoculars and a pocket calculator for tabulating exchange rates. And be sure to keep all valuables, such as a camera and expensive jewellery, in your carry-on luggage, as well as all prescription medicine and documentation,

Resort attire is suitable for daytime and casual-dress dinners.

such as your passport, tickets and a copy of your insurance policy. Last but not least, be sure to leave room in one of your suitcases for souvenirs.

Connecting with Home

Text messaging and e-mail are replacing phone calls as the most convenient way to reach someone while you're cruising. Most ships provide satellite-based broadband services that allow you to use your wireless devices while at sea anywhere on the ship. Bulk rates are usually offered on time used.

Most ships also have Internet cafes where passengers have access to on-line computers and are charged for their use on a per-minute basis. If you plan to send frequent e-mails while on your cruise, you may want to open a hotmail account upon embarkation.

With recent increases to bandwidth capacity and onboard wi-fi capability, some ships are now offering a flat daily rate for unlimited connectivity. On some ships, passengers can use their own lap-top computer or tablet to plug into the ship's connection.

Cell phones are the easiest way to call home but be sure to check with your service provider to get detail on your phone's roaming capability and the attendant roaming charges. A roaming package, if bought beforehand, can be more economical. One option, if you're carrying a smart phone, is to purchase a local pre-paid SIM card.

Calls can also be placed through the ship's radio office or by placing a direct satellite telephone call from your stateroom. This is expensive, however, and unless the call is urgent you may want to wait and place your call from a land-based phone. Refer to the map (below) to determine the time difference before placing a call.

An onboard Internet cafe

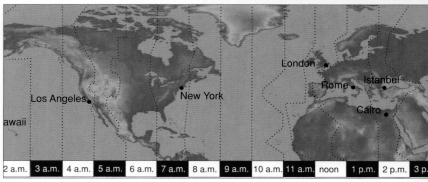

Vacation Photos

Digital images have largely replaced photographs, but the goal of capturing our holiday's highlights remains the same. If you're using a digital camera, be sure to pack an extra battery pack, which can be recharged in your stateroom. For print-quality reproduction, shoot at a fine setting and large size. Most onboard photo departments can develop digital images into prints.

Onboard photo galleries are a good place to purchase shots taken of yourself, friends and family members as you disembark at each port of call. These are nice mementos of your cruise. On formal nights, when everyone is looking their best, the ship's photographers are set up at locations around the ship to take studio-quality portraits which are displayed the next day in the photo gallery. There is no sitting fee and no obligation to purchase these prints but people often do because it's a convenient way to obtain a professional portrait.

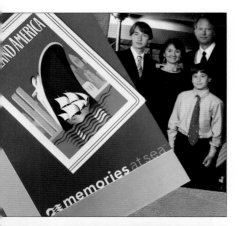

Security

While security is not a major concern when on board the ship, you should take some precautions when venturing ashore. Property crime can occur anywhere, but tourists are especially vulnerable because they carry large amounts of money, as well as cameras and other valuables. Keep all credit cards and most of your cash securely stowed in an inside pocket of your clothes or shoulder bag, and keep a few small bills in a readily accessible pocket to pay for small impromptu purchases.

Be aware of pickpockets. Many operate in pairs, with one creating a distraction, such as dropping a handful of coins, while the other lifts their victim's wallet. Don't wear expensive jewellery and don't wear a fanny pack because a professional pickpocket with surgical scissors can quickly snip the strap and lift your pack without your even noticing. An inside jacket pocket with a zipper or a money belt concealed beneath your clothes are more secure ways to carry money.

Situations requiring caution include any place where there are crowds of people. Always keep an eye on your luggage at airports and train stations. When hiring a taxi, watch to make sure every piece of luggage is loaded into the trunk, and never leave valuables in a rented car.

Shopping

Most stores and upscale shops accept all major credit cards, but it's best to have local currency (in most cases the euro) for small and impromptu purchases. Value Added Tax is attached to most purchases in Europe, and North American visitors can obtain a refund by first requesting a refund form in the store where they make their purchase, then having it stamped by customs staff in the airport prior to departure. Refunds can be obtained on the spot or after you are home, by sending the form to the appropriate office. Check with your travel agent or local customs office before leaving home to determine your duty-free allowances.

Europe is rich in centuries-old craftsmanship, and memorable souvenirs include hand-painted ceramics and decorative tiles. Woolen knitwear, embroidered linens and delicate laceware are other traditional crafts, as is amber jewellery.

Craftsmanship on display in Helsinki (top) and St. Petersburg (middle). (Right) A shopping street in Helsinki.

The waters of Northern Europe have been plied over the centuries by craft ranging from Viking longships to square-rigged frigates to dreadnought battleships. Naval power has been critical to the rise and fall of nearly every European empire, and a nation's merchant marine was usually the lifeblood of its trade-based wealth.

Modern ships navigating northern European waters must deal not only with the natural elements – strong currents, contrary winds and, in early spring, ice-clogged ports – but with the added challenge of heavy marine traffic. The North Sea and English Channel are among the busiest waters in the world, with over 400 ships using the Channel every day.

The constant flow of freighters, car ferries and other commercial traffic in the Channel and the Strait of Dover has resulted in serious ship collisions in the past and the movements of vessels are now monitored by coast guard radar stations in English and French ports. Using the Traffic Separation System, ships are always kept at a specific distance from one another while transiting these waters.

The Baltic Sea also has significant vessel traffic, but its waters are not as constricted, so separation of ships is not such an issue.

How Ships Move

Ships are pushed through the water by the turning of propellers, two of which are mounted at the stern. A propeller is like a screw threading its way through the sea, pushing water away from its pitched blades. Props are 15 to 20 feet in diameter on large cruise ships and normally turn at 100 to 150 revolutions per minute. It takes a lot of horsepower – about 60,000 on a large ship – to make these propellers push a ship along. The bridge crew can tap into any amount of engine power by moving small levers that adjust the propeller blades to determine the speed of the ship. Most modern ships use diesel engines to deliver large amounts of electricity to motors that smoothly turn the propeller shafts. Ship vibration is minimal using these sophisticated systems to deliver power. Some ships use electric motors mounted on pods hung from the stern of the ship, like huge outboard engines. These pods can swivel 360 degrees.

The average speed at which cruise ships travel is 21 to 24 knots. Distances at sea are mea-

Modern ships are designed for safety, passenger comfort and fuel efficiency.

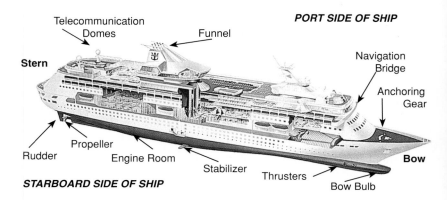

sured in nautical miles (1 nautical mile = 1.15 statute miles = 1.85 kilometres).

The majority of cruise ships currently deployed to Europe were built in the last decade or two. This proliferation of new-builds, along with ongoing retro-fitting and refurbishing of ships, has resulted in an ever-expanding array of shipboard amenities – from health spas and water slides to movie theatres and specialty restaurants. Cabins, formerly equipped with portholes, now are fitted with picture windows or sliding glass doors that open onto private verandahs.

Modern cruise ships are quite different from those of the Golden Age of ocean liners, which were designed for the rigours of winter storms in the North Atlantic. Ships built today are generally taller, shallower, lighter and powered by smaller, more compact engines. Although their steel hulls are thinner and welded together in numerous sections, modern ships are as strong as the ocean liners of yesterday because of advances in construction technology and metallurgy.

A ship's size is determined by measurements that result in a figure called gross tonnage (internal volume). There are approximately 100 cubic feet to a measured ton. Most new ships being built today are over 100,000 tons and carry several thousand passengers. At the stern of every ship, below its name, is the ship's country of registry, which is not necessarily where the cruise company's head office is located. Certain countries grant registry to ships for a flat fee, and ships often fly these 'flags of convenience' for tax reasons.

The Engine Room

Located many decks below passenger cabins is the engine room, a labyrinth of tunnels, catwalks and bulkheads connecting and supporting the machinery that generates the vast amount of power needed to operate a ship. A large, proficient crew keeps everything running smoothly, but this is a far cry from the hundreds once needed to operate coal-burning steam engines used before the advent of diesel fuel.

Technical advancements in the last 50 years have helped reduce fuel consumption and improve control of the ship. These include the bow bulb, stabilizers and thrusters. The bow bulb is just below the waterline and displaces the same amount of water that would be pushed out of the way by the ship's bow. This virtually eliminates a bow wave, resulting in fuel savings as less energy is needed to push the ship forward. Stabilizers are small, wing-like appendages that protrude amidships below the waterline and act to dampen the ship's roll in beam seas. Thrusters are port-like openings with small propellers at the bow and sometimes also at the stern, which push the front or rear of the ship as it is approaching or leaving a dock. Thrusters have virtually eliminated the need for tugs in most situations when docking.

A ship lying to anchor

The Bridge

The bridge (located at the bow or front of the ship) is an elevated, enclosed platform bridging (or crossing) the width of the ship with an unobstructed view ahead and to either side. It is from the ship's bridge that the highest-ranking officer, the captain, oversees the operation of the ship. The bridge is manned 24 hours a day by two officers working four hours on, eight hours off, in a three-watch system. They all report to the captain, and their various duties include recording all course changes, keeping lookout and making sure the junior officer keeps a fresh pot of coffee going. The captain does not usually have a set watch but will be on the bridge when the ship is entering or leaving port, and transiting a channel. Other conditions that would bring the captain to the bridge would be poor weather or when there are numerous vessels in the area.

An array of instrumentation provides the ship's officers with pertinent information. Radar is used most intensely in foggy conditions or at night. Radar's electronic signals can survey the ocean for many miles, and anything solid – such as land or other boats – appears on its screen. Radar is also used for plotting the course of other ships and for alerting the crew of a potential collision situation. Depth sounders track the bottom of the seabed to ensure the ship's course agrees with the depth of water shown on the official chart.

The helm on modern ships is

a surprisingly small wheel. An automatic telemotor transmission connects the wheel to the steering mechanism at the stern of the ship. Ships also use an 'autopilot' which works through an electronic compass to steer a set course. The autopilot is used when the ship is in open water.

Other instruments monitor engine speed, power, angle of list, speed through water, speed over ground and time arrival estimations. When entering a harbor, large ships must have a pilot on board to provide navigational advice to the ship's officers. When a ship is in open waters, a pilot is not required

(Above) The ship's captain on the bridge. (Below) A tender transports passengers ashore.

Tendering

At some ports, the ship will anchor off a distance from the town and passengers are tendered ashore with the ship's launches. People on organized shore excursions will be taken ashore first, so if you have booked an excursion you will assemble with your group in one of the ship's public areas. Passengers not on an excursion should wait 45 minutes to an hour before attempting to board a tender to avoid long line-ups.

(Above) Ships docked at Tallinn. (Below) A ship's hotel manager oversees all of the service staff.

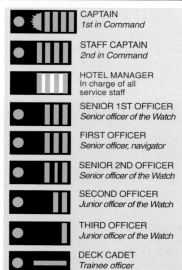

CAPTAIN	*1st in Command*
STAFF CAPTAIN	*2nd in Command*
HOTEL MANAGER	In charge of all service staff
SENIOR 1ST OFFICER	*Senior officer of the Watch*
FIRST OFFICER	*Senior officer, navigator*
SENIOR 2ND OFFICER	*Senior officer of the Watch*
SECOND OFFICER	*Junior officer of the Watch*
THIRD OFFICER	*Junior officer of the Watch*
DECK CADET	*Trainee officer*

Ship Safety

Cruise ships are one of the safest modes of travel. The International Maritime Organization maintains high standards for safety at sea, including regular fire and lifeboat drills, as well as frequent ship inspections for cleanliness and seaworthiness.

Cruise ships must adhere to a law requiring that a lifeboat drill take place within 24 hours of embarkation, and most ships schedule this drill just before leaving port. Directions are displayed in your cabin, and staff are on hand to guide passengers through the safety drill.

Hotel Staff

The Front Desk (or Purser's Office) is the pleasure centre of the ship. And, in view of the fact that a cruise is meant to be an extremely enjoyable experience, it is fitting that the Hotel Manager's rank is second only to that of the Captain. In terms of staff, the Hotel Manager (or Passenger Services Director) has by far the largest. It is his responsibility to make sure beds are made, meals are served, wines are poured, entertainment is provided and tour buses arrive on time – all while keeping a smile on his or her face. Hotel managers generally have many years' experience on ships, working in various departments before rising to this position. Most initially graduate from a college program in management and train in the hotel or food industries, where they learn the logistics of feeding hundreds of people at a sitting.

A Hotel Manager's management staff includes a Purser, Food Service Manager, Beverage Manager, Chief Housekeeper, Cruise Director and Shore Excursion Manager. All ship's staff wear a uniform and even if a hotel officer doesn't recognize a staff member, he will know at a glance that person's duties by their uniform's color and the distinguishing bars on its sleeves. The hotel staff on cruise ships come from countries around the world.

Checking In

Upon arrival at the cruise pier, you will be directed to a check-in counter and asked to offer up a credit card to be swiped for any onboard expenses. In exchange, you will receive a personalized plastic card with a magnetic strip. This card acts both as your onboard credit card and the door key to your stateroom. It is also your security pass for getting off and on the ship at each port of call. Carry this card with you at all times.

Life Aboard

Cruise ship cabins – also called staterooms – vary in size, from standard inside cabins to outside suites complete with a verandah.

Whatever the size of your accommodation, it will be clean and comfortable. A telephone and television are standard features in cabins, and storage space includes closets and drawers ample enough to hold your clothes and miscellaneous items. Valuables can be left in your stateroom safe or in a safety deposit box at the front office, also called the purser's office.

If your budget permits, an outside cabin – especially one with a verandah – is preferable for enjoying the coastal scenery and orienting yourself at a new port. When selecting a cabin, keep in mind its location in relation to the ship's facilities. If you're prone to seasickness, cabins located on lower decks near the middle of the ship will have less motion than a top outside cabin near the bow or stern. If you have prefer-

The front desk handles all passenger queries and accounts.

A standard outside stateroom with balcony. (Below) The main dining room on a large ship.

ences for cabin location, be sure to discuss these with your cruise agent when booking. Cruise lines often reward passengers who book early with upgrades to a more expensive stateroom.

Both casual and formal dining are offered on the large ships, with breakfast and lunch served in the buffet-style lido restaurant or at an open seating in the main dining room. Traditionally, din-

ner was served at two sittings in the main dining room and passengers were asked to indicate their preference for first or second sitting. While this traditional format is still offered on the large ships, open seating is also offered for passengers who want more flexibility. Luxury cruise lines usually have one open seating for dinner. Most large ships also offer alternative dining – small specialty restaurants that require a reservation and for which there is usually a surcharge (about $20-$30 per person). Room service is also available, free of charge, for light meals and in-between snacks.

Things to Do

There are so many things to do on a cruise ship, you would have to spend a few months aboard to participate in every activity and enjoy all of the ship's facilities. A daily newsletter will keep you informed of all the ship's happenings. If exercise is a priority, you can swim in the pool, work out in the gym, jog around the promenade deck, join the aerobics and

dance classes or join in the ping-pong and volleyball tournaments. Perhaps you just want to soak in the jacuzzi or treat yourself to a massage and facial at the spa.

Stop by the library if you're looking for a good book, a board game or an informal hand of bridge with your fellow passengers. Check your newsletter to see which films are scheduled for the movie theatre or just settle into a deck chair, breathing the fresh sea air. Your days on the ship can be as busy or as relaxed as you want. You can stay up late every night, enjoying the varied entertainment in the ship's lounges, or you can retire early and rise at dawn to watch the ship pull into port. When the ship is in port, you can remain onboard if you wish or you can head ashore, returning to the ship as many times as you like before it leaves for the next port. Ships are punctual about departing, so be sure to get back to the ship at least a half hour before it is scheduled to leave.

Children and teenagers are welcome on most cruise ships, which offer an ideal environment for a

A ship's specialty restaurant (above), celebrating a special occasion (below) and children's activities (bottom).

(Above) Power walking on the promenade deck. (Below) The view from a ship's lounge.

family vacation. Youth facilities on the large ships usually include a playroom for children and a disco-type club for teenagers. Supervised activities are offered on a daily basis, and security measures include parents checking their children in and out of the playroom. Kids can participate in activities ranging from ball games to arts and crafts, all overseen by trained youth staff. Each cruise line has a minimum age for participation (usually three years old), and some also offer private babysitting. Youth facilities and programs vary from line to line, and from ship to ship.

Extra Expenses

There are few additional expenses once you board a cruise ship. Your stateroom and all meals (including 24-hour room service) are paid for, as are any stage shows, lectures, movies, lounge acts, demonstrations and other activities held in the ship's public areas. If you make use of the per-

sonal services offered on board – such as dry cleaning or a spa treatment or a yoga class – these are not covered in the basic price of a cruise. Neither are any drinks you might order in a lounge. You will also be charged for any wine or alcoholic beverages you order with your meals.

Gratuities are extra, with each cruise line providing its own guidelines on how much each crewmember should be tipped – provided you are happy with the service. (On luxury lines, gratuities are usually covered by the all-inclusive fare.) Gratuities for your cabin steward, dining room steward, assistant waiter and head waiter were traditionally handed out individually in cash-filled envelopes on the last night of the cruise. However, most ships now offer a service that automatically bills an aggregate amount for gratuities (about $12 per passenger per day) to your shipboard account, which can be adjusted at your discretion. These gratuities do not cover bar bills, to which a 15% tip is automatically added.

Most ships are cashless societies in which passengers sign for incidental expenses, which are itemized on a final statement that is slipped under your cabin door during the last night of your cruise and settled at the front office by pre-approved credit card. It's best to check your account balance (which can usually be accessed on your stateroom television) before the last full day of your cruise and thus avoid long line-ups at the Front Desk should you need to clear up any discrepancies.

(Above) A ship's central atrium.
(Below) Sunset at the ship's rail.

water and occasionally causing severe winter weather in countries bordering the Baltic. The Arctic Ocean is capped by an ever-shifting ice pack and the dramatic increase in recent years of the region's summertime sea-ice retreat has opened up previously frozen waters. This environmental change has created a new race to the Pole – this time by the five nations which claim overlapping mineral rights to the Arctic seabed, namely Russia, Norway, Denmark (Greenland), Canada and the United States (Alaska). A recent U.S. Geological Survey has estimated that the Arctic contains 13% of the world's remaining undiscovered oil and up to 30% of its natural gas deposits.

The Arctic Ocean is an active area of seismic activity, with underwater earthquakes and ongoing eruptions of gas and molten lava from the numerous underwater volcanoes that rise from the seabed, their summits about four kilometres below the ice. Gakkel Ridge is an 1,800-km underwater ridge that extends from Greenland to Siberia and marks the boundary between two divergent plates of the earth's crust – the Eurasian Plate and the North American Plate. This fissure is a spreading ridge from which erupting molten rock produces new crust. A seven-mile-wide valley has formed where the two crustal plates are coming apart (at a rate of less than one centimetre per year) and it contains dozens of flat-topped volcanoes that erupted in 1999, depositing a layer of dark volcanic glass on the seabed.

The landscapes of Northern Europe range from densely populated cities to remote Arctic islands where seabirds are the sole inhabitants. The sea is the dominant force, with the North Atlantic Drift (a warm ocean current) bringing moderate weather to the coastlines of Britain and Western Europe. Even the northernmost coastline of Norway above the Arctic Circle is navigable for more than half the year due to warm ocean currents. Atlantic waters enter the North Sea through its northwest opening and, to a lesser extent, along the English Channel. The tide flows in a counter-clockwise direction along the edges of the North Sea and exits along the Norwegian coast.

Parts of the Baltic Sea, where the tidal range is much smaller, frequently freeze over in winter, cutting off the warmer Atlantic

Scientists studying the Arctic seabed are gathering data for their respective nations, which must substantiate any proposed extensions to their existing mineral rights in a submission to the UN's Commission on the Limits of the Continental Shelf. Under international law, a nation's territorial sea extends for 12 nautical miles from the coast, followed by a 200-mile-wide exclusive economic zone. This zone can be increased to 350 miles if a nation's continental shelf extends that distance, but no further. When the polar explorer Artur Chilingarov planted a titanium replica of the Russian flag on the North Pole's sea floor in 2007 (using a deepsea mini-submarine) this controversial 'land grab' garnered press headlines but the mat-

ter ultimately will be resolved under international law. The UN's International Seabed Authority reviews all boundary claims and an applicant country must prove the natural prolongations of its continental shelf with exhaustive geological studies.

As nations dispute their exclusive access to mineral rights in the Arctic, environmentalists are spotlighting the threat that oil and gas exploration could pose to the region's natural environment – which is already being affected by climate change. The melting of polar ice in summer and subsequent release of heat has destabilized the wintertime polar vortex – a huge circular flow of air that separates the Arctic's cold air from warmer air to the south,

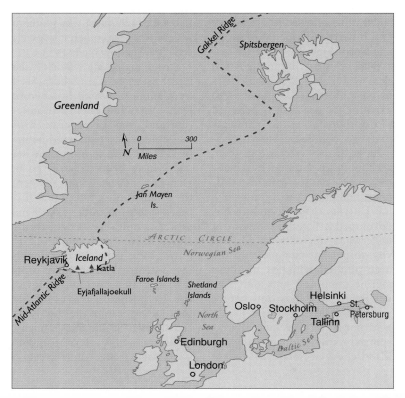

Wind turbines near Copenhagen.

and this has allowed jet streams to pull bitterly cold air into Europe and North America.

Seismic surveying in the North Sea, which involves geologists using underwater explosions to examine the sea bed, is believed to disorientate marine mammals that use echolocation to navigate. In British waters alone there are hundreds of beach strandings per year of whales, dolphins and porpoises. Fortunately, the University of Plymouth has developed a listening system of underwater microphones for survey ships that can pick up the high-pitched whistles of these marine mammals and alert surveyors to their position before setting off blasts.

Mineral wealth has always spurred exploration. During the Middle Ages, mariners were drawn to the Baltic Sea's coastline in search of highly prized amber, which is the fossilized resin of prehistoric trees. In the North Sea, in the 1960s, extensive natural gas reserves were discovered during test-drilling of the sea floor. The North Sea is politically divided into economic zones and Norway's zone contains the Ekofisk oil field of valuable, low-sulphur oil as well as the Troll gas field. The latter lies in the Norwegian trench – a band of deep water reaching depths of 1,000 feet (300 m) along Norway's southwest coastline. The rest of the North Sea is relatively shallow (except for Devil's Hole) and supports more than 230 species of fish, including cod, haddock, sole, mackerel and herring. These and other species of fish are caught mostly in southern waters where commercial vessels trawl the shallow banks.

Strong prevailing winds off the North Sea are being harnessed by Denmark, which is a world leader in wind energy production and aims to generate 75% of its electricity with wind power by 2025. Close to a dozen wind parks have been constructed in Denmark's coastal waters, where the blades of giant wind turbines spin high in the sky. Wind power is not a new concept, the Dutch having built windmills to power their canals' early pumping systems. With one-third of its land area lying below sea level, the Netherlands is vulnerable to flooding, as are the low-lying coastlines of Denmark, Germany, Belgium and eastern England whenever strong winds create a storm surge of high waves that coincide with a large tide.

One of the worst natural disasters of the twentieth century was the North Sea Flood of 1953, which claimed over 2,000 lives, mostly in Holland and along England's east coast. An intense low-pressure system had tracked across the Atlantic (a common occurrence in winter) then veered south into the North Sea where the combination of steep waves and a large tide created a deadly surge of water. Over a hundred ferry passengers perished when the *Princess Victoria* sank in the North Channel between Scotland and Northern Ireland after wave damage caused the vessel to take on water. The shocking death toll from this winter storm prompted Holland to build Delta Works – a system of dams, sluices and storm surge barriers designed to reduce and reinforce the country's exposed coastline. To protect London, which is vulnerable to flooding, the Thames Barrier (a moveable flood barrier located downstream of Central London) was completed in 1982.

The Baltic Sea has less pronounced tides than those of the North Sea but flooding is still a problem in some ports, such as St. Petersburg, which lies just a few feet above sea level and has experienced close to 300 major floods since its founding in 1703. When a low-pressure air mass over the Atlantic moves into the Gulf of Finland, bringing strong westerly winds and a storm surge of water to the mouth of the Neva, the river's outflow current is pushed back until it spills its banks.

The North Sea Flood of 1953.

In contrast to low-lying shorelines of mudflats and sandy beaches in the North Sea's southern waters are the sheer cliffs and deep fjords of coastal Norway and parts of Scotland. These rugged coastlines were formed by glaciers during the last Ice Age some 20,000 years ago. The final retreat of the ice sheet brought rising sea levels to the Atlantic Ocean, which flooded the European continental shelf to create the North Sea.

The deep Atlantic Ocean contains the longest mountain range in the world. Called the Mid-Atlantic Ridge, this sea-floor fissure starts at a junction with the Gakkel Ridge (Mid-Arctic Ridge) northeast of Greenland and includes the island of Iceland, which is a young basalt plateau straddling this volcanic submarine ridge. Iceland contains some

200 volcanoes, with new ones forming over nearby undersea vents. An erupting sea mount off Iceland's southern coast broke the sea's surface in 1963 to become Surtsey, an island named after Surtr, a giant from Norse mythology. The volcano didn't stop erupting until 1967, after which wind and wave erosion have reduced the island's original surface area of one square mile to about half that size.

Active volcanoes on Iceland's nearby mainland include the one lying beneath Eyjafjallajökull glacier. This volcano, which had previously erupted in 920, 1612 and 1821 to 1823, made front-page news in April 2010 when an explosive eruption sent a plume of ash 11,000 metres into the atmosphere. As high-altitude winds spread the cloud of ash and vapour eastward over Scandinavia and western Europe, commercial aircraft were grounded and air travel was disrupted, temporarily stranding thousands of passengers. (When a jet plane flies into volcanic ash, the finely ground rock is sandblasted onto the aircraft, clogging its engines and degrading its wing surfaces.)

Thousands of small earthquakes preceded the eruption of Eyjafjallajökull, which has in the past triggered the eruption of another subglacial volcano called Katla, located about 16 miles (25 km) west of Eyjafjallajökull. The potential eruption of Katla, with its larger magma chamber, would cause major flooding from glacial meltwater and send up plumes of ash that would once again disrupt air travel.

Eyjafjallajökull erupting in April 2010.

Arctic Flora & Fauna

The wildlife inhabiting the Arctic region includes polar bears, which roam the pack ice, as well as moose, reindeer and fox. The shaggy muskox, a grazing cousin of the bison, inhabits Greenland and islands of the Arctic. Its range was much larger in prehistoric times, but the population of muskox plummeted about 12,000 years ago at the end of the last ice age when a warmer, wetter climate arrived. In recent years, the melting of permafrost has again put the muskox and other species at risk in the Arctic. The region's marine mammals include several species of whale, as well as seals and sea walruses. Migratory birds arrive by the thousands each spring, and mosses, lichen and small flowering plants grow south of the permanent snow line during the short Arctic summer.

(Top to bottom) Atlantic puffin, reindeer, Northern Gannet, wildflowers, walruses.

The Ancients

Western Europe's earliest inhabitants were a Bronze Age people about whom we know very little but who left behind one of the world's great wonders – Stonehenge. These megalithic stones, weighing up to 50 tons each, were somehow transported, upended and arranged within a circular trench on Salisbury Plain in southern England. There they have stood since before 2000 BC, strangely out of context amid the sheep pastures and dairy farms of modern-day Wiltshire.

The earliest Celtic invaders of the British Isles arrived in the 5th century BC, bringing an Iron Age culture with them. Next were the Romans, who named the island

Stonehenge on Salisbury Plain.
(Below) An early Viking ship.

Britannia. The rise of Rome, from city-state to empire, was led by Julius Caesar. Born into one of the oldest patrician families in Rome, Caesar left his mark across Western Europe, from the Alps to the Atlantic. Between 58 and 49 BC he fought in the Gallic Wars, by the end of which all of Gaul – the seed of modern France – had fallen under Roman control. Caesar also led a military campaign to the British Isles, aimed at preventing the Celts from launching incursions across the English Channel into Gaul. A full-blown conquest soon followed, with the Romans building roads and developing towns to support their military occupation.

When the crumbling Roman Empire withdrew its troops from outposts such as Britain, the Germanic tribes of Northern Europe (the Angles, Saxons and Jutes) began their first raids, followed by great waves of invasion and settlement in the 5th century AD. As the Celts retreated into Wales and Cornwall, the Anglo-Saxons established seven small kingdoms in England – Kent, Sussex, Essex, Wessex, East Anglia, Mercia and Northumbria.

The Vikings

Arable land is scarce and the climate is harsh in much of Scandinavia, which prompted the Vikings' forays into other lands in search of more hospitable living conditions. The Danish and Norwegian Vikings headed west, while the Swedish Vikings travelled into what is now Russia. Their mode of transportation was the longship – a remarkably advanced craft that was fast, sea-worthy and navigated with precision. A typical longship had a high prow and stern, the former adorned with an animal figure. Seating up to 30 oarsmen and carrying an average crew of 90, the long ship was elaborately carved and decorated, with rows of painted round shields hung along both sides of the hull and its square sails dyed with coloured stripes. Epic voyages to North America (between 985 and 1011) were possible, in part, due to the Vikings' ability to provision these open ships with dried and salted cod that could be stowed compactly in the hull.

When the Vikings landed on a foreign shore, their arrival triggered panic amongst local populations who feared for their lives, possessions and property. However, according to modern historians, the Vikings have been given a bad rap. New evidence suggests that although the arrival of the Vikings was initially disruptive to the established society, these newcomers (who were mostly from the upper classes) were looking for a better life and they quickly became model immigrants as they settled into new careers as farmers, craftsmen and traders. And they weren't hairy goons with funny horned hats but were actually quite snappy dressers. The Swedish Vikings in particular liked to combine oriental ornateness with Nordic styles, and the women dressed provocatively, adorning themselves in vivid colours and ornamenting their dresses with silk ribbons and glittering decorations. This early

Pagan Practices

Prior to the introduction of Christianity and the adoption of the Roman alphabet, the runic alphabet (its characters called runes) was used in Scandinavia. Rune stones (bearing inscriptions) were raised beside the graves of deceased kings and queens, who were interred in burial mounds. The days of the week (except for Saturday) were named for Norse gods: Sun's day, Moon's day, Tyr's day, Odin's day, Thor's day, Freyja's day. Festivals were held at midsummer and midwinter, the latter eventually blending with Christmas as pagan worship was replaced with Christian beliefs. Many of the pagan traditions are still part of Christmas, including the Yule log and the hanging of mistletoe, and summer solstice is still celebrated throughout Scandinavia with a public holiday (Midsummer's Day) of outdoor festivities centred around civic parades and the lighting of a bonfire.

Scandinavian style eventually gave way to medieval Christian fashion, which was much more conservative.

The Norman castle in Arundel, England. Portrait of Henry VIII.

The Britons

Late in the 8th century, the Vikings began their raids on coastal England, followed by a full-scale assault in 870 which was met head-on by the Saxon king, Alfred the Great. His successors formed a united England, but ensuing Danish invasions eventually overcame the English until the Wessex dynasty under Edward the Confessor regained the throne in 1042.

When Edward died in 1066, his cousin William, Duke of Normandy, laid claim to the British throne. He is best known as William the Conqueror and the Norman conquest he led was the last foreign invasion of Britain. He is also known for introducing taxation when the country's first census, The Domesday Book, was conducted.

Over time, a formidable nation was shaped by ongoing political struggles between powerful barons and their monarch, between church and state, and between rival claimants to the throne of England. Momentous events in the nation's history include King John's signing of the Magna Carta at Runnymede in 1215, which officially recognized the division of power between the monarch and the landed gentry. The king was now required to convene parliament in order to raise tax money for projects, such as building new ships or castles.

Still, the British monarchy became even more powerful under the rule of Henry VII, a Welshman whose claim to the throne was tenuous but who

Mary, Queen of Scots

The only child of James V of Scotland, Mary Stuart was just six days old when she became Queen of Scotland upon her father's death in 1542. Her mother, Mary of Guise, was a French aristocrat who made no secret of her desire to bring France and Scotland together. As regent of Scotland, she betrothed her infant daughter to the French dauphin (future king) and five-year-old Mary was sent to France where she was raised by her powerful relatives until she turned 15, at which time her arranged marriage took place. Her husband was crowned Francis I a year later but soon died. Mary's Guise uncles fell from power with the ascent of a new French king and Mary returned to Scotland. Not yet 20, the beautiful young queen faced a nation of hostile subjects due to her being French and a Catholic, but she quickly charmed many of her Scottish lords. She reassured her people that there would be no further French interference in Scottish affairs, and she officially (but not privately) accepted the establishment of the Presbyterian Church.

Mary, Queen of Scots

Mary's driving ambition was to rule England, and she strengthened her claim to the throne by marrying her cousin Henry Stuart (Lord Darnley), both of whom were grandchildren of Margaret Tudor (sister of Henry VIII). Mary soon grew to dislike Darnley and refused to share power with him. When an Italian court musician named David Rizzio became Mary's confidante, Darnley joined a plot to murder Rizzio and seize the Scottish throne. He and a band of nobles broke into the queen's apartment at Holyrood Palace in Edinburgh and killed Rizzio in Mary's presence. The quick-thinking queen averted the coup attempt by talking Darnley over to her side, after which she escaped. Three months afterward she gave birth to Darnley's son James. She also fell in love with the Earl of Bothwell, one of her loyal nobles, and a short while later Darnley was found strangled to death.

Bothwell was charged but acquitted of the murder, and he quickly whisked Mary to Dunbar Castle where they were married. This flagrant behavior triggered a rebellion and Mary fled to England where she was welcomed by her cousin Queen Elizabeth I, who refused to hand Mary over to the Scottish government.

A privileged prisoner of the English government for the next 16 years, Mary schemed repeatedly with various nobles to depose Elizabeth. After several murderous plots were uncovered, Elizabeth – at the urging of Parliament – reluctantly ordered Mary's execution. Mary's 21-year-old son, James VI of Scotland, who had allied himself with Elizabeth to improve his prospects of succeeding to the English throne, did not intervene. His mother was beheaded at Fotheringhay Castle in February 1587 and when Elizabeth died in 1603, he became King James I of England, thus uniting Scotland and England under one crown. One of his acts as king was to move his mother's body to Westminster Abbey where he had a magnificent tomb built for her. A controversial figure in her lifetime, Mary Queen of Scots gained legendary status after death as a Catholic martyr and Scottish heroine.

married Elizabeth of York and united the House of Lancaster with the House of York, thus ending a longstanding feud between two powerful dynasties. His son, Henry VIII – a charismatic and much-loved king (before he became a bloodthirsty tyrant) – failed to produce a male heir with his first wife Catherine of Aragon. His determination to marry Anne Boleyn and produce the much-coveted male heir triggered a power struggle between the English king and the Catholic pope in Rome, who refused to grant King Henry an annulment of his first marriage. Henry's response was to break away from the papacy and make himself the supreme head of the Church of England, thus asserting the divine right of kings. Never had an English king been so powerful

– or paranoid. The Tudor claim to the throne was under constant threat by rival heirs and factions, and Henry's response was to charge anyone who was suspect with treason and send them to the Tower.

A well-known jingle may be sung about Henry VIII and his six wives, but an entire period of history – the Elizabethan Age – is named for the daughter he shared with Anne Boleyn. Elizabeth I's glorious reign brought prestige and prosperity to England, her royal coffers filled with riches captured from Spanish treasure ships by daring privateers such as Walter Raleigh and Francis Drake, who led the British fleet to victory against the Spanish Armada. Elizabeth successfully occupied the religious middle ground between the Catholics and the Puritan Protestants, but religious tensions returned under the Stuart kings, who officially recognized the Church of England but privately practised Catholicism.

Charles I, whose treasonous activities brought about a civil war, was executed and Oliver Cromwell became Lord Protector of a short-lived republic. When Cromwell died, the Stuart line was restored but once more resented under the kingship of James II, an avowed Catholic. Unpopular and autocratic, he was eventually run out of England during the Glorious Revolution and his Protestant daughter Mary and her husband William of Orange were offered the crown.

Elizabeth I of England

When the Stuart line ended with the death of Mary's sister Queen Anne in 1701, an Act of Settlement was drawn up which states that only Protestants can hold the throne. This act, which remains in effect to this day, ushered in the Hanoverian line of British monarchs (German-born George I was 52nd in line to the throne but the nearest Protestant). Queen Victoria, who was the last of the Hanoverian monarchs, married Prince Albert of the House of Saxe-Coburg-Gotha and their son, Edward VII, belonged to his father's line. In 1917, the Royal Family changed their official name to Windsor by a proclamation of George V, grandfather of Queen Elizabeth II.

The Russians

The lands that would eventually comprise Russia were initially invaded and settled by Finnic and East Slavic tribes which warred against each other. The origin of the Russian state is credited to the arrival of Scandinavian traders and warriors who were members of a noble Viking class called Varangian – also known as Rus. According to tradition, a Varangian prince named Rurik founded a ruling dynasty at Novgorod in 862. This new state became Kievan Russia when Rurik's successor moved the capital to Kiev.

In 988, Prince Vladimir the Great adopted Orthodox Christianity as the state religion, and this synthesis of Slavic and Byzantine influences would come to define Russian culture.

Russia's first czar, Ivan IV

In the 13th century, Turkish-speaking Mongol tribes invaded and founded the short-lived Empire of the Golden Horde, which collected taxes for the khan and introduced Asian and Muslim traditions to Russia.

Moscow eventually became the capital of the Russian national state and in 1547 Grand Duke Ivan IV was the first to assume the title of czar. Known as Ivan the Terrible, he also diminished the powers of the upper nobility by confiscating their lands in a reign of terror. His tyranny extended to personal relations. In one of his infamous fits of rage he accidentally killed his eldest son. Ivan himself was murdered by poisoning.

The Rurik dynasty ended shortly after the death of Ivan's sickly son and heir Feodor, and was followed by the Time of Troubles, in which several pretenders laid claim to the throne. Then, in 1613, a teenaged grandnephew of Ivan the Terrible was elected czar. His name was Michael Romanov and the dynasty he founded would rule Russia for the next three centuries.

The Romanov line included Peter the Great, who ruled from 1682 to 1725, and whose grand vision and constant wars with Sweden and the Ottoman Empire transformed Russia from nation to empire.

The Middle Ages

The Middle Ages, between the fall of Rome and the beginning of the Renaissance, were once viewed as a thousand years of darkness. The designation of Dark Ages now refers strictly to the Early Middle Ages (c. 450-750), when the collapse of the West Roman Empire plunged western Europe into turmoil as it endured waves of Germanic invasion by the Visigoths, Vandals, Franks, Ostrogoths and Lombards. Amid the political and social upheaval of western Europe, in which the Germanic and Roman cultures were assimilating, Christianity became a unifying force, despite an ongoing dispute between the pope in Rome and the patriarch in Constantinople, both of whom claimed leadership of Christendom.

In 800, Charlemagne, the Carolingian king of the Franks, was crowned emperor of the West by the pope in Rome, and this symbolic ceremony introduced a new concept: the interdependence of church and state. Such sharing of power did not exist in the Orthodox East, where the emperors embodied both spiritual and secular authority, regularly installing patriarchs of their choice. Charlemagne's splendid court was located not in Rome but in Aachen (now part of West Germany near the Belgian and Dutch borders), and the centre of civilization in western Europe shifted northward.

Feudalism, originating in the empire of Charlemagne, spread to neighbouring countries and provided protection from attack by plundering Germanic bands. An agricultural-based system of distributing wealth, feudalism was based on a hierarchy of king, nobility and peasantry. The nobles, who

Detail from the Bayeaux Tapestry depicting the Norman invasion of England in 1066.

held land directly from the king, provided protection to the serfs who worked the land. Chivalry, a fusion of Christian and military concepts, grew out of feudalism and inspired the Crusades – an attempt by western Europeans to regain the Holy Land from the Muslims. Monastic orders of knights were sworn to uphold the Christian ideal, and tournaments were staged in which knights could prove their chivalric virtues.

The Holy Roman Empire, successor state to the empire of Charlemagne, was established in 936, but its emperors, who were initially elected by German princes and crowned by the pope, were constantly struggling to assert their control over a fragmented western Europe. The papacy, surrounded by corruption, was weakened in 1083 when Rome was sacked by the Normans. In 1305, Pole Clement V moved the papal court to Avignon, where it came under French control until its return to Rome in 1378.

By the late Middle Ages, feudalism was firmly entrenched in France, but not in northern Italy, where the rise of the city state and the ascent of the merchant class eventually brought about the demise of feudalism, marking the end of the Middle Ages and the dawn of the Renaissance.

The Origins of Surnames

For centuries surnames in Europe were based on the father's first name. Eric, son of John, became Eric Johnson, or John, son of Eric, became John Ericsson. In Scotland, the prefix 'mac' meant son. Thus MacDonald meant son of Donald.

In Ireland, the Anglo-Norman prefix of 'fitz' ('son of') was widely adopted. Thus, Fitzgerald meant son of Gerald. (In the case of British royalty, Fitzroy meant 'son of the king' and the royal use of 'fitz' often implied illegitimacy.) In Ireland, the 'O' in names such as O'Brien meant 'grandson' or 'descendant of'. 'Van' is a widely used preposition in Dutch names (i.e. Vincent van Gogh) and it means 'of' or 'from'.

Until the Norman invasion of England in 1066, surnames were virtually unknown and were introduced by the Normans during the writing of the Doomsday Book. Over time, the need of new surnames resulted in the use of the father's occupation for his children. In Britain, common examples are Smith, Draper, Weaver, Thatcher and Baker. People who worked for the nobility acquired a surname reflecting this, such as Duke or Knight. Some surnames described the features of the landscape where the family lived, such as Hill, Marsh or Ford.

The tradition in Scandinavian countries, until it was abandoned in the 19th century, was for a newborn son to be granted a surname incorporating his father's first name and the suffix 'son' or 'sen' (eg. Jonson). Baby girls used the suffix 'dottir' (Jonsdottir). Today only Iceland has retained this tradition, which is why Icelanders commonly refer to each other by only their first names.

In Russia the ending of a person's surname differs between males and females, eg. Karenin (male) and Karenina (female). Middle names are derived from the father's first name and end with 'evich' or 'ovich' if a boy, and with 'ovna' or 'evna' if a girl. For example, children whose father is named Mikhail would be given the middle name Mikhailovich (boy) or Mikhailovna (girl). Ilyena Lydia Vasilievna Mironoff is the birth name of British actress Helen Mirren, whose father was Russian. His father was a czarist diplomat stationed in London when the revolution broke out and was unable to return home.

SPE ERIT   FORTITVDO

The Renaissance and Reformation

Called the *rinascita* in Italian and the *renaissance* in French, this 'rebirth' of classical antiquity's arts and sciences not only produced an outpouring of creativity never before seen, it ultimately ushered in modern civilization. The Renaissance, which originated in Italy, did not begin with a single momentous event but began as an artistic and intellectual movement that gradually gained momentum and eventually spread across Western Europe to Great Britain, where humanist thought influenced the works of writers Ben Jonson and William Shakespeare.

The seeds of the Renaissance's flowering were planted during the late Middle Ages, when a rediscovery of Greek and Roman literature led to the eventual development of the humanist movement. The Italian poet Petrarch, who lived from 1304 to 1374, is considered the first modern poet and the father of humanism. By proclaiming pagan antiquity as the most enlightened stage of history, and the centuries that followed as a time of darkness, he set in motion the pursuit of learning based on a secular rather than a religious framework. This humanistic challenge to scholasticism advocated not a pre-Christian paganism but a reconciliation of classical antiquity's artistic and intellectual achievements with Christian beliefs.

As medieval courtliness and codes of conduct gave way to a new era that focused on expressiveness and emotionalism, the social status of the artist was elevated. Stressing human values and capabilities, humanism's rejection of medieval religious authority climaxed in 1517 when the German cleric Martin Luther sparked the Protestant Reformation with his open attack on the doctrines of the wealthy and corrupt Catholic church. Condemning such practices as the sale of indulgences (pardons for sin), Luther believed that individuals could communicate directly with God and could seek salvation by reading the Bible, obtaining grace not through the sacraments (religious ceremonies conducted by priests) but through faith.

The growth of literacy, education and middle-class wealth

Martin Luther initiated the Protestant Reformation.

Rule Britannia

When Britain's Royal Navy defeated the combined French and Spanish fleets at Trafalgar in October 1805, this decisive naval battle ushered in an era of British supremacy at sea that remained unchallenged for over a century. At its height in the early 1900s, the British Empire comprised nearly one-quarter of the world's population and area. Its former colonies include the United States of America, Canada, Australia and New Zealand.

The iconic status of the Royal Navy endures to this day in Britain, where naval officers gather annually at the Portsmouth Historic Dockyard to pay homage to Admiral Horatio Nelson on the anniversary of his death at the Battle of Trafalgar. Nelson was felled on the deck of HMS Victory while commanding the outnumbered British fleet to victory, thus lifting the threat of invasion by Napoleon's armies. He died belowdecks and his body was preserved in a barrel of rum and transported back to England, where he was buried at St. Paul's Cathedral.

To honour their greatest naval hero and his victory at Trafalgar, the British staged a year-long 200th anniversary celebration in 2005, which included a re-enactment of Nelson's waterborne funeral procession up the River Thames.

provided a fertile environment for the new Protestant culture, which adopted an austere taste in Christian art, in contrast to the worldly opulence of Rome. Secular art was, however, patronized and new subject matters – landscapes, still lifes and scenes of daily life – formed part of the Renaissance taste in personal artwork, as did portraiture. Wealthy private collectors commissioned painters to decorate the walls, chests and other objects of their private palaces.

The scientific and intellectual achievements of the Renaissance, along with seaborne exploration and the discovery of new lands and cultures, fostered further learning in the 17th century. The rationalism of Descartes, the empiricism of Francis Bacon and John Locke, and the groundbreaking achievements of Sir Isaac Newton, widely considered the greatest scientist of all time, reflected an intensifying belief in natural law, universal order and human reason. The Renaissance also set the stage for an emerging middle class, which originated with the merchants and craftsmen in medieval towns and which eventually spearheaded the revolutionary upheavals of the 18th century.

Age of Enlightenment

The 18th century in Europe was called the Age of Enlightenment, an era marked by colonial expansion, scientific discoveries and mechanical inventions. The first

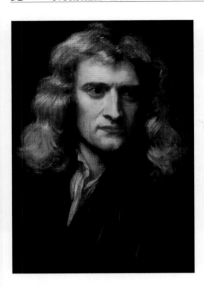

Isaac Newton, reputed as the greatest scientist who ever lived.

geographical survey was undertaken in France, as was the first flight in a hot-air balloon. Captain James Cook and other explorers opened up new territories across vast expanses of the Pacific Ocean, while Wolfgang Amadeus Mozart entertained the courts of Europe. Rational and scientific approaches were now applied to all issues – whether social, economic, religious or political. Amid a stimulating atmosphere of skepticism and idealism, Christianity was questioned and classical teachings were scrutinized. The French philosopher Voltaire even dared to declare that Plato "wrote better than he reasoned."

The most cataclysmic event of 18th-century Europe was the French Revolution, which began in 1789 and eventually affected the entire world as it tore down the medieval structures of Europe and made way for 19th-century liberalism and nationalism. France, not yet free of feudalism, was ripe for rebellion. The country was still ruled by two privileged classes, the nobility and the clergy, and a simmering resentment among the oppressed bourgeoisie and working classes led to widespread violence and anarchy. A Parisian mob's storming of the Bastille, a prison fortress, symbolized the revolt of the lower classes. In 1793, to the horror of other European monarchs, the king of France was beheaded, along with hundreds of aristocrats.

The army general Napoleon Bonaparte rose to dictatorial power in 1799 and had himself crowned emperor in 1804. Although the British navy defeated the French at Trafalgar in 1805, Napoleon soon controlled the European continent. The Holy Roman Empire dissolved in 1806, and Napoleon installed his brothers on the thrones of Europe. When Napoleon's massive army invaded Russia in 1812, it was repulsed and nearly annihilated by Russian forces in the winter of that year. This victory made Russia one of the leading powers of continental Europe and Czar Alexander I was a national hero. Napoleon was ultimately defeated by the allied forces of Britain, Prussia, Sweden and Austria in 1814 and exiled to the island of Elba off the coast of Italy, but he returned a year later, only to be defeated in the Waterloo Campaign and sent as a prisoner of war to the isolated British island of Saint Helena in the south Atlantic, where he died six years later.

The French monarchy was

restored, but unrest and rebellion continued, culminating in a bloody insurrection in 1848. The collapse of the French monarchy and the establishment of a new republic caused a chain reaction across Europe, spawning public demonstrations and a general cry for the overthrow of monarchies as an urban bourgeoisie called for constitutional, representative government. The most glaring exception was Russia. Alexander I had begun his reign with liberal reforms but became increasingly conservative, prompting the formation of secret political societies whose members, called Decembrists, were officers who had served in Europe during the Napoleonic Wars and had adopted western ideals of representative democracy. Alexander's brother Nicholas I came to power in 1825 while rumours swirled that Czar Alexander had not died but had fled to Siberia to become a hermit. Amid the confusion, a failed insurrection by Decembrists resulted in five of their leaders being executed.

It seemed at last that democratic reform would come to Russia with the ascent of Alexander II. He abolished serfdom in 1861 and freed 23 millions serfs (of a total Russian population of 62 million). However, the terms were so unfavourable that the liberated serfs were in effect thrown into lives of poverty and hopelessness. Many moved to St. Petersburg to work in the factories, where crowded and unsanitary living conditions festered discontent and stoked revolutionary sentiments. In 1880, Alexander II was nearly

Emperor Napoleon Bonaparte

Schleswig-Holstein

For centuries, the ongoing power struggles and changing alliances in Europe resulted in the swapping of territories and shifting of borders. One example of this is the border between Germany and Denmark on the Jutland peninsula. This area of fertile farmland and natural harbours changed hands numerous times over the centuries, prompting the 19th-century British statesman Lord Palmerston to state, "The Schleswig-Holstein question is so complicated, only three men in Europe have ever understood it. One was Prince Albert, who is dead. The second was a German professor, who became mad. I am the third and I have forgotten all about it." Dubbed Lord Pumice Stone for his abrasive and outspoken gunboat diplomacy, Palmerston also famously said, "Nations have no permanent friends or allies, they only have permanent interests."

killed when an infiltrator planted a bomb two floors beneath the main dining room at the Winter Palace. The czar and his family were late coming to dinner the evening the bomb exploded and they escaped injury, although Alexander was later assassinated in the streets of St. Petersburg.

The Grand Tour

Propelling the social and political upheaval of Europe was the Industrial Revolution. Originating in England in the mid-1700s, it marked Europe's transition from an agricultural-based society to a modern industrialized society. The steam engine was invented in England in 1698 and by 1814 the steam locomotive was being used to power early rail travel, followed by the first steamship crossing of the Atlantic in 1819. Europe began rapidly industrializing, building roads and rail lines. The railroad revolutionized travel, for people could now journey across the continent in a fraction of the time it had once taken. Leisure travel, formerly the reserve of the privileged wealthy, would soon become the domain of the masses.

Leisure travel to the Continent originated with the grand tours of the British aristocracy. By the mid-18th century, it was commonplace for the young men of Britain's upper classes to embark on an educational tour of Europe to acquaint themselves with famous classical ruins and the Renaissance art of Rome and other Italian cities. Although politically fragmented and in a state of economic decline, Italy was still considered the heart of western culture. Britain had become the wealthiest nation in the world due to its colonial trade, but its privileged classes, who were schooled in Latin and the classics, felt isolated from the cultural riches of Europe. Thus, a Grand Tour was considered necessary for a person to become a fully educated member of elite society.

The French Revolution and the Napoleonic Wars interrupted continental touring by the British, but the defeat of Napoleon at Waterloo in 1815 brought peace to the continent. One of the first postwar travellers into mainland Europe was Lord Byron, followed by Keats and Shelley. These Romantic poets' literary works spawned a fresh British interest in the antiquities of continental Europe, and the first modern guidebooks appeared around this time. William Thackeray, Charles Dickens and Mark Twain were among the popular writers given free passage on steamships in exchange for writing a book about their travels. By the end of

A British tour group poses for a photograph at Pompeii.

the 19th century, the Americans were second only to the British in terms of numbers touring Europe.

In 1841, an English cabinet maker named Thomas Cook organized the first group excursion when he obtained reduced train fares for members of his temperance society, who were travelling to a regional meeting. His organizational skills soon led to a new concept – the guided tour. These packaged holidays appealed to average Britons of modest means who wanted to travel abroad and see the sights previously enjoyed only by the wealthy, who would spend months, even years, completing their grand tours.

As British and American tourists began travelling through continental Europe in steadily increasing numbers, the wealthy elite sought ever more exclusive and exotic destinations. Luxury travel, in the form of Pullman rail cars, grand hotels and palatial steamships, enabled the wealthy to isolate themselves from the travelling masses. By the end of the industrial revolution, the 'high bourgeoisie', consisting of rich industrialists and bankers, were distinguishing themselves from the 'petty bourgeoisie', which comprised tradespeople and white-collar workers. The bourgeoisie's preoccupation with status and material gain had long been ridiculed, beginning in the 17th century with witty satires by the French playwright Moliere, who was himself the son of a merchant, but some of society's commentators rose to the defence of working men and women, including Karl Marx, who interpreted attacks on the upwardly mobile classes as an effort to subdue the wage-earning proletariat.

Another movement, fostered during the Age of Enlightenment, was the construction of art museums, galleries and academies, including the famous British Museum, which was established in 1753 and began occupying its present buildings in 1829. The Athenian monuments of ancient Greece sparked public interest in England when Lord Elgin, the British ambassador to Turkey (which at that time ruled Greece), removed numerous marble sculptures from the Parthenon. Byron was among those critical of Elgin, who defended his actions in a pamphlet he wrote in 1820, claiming he wanted to protect the Greek sculptures from destruction under Turkish rule. In any event,

Faux-Egyptian sphinxes flank Cleopatra's Needle – an ancient obelisk given by Egypt to Great Britain and installed on the Thames Embankment in 1878.

the 'Elgin marbles', currently in the British Museum, stimulated a strong interest in ancient Greece among the English Romantic poets and became the subject of a poem by John Keats entitled 'On Seeing the Elgin Marbles.'

Egypt also became a source of historical interest when the Rosetta Stone, a slab of black basalt engraved with hieroglyphics, was discovered at the mouth of the Nile by scientists accompanying Napoleon on his Egyptian campaign of 1798. Deciphered a quarter of a century later by the French scholar Jean Francois Champollion, the Rosetta Stone's inscriptions provided the first key to understanding the language and lives of the ancient Egyptians. Scientific findings from Napoleon's Egyptian campaign were published in 21 volumes over a 20-year period, thus launching Europe's fascination with ancient Egypt.

Museums began indiscriminately collecting Egyptian antiquities, as dozens of explorers and collectors dug through the desert sands in search of treasures. Eventually a more systematic process was enforced following the British occupation of Egypt in 1882, with all excavated objects recorded and catalogued. Meanwhile, the Egyptian government had made diplomatic gifts of several New Kingdom obelisks, presenting France with one from the Luxor temple, which now stands in the Place de la Concorde in Paris, and sending one of Cleopatra's Needles to England where it was re-erected on the Thames Embankment.

By the end of the 19th century, advancements in science, mathematics and engineering had produced the diesel and turbine engines, the electric motor, the automobile, the light bulb and the camera. The invention of photography introduced a new medium to the visual arts, and helped fuel the growth of tourism, as people were increasingly exposed to photographic images of faraway lands and exotic cultures.

The British Museum houses famous ancient artifacts.

The Rise and Fall of the Soviet Union

The last Russian czar, Nicholas II, had already moved with his family to Alexander Palace outside St. Petersburg when thousands of downtrodden factory workers staged a peaceful protest march one cold Sunday in January 1905 to petition their czar for reforms. As they approached the Winter Palace, singing patriotic hymns and clutching religious icons, the response from the Imperial Guard was to gun them down. This act of barbarism was the catalyst for the 1905 Revolution, spurred by widespread discontent and the disastrous Russo-Japanese War which revealed the corruption and incompetence of the regime. The outcome was that Czar Nicholas was forced to govern with a parliamentary body – the Duma – but repression continued until 1917 when, amid the chaos of World War I, the February Revolution forced the abdication of Nicholas II. In October of that year, the pro-

Czar Nicholas II and his family shortly before their arrest.

visional government was toppled when the Bolsheviks, led by their founder Vladimir Lenin, stormed the Winter Palace. The former czar and his family were placed under house arrest and eventually relocated to a mansion in Yekaterinburg in Central Russia where, in July 1918, they were herded into a cellar and murdered by a squad of Bolshevik gunmen and Hungarian prisoners of war, the latter used in case Russian soldiers refused to shoot.

A civil war raged between the Bolshevik (Red) and anti-Bolshevik (White) forces until 1920. The Bolsheviks emerged victorious and Lenin was now the undisputed leader of a new communist regime that would prove to be as repressive as Czarist Russia. When Joseph Stalin succeeded Lenin as head of the USSR in 1924, he embarked on a reign of terror in which millions of

Russians, many of them political prisoners, were exiled, imprisoned or executed in his infamous purges. He also led Russia to victory in the Second World War, a feat for which he is still hailed as a hero by many Russians, despite the atrocities he inflicted on his own people.

The USSR had signed a non-aggression pact with Nazi Germany in 1939 but two years later Hitler launched a surprise attack. St. Petersburg endured a 900-day siege of bombings and food shortages, with over half a million residents dying. It's estimated that a total of 20 million Russians – soldiers and civilians – lost their lives repelling the German invasion, many dying of starvation. Following the war, the USSR's relations with the United States of America deteriorated into the cold war era of massive military build-ups on both sides as an "iron curtain" descended between the West and the Communist bloc.

The situation came to a head in the 1980s when American President Ronald Reagan embarked on an arms race with the Soviets. In the end, the United States defeated its Cold War adversary because the Soviet economy was no match for the Americans

(Top to bottom)
Lenin; Stalin with
German minister
von Ribbentrop
at signing of non-
aggression pact;
Gorbachev and
Reagan.

who outspent their foes until they capitulated. Warmer relations prevailed as the Soviet leader Mikhail Gorbachev focused on resuscitating his nation's moribund economy by introducing a new openness (*glasnost*) and sweeping out government corruption and abuse of power. His ambitious restructuring plan – called Perestroika – was met with resistance, and even his supporters criticized him – for setting too slow a pace. These included Boris Yeltsin, a populist advocate of radical reform who emerged a national hero in August 1991 when members of the Communist Party placed Gorbachev under house arrest at his villa in the Crimea and sent army tanks to the Russian Parliament in Moscow to arrest Yeltsin. A defiant Yeltsin, supported by armed and unarmed civilians who had surrounded the building, climbed onto a tank and delivered a plea to the Russian soldiers who then turned to join Yeltsin's supporters and peacefully ended the stand-off.

The reigns of power were now in Yeltsin's hands and by year's end the USSR no longer existed. Gorbachev resigned and Yeltsin, now president of the Russian Federation, faced economic turmoil created by the collapse of the Soviet Union. As poverty swept across Russia, Yeltsin's democracy became as corrupt as had Soviet communism or czarist imperialism. Under Yeltsin's drive to privatize industry, a small number of entrepreneurs – called oligarchs – acquired vast state interests. Their excessive and ill-gained wealth was in stark contrast to the dire conditions of the average Russian, and public support for Yeltsin plummeted.

Yeltsin's hand-picked successor, Vladimir Putin, was everything the gregarious and erratic Yeltsin was not. A former KGB agent, Putin displayed the authoritarianism traditionally valued in Russian leaders as he restored economic order and national pride to his country. Criticized by western observers for backtracking on democratic reforms, Putin enjoys tremendous popularity with the Russian people. When Russia's wealthiest oligarch, oil tycoon Mikhail Khodorkovsky, began challenging Putin's monopoly on power, he was arrested at gunpoint on charges of fraud and tax evasion. He futilely defended himself from a cage at his year-long trial and was sentenced in 2005 to nine years in prison, all of which cast doubt on the rule of law in Russia but was applauded by many Russians who approved of Putin's crackdown on corruption.

Vladimir Putin

CHURCHILL

Sir Winston Churchill once wrote, "History will be kind to me, for I intend to write it." He could also have said "for I intend to make it." In his long life he achieved distinction as a soldier, politician, journalist and historian, winning the Nobel Prize for Literature in 1953 for his epic History of the Second World War. He was a political maverick, deeply distrusted by many politicians and voters, but just when his career seemed finished he emerged, at the age of 65, to lead his country as Prime Minister through the greatest conflict in its history.

Winston Leonard Spencer-Churchill was born in 1874 into one of the Britain's leading aristocratic families, a grandson of the Duke of Marlborough. His mother, Jennie Jerome, was the daughter of an American business tycoon, and throughout his life he enjoyed a special relationship with the United States. After an unhappy childhood and school days in which he showed ability only in English and history, he was commissioned as an army officer and saw service in the British Empire's campaigns on the Indian Northwest Frontier and in Sudan. There he discovered a talent for war reporting, and his escapades as a correspondent during the South African War made him a minor national hero and helped launch a political career.

Four years after his election as a Conservative Member of Parliament he scandalised the political establishment by crossing over to the Liberal Party. At the start of World War I he was in charge of the Royal Navy as First Lord of the Admiralty, but his decision to stage an amphibious landing at Gallipoli in 1915 led to a military disaster and his resignation. He then served as a junior army officer on the Western Front but was later recalled to government. He was a minister in British governments of the 1920s, and survived the controversy caused by his changing political sides again, back to the Conservatives, but his economic, social and foreign policies were full of serious shortcomings — as he later admitted.

During the 1930s Churchill foresaw the growing threat to world peace and realised Britain's lack of preparedness for war. However, his earlier political blunders made it easy to ignore his advocacy of rearmament. When war broke out in 1939 Churchill was appointed again as First Lord of the Admiralty and

Churchill proposed to his wife Clementine Hozier (left) at his family's ancestral home of Blenheim Palace (below) near Woodstock.

CHURCHILL

the Royal Navy sent out the signal "Winston is back." Early British defeats and failures led to the fall of the Chamberlain government, and in 1940, with Chamberlain's support, Churchill was called on by the King to head a national, all-party government to fight the war.

Churchill's unswerving refusal to surrender or to seek a dishonourable peace, even during the darkest moments of the war, and his establishing a close relationship with President Roosevelt and the United States, were key factors that enabled Britain to hold out until the tide of the war turned. Above all, his gift for oratory raised the morale of the British and their allies. His first address to the nation on becoming Prime Minister contained the legendary words "I have nothing to offer but blood, toil, tears and sweat."

On May 8, 1945 Germany surrendered and Britain celebrated Victory in Europe Day. Churchill told a huge crowd in Whitehall, "This is your victory." The people shouted back, "No, it's yours." But he was soon voted out of office by a population that preferred less conservative views on issues of reform and social welfare. Churchill remained influential, however, and in 1946 he coined the phrase "the Iron Curtain" to describe the advance of Soviet Communism in Europe. He was returned to power in 1951, but ill health forced him to retire from government a few years later. When Churchill died in 1965 at the age of 90, he was granted a state funeral (a rare honour for a non-royal) and representatives of more than 100 countries came to pay their respects. Winston Churchill's life was full of controversy and contradictions, but in 2002 a BBC poll of his fellow-countrymen voted him 'the greatest Briton of all time.'

(Top) Churchill in 1942. (Middle) Churchill surveys the ruins of Coventry Cathedral, 1941. (Bottom) Churchill, Roosevelt and Stalin at Yalta in 1945.

Modern Europe

The 20th century began with optimism, preceded by a long era of relative peace. However, the decaying Ottoman Empire had left the Balkan territories susceptible to diplomatic intrigue among the European powers of Austria, Britain, Germany, Russia and France. The imperialistic, territorial and economic rivalries of these countries, along with a rampant spirit of nationalism, all contributed to the outbreak of World War I. Called the Great War, it was the largest war the world had yet seen, fought chiefly in the trenches of France and Belgium. When the First World War ended on November 11, 1918, without a single decisive battle having been fought, at least 10 million people had been killed and 20 million wounded, with additional deaths from starvation and epidemics in the war's aftermath.

The face of Europe had radically changed, and a general revulsion to the destruction and suffering of war was symbolized by the creation of the League of Nations. Still, a fervent nationalism soon resurfaced in several countries where the hardships of the Great Depression made the masses vulnerable to the promises of demagogues. Adolf Hitler rose to power in Germany in 1933 and promptly began rebuilding the German army in preparation for a war of conquest. When Germany invaded Poland on September 1, 1939, the democratic governments of Britain and France declared war. Soon all of Europe was pulled back into the war, with Germany quickly occupying Poland, France, Denmark, Norway and Sweden.

The great war leader Winston Churchill, who is widely regarded as the personification of British fortitude, led Britain through her

(Top) Hitler saluting troops in Warsaw at the start of World War Two. (Left) Home Guard in London watches for enemy aircraft during the Battle of Britain.

darkest hour when the nation faced imminent invasion by Nazi Germany in 1940. The British airforce was victorious in the Battle of Britain, which was waged in the skies over the English Channel, but the major turning point came with Japan's surprise attack on Pearl Harbor in 1941. This devastating blow propelled the United States into the war in Europe as well as the Pacific. America mobilized and within three years had amassed huge armies in England alongside British and Canadian troops.

On June 6, 1944, D-Day – the Allied invasion and liberation of occupied Europe – began. German resistance continued until Hitler's suicide in April 1945, with Germany surrendering to the Allies in May 1945. An Allied victory in the Pacific brought the war to an end in August of that year, but the devastation it had wreaked remains horrifying to contemplate. Europe, the cradle of Western civilization, had become the most uncivilized place on earth. Modern warfare had brought upon the world a barbarism of such scale that previous wars paled in comparison. The blanket bombing of cities and Germany's systematic attempt to exterminate entire racial groups had terrorized civilians as well as soldiers and caused millions to die. In the war's aftermath, a vanquished Germany was partitioned into four zones – American, British, French and Russian. The Russian zone became East Germany when the Iron Curtain descended, dividing Europe into the Soviet bloc of communist countries and the Western bloc of free democracies.

In post-war Europe, a widespread aversion to the national rivalries that had provoked such bloodshed and destruction prompted the idea of a united Europe as a way to provide strength and security to the wartorn region and prevent further hostilities. The European

American troops landing at Omaha Beach on June 6, 1944.

The European Central Bank in Frankfurt governs the Eurozone's monetary policy.

Economic Community (known informally as the Common Market and today called the European Union) was established in the 1950s as an economic and political confederation of European nations. Its original members were West Germany and France, soon joined by Belgium, Luxembourg, the Netherlands and Italy. Great Britain, Ireland and Denmark joined the EU in 1973. A central banking system was provided by the 1992 Maastricht Treaty, and the gradual introduction of a common currency – the euro – was completed in 2002, the national currencies of 300 million Europeans replaced with 10 billion new bills and 50 billion new coins. Not since the 8th century, when Charlemagne circulated his own silver coinage throughout his empire, had Europe used a common currency. Its introduction created the practice of 'rounding up' prices, thus making some things more expensive for locals.

Joining the European Union has been a hotly debated issue for the citizens of Europe, in both its member and candidate nations. Fierce national rivalries remain, as do economic disparities, which were painfully revealed by the debt crisis that swept across much of Europe following the global recession of 2008. Some member nations, including Britain, Denmark and Sweden, have not adopted the euro as their unit of currency.

The 21st Century

Europe's societies have become increasingly diverse in recent decades, with several countries – including England, France and the Netherlands – now containing substantial Muslim minorities. These nations, in which social tolerance and freedom of speech are core values, have experienced cultural tensions as these newcomers assimilate, and several high-profile crimes by religious extremists have polarized the issue of immigration.

Western Europe's first suicide bombings took place in London, in July 2005, when the city's transit system was targeted by British-born militant Muslims. This was the deadliest attack on London since the Second World War, with the bombs killing 52 people and injuring more than 700.

Royal Foot Guards

The military uniform of the Queen's Guards in England is distinctive for its bearskin helmet. Made from the fur of Canadian black bears, these busby hats have been worn by the Regiments of Footguards since the defeat of Napoleon in 1815. However, in recent years animal rights activists have protested the use of real fur and pressured the British Army to find a synthetic replacement. Traditionally, the bear pelt is stretched over a bamboo frame to create a water-repellant and long-lasting hat. The outer layer of course fur keeps rain out and the layer of fine fur underneath retains warmth. Finding a substitute has been challenging, with nylon losing its shape, becoming spiky when wet and standing on end with static electricity in certain weather conditions.

As Europe faces a new war against terrorism, old scores are still being settled. Efforts to regain the spoils of Holocaust plunder have intensified, with governments and individuals pressuring museums to return Nazi-looted artwork to their rightful owners, who are often descendants of the original owner.

The question of rightful ownership is a contentious issue. In the case of the disputed Eberswalde Hoard – a collection of Bronze Age artifacts removed from a Berlin museum by Soviet troops during WWII – the Russian government regards these treasures as part of reparations for the damage inflicted by Hitler's troops when they invaded Russia.

Similar disputes have arisen long before WWII. The Greek government has pleaded for decades with the British Museum to return marble sculptures taken from the Parthenon in 1802 by Lord Elgin, British ambassador to Greece when it was under Turkish occupation. Meanwhile, Egypt has sought the return of the Rosetta Stone, also in the British Museum. But these attempts to repatriate cultural property have clashed with the mandate of museums, which is to preserve artifacts that might otherwise have been lost or damaged.

In Britain, where people are still discovering ancient treasures in their back gardens, relic hunting is a popular hobby. In 2002, an amateur archeologist armed with a metal detector was sweeping a farmer's field near Sandwich, Kent, when he discovered a Bronze Age artifact. This hand-beaten gold-and-silver cup dating from about 1700 BC was buried less than half a metre in the ground and had been struck by a plow. Whenever anyone in

Britain finds a treasure — defined under Britain's 1996 Treasure Act as an object consisting of at least 10% gold or silver and buried at least 300 years ago – its value is assessed by an independent panel of experts and the money is split between finder and landowner.

Treasure is not the only thing found in the ground. In 2012, a skeleton discovered under a Leicester parking lot was identified through DNA tests, bone analysis and other scientific scrutiny as that of King Richard III, who was killed in battle in 1485 and quickly buried without a coffin in a church that was later demolished.

One of the largest archeological digs is taking place in the British capital alongside work crews tunneling deep beneath city streets with huge boring machines to build the new underground Crossrail line. Excavations have unearthed the remains of a Roman road dotted with ancient horseshoes made of metal and fastened to the animals'

SPY VS SPY

The Cold War might be over but the business of spying continues to thrive, especially on the streets of London. With more than 66,000 Russian nationals on the run abroad, Kremlin officials are pointing the finger at 'Londongrad' for harbouring some of Russia's most prominent exiles. Among those who found sanctuary in Britain was billionaire oligarch Boris Berezovsky, wanted on embezzlement charges in Russia but granted political asylum by British authorities. The controversial tycoon hanged himself in his Berkshire mansion in 2014.

Meanwhile, Russia has refused to extradite ex-KGB agent Andrei Lugovoi, who is wanted in Britain in connection with the 2006 murder by poisoning of former Russian agent Alexander Litvinenko, who was an outspoken critic of Vladimir Putin and, according to his widow, an agent working for MI6. A lethal dose of radioactive isotope polonium 210 was slipped into Litvinenko's cup of tea while meeting with Lugovoi at a Mayfair hotel, and doctors were unable to save him from a slow death in a London hospital.

Secrecy once surrounded the location of Britain's external secret intelligence service – MI6 – but today the location of its headquarters is public knowledge, as is the identify of its chief (known as 'C' during the Cold War era of the 1950s and '60s when the James Bond movies adopted 'M' as their chief). MI6's fortress-like building is situated at 85 Albert Embankment, next to Vauxhall Bridge. Although no longer shrouded in secrecy, its walls are bombproof and its windows block electronic spying. And no visitors are allowed.

MI6 headquarters in London

All in the Family

When Queen Elizabeth II hosts a family reunion, invitations go out to most of the remaining monarchs of Europe. Following centuries of arranged marriages among Europe's royal houses, their family trees have more interconnecting branches than a banyan tree. Distant cousins invited to the Queen's Golden Jubilee celebratory dinner at Windsor Castle in 2002 included King Harald of Norway, Queen Beatrix of the Netherlands, Queen Margrethe of Denmark and King Carl XVI Gustav of Sweden.

Such ceremonial gatherings of constitutional monarchs is more about pomp and pageantry than political power, but it was a different matter a century ago when the crowned heads of Russia and Germany still governed their countries.

Three European monarchs, all grandchildren of Queen Victoria, were central players in the chaos that descended on Europe in the early 20th century. The German kaiser, Wilhelm II, who was self conscious about his deformed arm, felt snubbed by his British royal cousins, who in fact had more German than English blood flowing in their veins.

Nonetheless, Wilhelm was compelled to build a navy that would prove Germany's superiority over the British. If only Wilhelm hadn't taken it personally, for George V was also ambivalent toward his Russian cousin

Queen Elizabeth and Prince Philip at Trooping the Colour

Nicholas II, refusing the deposed czar and his family safe haven in England for fear it would alienate his British subjects.

hooves with leather straps. Other finds range from pre-historic mammoth bones to medieval ice skates. One of the most important finds are the human skeletons of victims of the Black Death, which wiped out more than half of the city's population. Scientific analysis of these remains is shedding new light on the cause of this 14th century plague.

Elgin Marbles, British Museum

Prehistoric & Ancient Art

Prehistoric rock carvings at Tanumshede in Sweden.

The countries of Northern Europe are rich in prehistoric artifacts and monuments such as rock art, cave paintings and massive standing stones. By the 5th century BC, Celtic tribes inhabited southern Germany and eastern France. As these tribes dispersed throughout Europe and the British Isles, they developed an artistry that featured geometrical and intertwining patterns, and stylized plant and animal forms. Celtic artisans decorated the surfaces of weapons, vessels and utensils, producing highly ornamented items of craftsmanship.

When the Roman Empire began spreading westward, it brought to these faraway lands a new influence – the art and architecture of Classical Greece. The Romans, who were great admirers and imitators of Greek art and culture, were also great builders and architectural engineers, their designs stressing power and boldness in contrast to the Greek emphasis on harmony and beauty. By perfecting the use of brick and concrete, the Romans were able to use arches and vaults to create large buildings with complex and spacious interiors. They embarked on vast construction projects throughout their growing empire, building roads, aqueducts and bridges, and laying out new cities and towns according to a logical plan with an emphasis on drainage, water supply and zoning. Each urban centre had a forum – an open public square surrounded by temples, exchanges and basilicas (law courts).

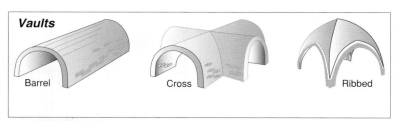

Vaults

Barrel   Cross   Ribbed

The Romans erected free-standing commemorative columns (similar to the obelisks of Ancient Egypt) and built triumphal arches to honour an emperor or commemorate a military triumph. These arches were built throughout the empire and would often span a road. Roman roads were usually built in a straight line, their uppermost layer of pavement made with concrete or pebbles set in mortar.

Roman art was highly imitative and eclectic, reflecting the various cultures encompassed by its far-reaching empire. Pseudo-Egyptian statuary were popular, but it was Greek art that thoroughly permeated Roman tastes. Modifications were made to reflect the Roman emphasis on action and strength, and a distinct Roman style of portraiture developed which combined Greek idealism with Roman realism. Then, in about 200 AD, just as Roman art was fusing with Greek, the doctrines of Christianity, including denunciation of all pleasures of the flesh, shattered the synthesizing process.

Celtic Parade Helmet (c. 350 BC) found buried in a cave in France. (Below) Portland Vase.

The Portland Vase

The famous Portland Vase (1st century BC) was excavated near Rome in the 17th century. Made of dark blue glass overlaid with white cameo relief, the vase was widely copied, most notably in jasper ware by Josiah Wedgwood. It was eventually acquired by the Duke of Portland, who lent it to the British Museum. In 1845, a deranged museum visitor smashed the priceless vase to pieces, but it was skillfully restored and remains on display.

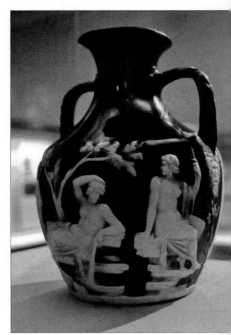

arcade – a series of arches supported by piers or columns; called a 'blind arcade' when attached to a wall.

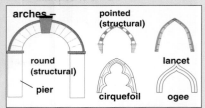

a r t categories – fine art is any painting, drawing or sculpture that is aesthetically beautiful. In free art, the object is purely ornamental. Decorative art adorns a useful object, such as a flower painted on a plate. The applied arts are functional and include the crafts of weaving, furniture-making, glassmaking and ceramics.

balustrade – railing supported by short pillars, called balusters.

basilica – in ancient Rome, a large rectangular building containing the law courts and serving as a public meeting place. Elements of the Roman basilica were later implemented in Christian churches

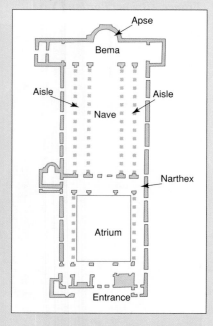

(see illustration below). Differing from the longitudinal, basilica-plan church is the central-plan church (also called Greek-cross church) which has four arms of equal length.

battlement – a parapet punctuated with open spaces (crenels).

caryatid – a sculptured female figure serving as a structural support, used in Egyptian and Greek architecture. A celebrated example is the Porch of the Caryatids atop the Acropolis in Athens.

cathedral – church in which a bishop resides (see illustration below). Important cathedrals include Notre-Dame in Paris, St. Paul's in London, Canterbury Cathedral in Kent, St. Isaac's in St. Petersburg and Trondheim Cathedral in Norway.

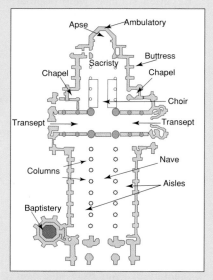

clerestory – an upper row of openings or windows that is higher than the rest of the structure. Implemented in certain Egyptian temples, this feature was later used in the great halls of Roman basilicas and became a characteristic element of Gothic churches.

colonnade – a row of columns supporting either an entablature or a series of arches.

TALKING ART & ARCHITECTURE

crenellation – a style of fortification in which a battlement contains open spaces (crenels) for firing.

fresco – the Italian word for 'fresh'; a technique of painting on wet plaster so that the paint becomes part of the wall.

frieze – a continuous band of painted or sculptured decoration.

gold leaf – gold beaten into very thin 'leaves' and applied to illuminated manuscripts and panel paintings.

icon – small panel painting of a sacred image, usually Christ, the Virgin Mary or a saint.

keep – innermost and strongest tower of a medieval castle, often containing living quarters.

loggia – an open-air, covered arcade, either free-standing or running alongside a building.

lustreware – pottery finished with an overglaze containing copper and silver to create an iridescent effect. Initially used by Islamic potters, the technique was practiced in Moorish Spain and later adopted by Josiah Wedgwood in 18th-century England.

majolica – a technique of decorating and glazing pottery that was highly developed in medieval Italy, beginning in the 11th century, and named for the island of Majorca where the craft was first introduced by Muslim artisans.

mosaic – decorative work in which surfaces are covered with small pieces of colored materials, such as marble or glass, that are set in plaster or concrete.

orders of architecture – a system devised in Roman times to categorize architectural styles. The three main orders are Doric, Ionic and Corinthian (see illustration on page 78). Tuscan is a simplified version of Doric, with unfluted columns. Composite combines Ionic and Corinthian. Colossal is any order with columns or pillars rising above one storey.

palazzo – stately residence or government building.

pantheon – temple dedicated to all the gods.

parapet – low wall on the edge of a platform such as those atop a fortress wall.

parquetry – geometrically patterned wood, laid especially for floors.

pediment – triangular area formed by a gabled roof. A feature of Greek temples, it later became a decorative motif as well, used chiefly over doors and windows. lap.

pillar – general term for upright structural supports, including columns (which are cylindrical), piers (which are square or rectangular) and pilasters (which are piers that project from a wall surface and are generally decorative rather than structural).

portal – a monumental door or gate.

portcullis – a heavy iron gate at a castle's entrance.

portico – a columned porch.

relief – figures carved from a flat surface. High relief is deeply carved so that the figures are almost fully detached from their support. Bas-relief consists of low sculptures that barely protrude.

rose window – a large circular window of stained glass and ornamental stonework (tracery), frequently used in Gothic churches.

rustication – a masonry technique that creates a roughly textured surface by projecting blocks of stone beyond the mortar joints.

tempera – form of painting used before the development of oil painting, in which pigments were mixed with egg yolk and water.

terracotta – Italian word for 'baked earth'; a fired, unglazed clay of varying colour (depending on the type of clay), but often a shade of red. One of the oldest known building materials, it is used for pottery and architectural ornament.

turret – a small lookout tower atop a larger tower or structure.

trompe-l'oeil – French for 'deceives the eye'; painting style that utilizes realism and perspective to create the illusion that what is depicted actually exists, i.e. a door or window painted on a wall.

The Medieval Period

Medieval cities, facing barbarian invasions and pirate attacks, were designed with security in mind and were protected by thick walls. The only open areas amid the narrow winding streets were municipal or church squares. Fires were devastating, spreading quickly through closely spaced timbered and thatched buildings. Fortresses, castles, even monasteries were built for defence.

It took about ten years to construct a

Dover Castle (above) and Tallinn's medieval walls (below).

castle, employing hundreds of stonemasons, carpenters, blacksmiths and labourers, all under the charge of a master mason. Walls were built with an outer and inner skin of fine stone, in between which was poured rubble and mortar (lime mixed with sand) to form a thick solid wall. A moat usually surrounded the castle, which was accessed by a drawbridge that could be raised and lowered on a winch. The portcullis, a heavy grilled gate, could be dropped in an instant to bar entry. The castle's outer wall was usually about 30 feet (9 m) high and punctuated with massive watch towers. It encircled the castle keep – the great tower – which contained the lord's living quarters, including a banquet hall. Winding stone staircases led to the top of the keep's watchtowers where turrets provided archers with a commanding view of the approaches to the castle.

Early churches, inspired by Imperial Rome, were basilican in design and decorated with Byzantine-style mosaics. Eastern influences had been introduced during the time of Constantine, who moved the Roman Empire's capital from Rome to Byzantium and renamed it Constantinople. In Russia, the earliest painters of religious art were Greeks or Greek-trained Russians of the Byzantine school of iconography.

The 9th century's Carolingian style, so named for the Frankish emperor Charlemagne, was followed by the Romanesque ('in the manner of the Roman') and its variants, such as Norman and Gothic. Local styles developed under the generic name Romanesque, but common features included the rounded arch and vault, as well as heavy walls and piers for structural support.

A visitor ascends a winding stone staircase in the Tower of London. (Below) Urnes stave church in Norway.

In Scandinavia, the early churches were built entirely of wood using a simple post construction which evolved into an architectural style called *stavkirke* or stave church (stave means 'post' in Old Norse) which brought together Celtic art, the Viking use of animal forms and Romanesque spatial structuring. In Russia the early churches also were made mostly of wood and bore strong Norse stylistic influences. The distinctive onion-shaped domes of Russian churches began appearing in the mid-12th century.

The Gothic style originated in France in about 1150 and flourished until 1450, especially in the cathedrals of northern Europe. Churches became airy and soar-

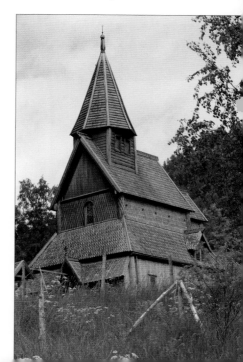

(Above) Beautiful stained glass in Notre Dame Cathedral, Paris. (Below) Leonardo da Vinci's Madonna and the Child, safely behind glass at the Hermitage.

ing, with pointed arches and vaults, slender piers and counter-balancing flying buttresses. Walls were thin and windows were large to allow a mystical and wondrous light to filter through their panes of stained glass. The sculpting of gargoyles in the form of beasts and grotesque human forms reached its peak in the Gothic period, after which the use of these ornate waterspouts was gradually replaced with lead drainpipes. All other visual art forms were dominated by architecture during the Gothic period, with sculpture and stained glass integrated into the churches.

The Renaissance

The Italian Renaissance, which began shortly after 1400 in Florence, ushered in a new and exciting age. Whereas medieval towns were built with moats, fortresses and high walls for protection from marauding bands, Renaissance cities were built with monumental views provided by wide avenues and long approaches. Palaces replaced fortified castles as royal residences, their gated grounds containing manicured gardens. New World discoveries contributed to the joy of expansion, but it was a revival of classical antiquity that formed the basis of Renaissance art.

In painting, as in the other visual arts, the Renaissance artist sought perfection. Three staggered planes – foreground, middle distance and background – were used to achieve perspective depth, and the painting's figures were harmoniously arranged, their expressive gestures achieving a heightened emotional intensity. In sculpture, the freestanding nude figures of the Renaissance marked the end of a medieval interdependence of architecture and sculpture. In architecture, the classical ideals of order, symmetry and unity were adopted. Rome's structural elements – arches, vaults and domes – were used in original combinations, with the dome symbolizing Renaissance man's pursuit of both learning and clarity.

Although the Renaissance artist was liberated from medieval convention, with pagan symbols reappearing alongside symbols of the Christian faith, the challenge of reconciling rational thought with religious belief was personified in the tormented genius of Michelangelo. A master of the three major visual arts – sculp-

Church domes, such as the one crowning St. Paul's Cathedral in London, symbolized the ideals of the Renaissance.

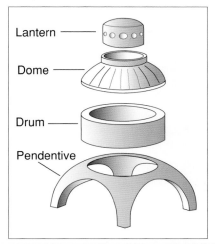

Lantern

Dome

Drum

Pendentive

ture, painting and architecture – he transcended conventions and traditions, and is considered the first truly modern artist.

On the heels of the High Renaissance came mannerism, a term coined to describe the painting of this period (1520 - 1600). The mannerist schools of painting produced nativity scenes in which signs of poverty were erased from the manger and the newborn Christ child was transformed into a cherub-like one-year-old perched on the lap of a rosy-cheeked Madonna. This less reverent and more intimate attitude was also reflected in the artists' penchant for painting themselves and fellow artists into scenes – positioning themselves not modestly to one side, but squarely in the centre of the canvas. The jubilant and joyous nature of mannerist art was criticized by austere theologians, but the last glorious outburst of Christian art was yet to come in the form of baroque, the dominant art of the 17th century.

Baroque

The baroque style harmoniously united painting, sculpture and architecture. The latter became fluid, like sculpture on a massive scale, with curving forms and undulating facades. Sculptures set within this elaborate architecture seem to spill from their niches or soar heavenward. Baroque painters used illusionist effects to create a deep sense of space, and its masters included Rembrandt, Rubens and van Dyck. In the late phases of baroque, the centre of the movement shifted from Italy to France, due largely to the patronage of Louis XIV.

As the vitality and force of baroque spilled into the 18th century, its final flowering became known as rococo. Originating in France and lasting from 1700 to 1750, the rococo style, with its light lines and exquisite refinement, was especially popular for interiors and the decorative arts. It was an unfettered style of excessive ornamentation and embellishment, with frescoes travelling across entire walls and ceilings, often multiplied in wall mirrors and reflected in polished parquet floors.

(Opposite) Rococo ballroom in the Grand Palace, Peterhof. (Below) Baroque facade of St. Petersburg's Winter Palace.

Revival Movements

The first of a series of overlapping movements and counter-movements began in the mid-18th century. These 'revival' movements were manifested mostly in architecture and began with Neoclassicism, which was inspired by the discovery of the ancient Roman ruins of Herculaneum and Pompeii on the Bay of Naples.

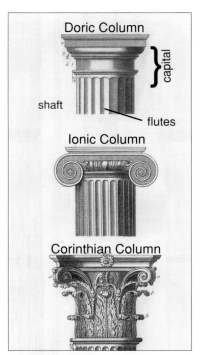

The Empire Style, considered the second phase of Neoclassicism, originated during the Napoleonic years of the early 19th century. Called the Regency style in Britain and the Karl Johan style in Sweden, its famous monuments emulate those of the Roman Empire and include the Vendome column and Arc de Triomphe du Carrousel in Paris. In St. Petersburg, the Alexander Column, Kazan Cathedral and Narva Triumphal Gate were raised to commemorate Russia's victory over Napoleon. In tandem with the classical revival was the Gothic revival, its largest monument being the Houses of Parliament in London.

The final revival phases were the neo-Renaissance and neo-baroque, which dominated from 1850 to 1875 and lingered through the turn of the century. Neo-baroque buildings favoured a profusion of ornament, creating an excess of opulence that appealed particularly to the newly rich and powerful of the Industrial Revolution. New building techniques made use of iron, which was used extensively in the construction of railroad stations, exhibitions halls and pub-

lic libraries. The Eiffel Tower, erected at the entrance to the Paris World's Fair of 1889, became a famous symbol of 19th-century technology.

Narva Triumphal Gate in St. Petersburg. (Below) Eiffel Tower.

Art nouveau, a decorative arts movement lasting from the 1880s to World War I, was originally meant to produce art for the masses. As a reaction to the historical emphasis of mid-19th century art, this new style incorporated organic, plant-inspired motifs and flowing lines. The movement was called Jugendstil ('youth style') in Germany. Another turn-of-the-century style was associated with the Ecole des Beaux-Arts in Paris and became fashionable both in Europe and North America. Beaux-arts buildings were an eclectic mix of styles, often incorporating Greek, Roman and Egyptian elements.

In the art of painting, the Romantic movement (which

arose in Western Europe in the late 18th century) revered nature and the individual's freedom to act naturally. Famous artists of this movement include the English landscape painters Turner and Constable. After Romanticism, most painters rejected traditional subjects taken from the Bible, the classics or the life of the courts, and turned instead to everyday scenes around

them. No single movement has dominated modern western art for long periods of time since the 18th century, and there has been a speeding up of successive styles and ideas. The impressionist movement, originating in late-19th century France, rejected the romantics' emphasis on emotion and instead pursued objectivity when painting visual impressions, often directly from nature.

(Left) Turner's 'The Fighting Téméraire' (National Gallery, London)
(Below) Monet's 'Poppies Blooming' (Musée d'Orsay, Paris)
(Opposite) Rodin's 'The Thinker' (Musée Rodin, Paris)

Following the impressionist movement, artists sought new inspiration in fresh landscapes. Fleeing Europe's industrial north, Vincent van Gogh headed to the south of France to be 'near Africa' and Gauguin, who had worked as a stock broker in Paris and Copenhagen, moved to Tahiti to pursue primitivism in his painting. Van Gogh's dark and sombre early paintings gave way to swirling brush strokes and the intense yellows, greens and blues found in his later works, these representing the archetype of expressionism's emotional spontaneity in painting.

Auguste Rodin, born in Paris in 1840, is considered the most influential sculptor of the 19th century. His unconventional works departed from themes of mythology and embraced realism.

20th Century Art

(Below) National Bank of Denmark, designed by Arne Jacobsen.

Artists in the early 20th century, attempting to express an inner vision, intensified their search into the subconscious. The French painter Henri Matisse began using strong primary colours and became a leader of Fauvism, a style that emphasized the use of vivid colour. Pablo Picasso, who played a leading role in most of the 20th-century art movements, created cubism's most significant work when he painted *Les Demoiselles d'Avignon* in 1907. Surrealism, an artistic and literary movement founded in Paris in 1924 and influenced by Freudian theories, used dream-inspired symbols and near-photographic realism.

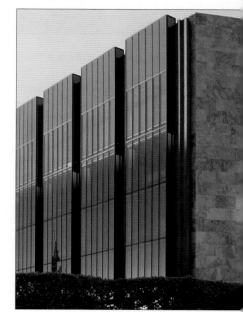

Norman Foster's 'Gherkin'

In the 1950s, Danish architect and designer Arne Jacobsen pioneered the total concept of design in which the building, furniture and other interior decor are all integrated. His interpretation of functionalism, in which a building's form is determined by its function, became known as Danish Modernism. Features of this style include straight angles, flat roofs, repetition of modular units and minimal ornamentation

Artistic works produced since the 1970s are usually classified as contemporary or post-modern. They include the controversial works of British conceptual artist Damien Hirst whose formaldehyde-preserved sharks and diamond-encrusted skulls fetch millions of pounds. Prince Charles is an outspoken critic of contemporary architecture, but Londoners have embraced some of the recent additions to the city's famous skyline, including Greater London's City Hall (resembling a glass beehive) and the City's pickle-shaped office tower known as The Gherkin. Its exterior clad with two-tone glass and wrapped in steel lattice, this 40-storey structure was designed by the British architect Norman Foster, who also designed the new glass dome atop the Reichstag in Berlin.

In Paris, the post-modern Pompidou Centre was designed in the 1970s by an international team of architects and structural engineers which included Renzo Piano and Richard Rogers. Considered an icon of the high-tech style of architecture, this structure features an exposed skeleton of brightly coloured tubes containing the building's mechanical systems. The Louvre Pyramid, designed in the 1980s by Chinese-born American architect I.M. Pei, was controversial when first unveiled. Critics felt the futuristic structure was out of place next to the classical architecture of the Louvre, yet the glass pyramid has become a Paris landmark.

Preserving & Restoring Art

Art museums take extraordinary precautions to preserve their priceless works, using climate control systems that filter dust and chemical pollutants from the air, and sensors that monitor temperature and humidity. Even the wrong kind of carpet, when walked on, can produce dust and lint that settles onto paintings.

Art restoration is as old as art itself, with early restorers using varnishes made of animal glue to temporarily brighten fresco paintings. When modern restorers clean frescoes, their painstaking methods involve washing an area with de-ionized water and an organic solvent, then sponging ammonium carbonate onto the area through layers of absorbent paper, which are left in place for several minutes before being removed. Any loosened dirt is wiped away and the area given a final rinse with water.

When paintings travel to other museums, there is always the risk of damage, despite careful handling by white-gloved workers and the use of custom-designed metal cases fitted with high-density foam. Concerns include potential damage from jet engine vibrations, which can gradually shiver paint from a fragile canvas, and sudden decreases in humidity, which can cause a canvas to shrink and possibly crack.

Wars create special challenges for art curators. In London in August 1939, the National Gallery's entire collection was evacuated and secretly shipped to Wales. There the paintings were stored in various buildings until France fell in May 1940, after which the paintings were moved in crateloads to Manod Quarry – a slate mine dug into the mountains above the remote Welsh village of Ffestiniog. Here the priceless paintings were hidden for the duration of the war, shielded from German bombs by two hundred feet of solid rock. The Tate Gallery (now called Tate Britain) also evacuated their collection. However, a large Stanley Spencer was deemed too large to move, so a brick wall was erected in front of it to protect it from potential bomb blasts.

Preserving outdoor monuments is another challenge. Marble monuments are threatened by air pollution, as well as microorganisms like algae, lichens and fungi, which discolour surfaces and burrow beneath the surface. Scaffolding is a fact of life in Europe, where restoration work by skilled marble masons is time-consuming and extremely costly.

Some of Europe's most famous cathedrals are now charging admission to finance their upkeep. In the case of York Minster, which receives over a million visitors annually, the city of York had no choice when faced with a million-dollar deficit incurred by maintaining this historic structure. Other major cathedrals in England, including St. Paul's and Canterbury, also charge admission. Some allow film crews to shoot interior scenes, such as Gloucester Cathedral, which served as Hogwarts School in the Harry Potter movies.

Gardens have been cultivated since antiquity. During the days of the Roman Empire, landscape gardening was highly developed and the formal gardens enjoyed by emperors at their country villas were often terraced and adorned with statuary and fountains. Roman subjects grew herbs and vegetables in simple garden plots, a practise that continued throughout the Middle Ages.

A new type of garden was introduced to Europe with the arrival of the Renaissance and its ideals of harmony and order. As scholars unearthed descriptions of antique Roman villas and gardens, leading artists of the day were commissioned to design elaborate hillside gardens of

French formal gardens were once favoured throughout Europe. (Above) Tsarina Alexandra's private garden at her summer pavilion on the grounds of the Peterhof estate near St. Petersburg, Russia. (Right) Royal gardens at Fredensborg Palace near Copenhagen, Denmark. (Opposite) A garden path leading to Peterhof's Grand Palace.

fountains, waterfalls and reflecting pools, mingled with statuary and topiary, often in geometrical designs. In France, the formal garden, based on the principal of imposing order over nature, attained its greatest expression with the Gardens of Versailles. These splendid gardens were widely copied by the other courts of Europe and inspired Russia's

Peter the Great when planning his summer palace and gardens at Peterhof.

The Golden Age of summer palace gardens gradually came to an end in the 18th century as Europe replaced the rigid symmetry of classical gardens with the English garden. Also called the English landscape park, this style was used for public parks

and royal estates throughout Europe. The English garden presented an idealized view of nature and usually included an ornamental lake, gently rolling lawns, groves of trees and copies of classical temples.

(Top) The gardens at Oslo's royal palace. (Left) A garden enclave at Peterhof. (Below) An Oxford college's garden.

PART II

THE VOYAGE AND THE PORTS

The British Isles

The British Isles are packed with ports of call and England is a major hub for cruise passengers. Three base ports are within two hours by road or rail of London and the city itself is a port for small cruise ships, which dock on the River Thames. Southampton, on the south coast, is the largest of England's cruise ports and is home port for Queen Mary 2's transatlantic sailings to New York. Dover, on England's southeast coast, and Harwich, situated northeast of London on the Essex coast, are also base ports for Northern Europe cruises. Other English ports, such as Liverpool, are gaining popularity as ports of call and are sometimes included in a British Isles itinerary, as are various ports in Scotland, the Channel Islands and Ireland.

This section contains information on England, with detail on London, along with Wales, Scotland, the Channel Islands and Ireland. To quickly find information on a specific port, please refer to the Index at the back of this book. For a history of Great Britain, please turn to the History section in Part I.

London's Houses of Parliament
Photo: David Iliff

ENGLAND
WALES & CHANNEL ISLANDS

England is a country that prides itself on tradition, pomp and pageantry. The national anthem is 'God Save the Queen' and a royal presence permeates English society. The sovereign's coat of arms appears everywhere – from government documents to boxes of biscuits – and the presence of the red Royal Mail bags raises the nation's postal service to a level of gentility not usually associated with receiving monthly bills in the post.

In spite of its pivotal role, the British monarchy has been reduced over the centuries to a largely ceremonial institution, and the country's age-old class system – based on inheritance of landed wealth – has been challenged in recent decades by a new breed of Briton whose status is based on merit. Yet, as industrialists and rock stars ascend the social ranks, purchasing country estates next door to earls and countesses, they are merely adding another layer of history to a country built upon a rich and remarkable past.

England at a Glance

England occupies two-thirds of the island of Great Britain, which it shares with Scotland and Wales. The population of England is approximately 53 million, with

Pomp and pageantry at Horse Guards Parade in London.

London the capital. England is governed by a constitutional monarchy.

England's currency is the pound sterling (GBP) divided into 100 pence. Value Added Tax (VAT) is charged on most goods sold in the UK; stores provide refund forms for foreign visitors. A 12.5% service charge is usually included in the bill at hotels and restaurants. Taxi drivers should be tipped 10-15%. Britain's country code is +44 when calling internationally.

Arriving by Air

The distance from Heathrow Airport to Central London is about 16 miles (26 km). The taxi fare from Heathrow to Central London is £45-£70. The one-way Heathrow

Express train (15 minutes from Heathrow to Paddington Station) costs £21-£29 per person one-way and is the fastest link between Heathrow and London. However, if there are three or more people in your party, hiring a taxi might be more convenient. Also, unless your hotel is close to Paddington Station, you will likely still need to hire a taxi to get you and your luggage from the train station to your hotel. The regular Piccadilly Line train from Heathrow to Central London (a 50-60 minute trip) is the cheapest mode of transport

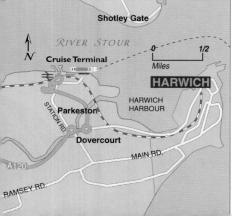

(£10). It makes numerous stops but is a good option if your hotel is located close to one of the stops. For more detail on your options for getting from Heathrow to Central London, visit heathrowairport. com.

Gatwick Airport is located 33 miles (53 km) south of Central London. The express train from Gatwick to Central London's Victoria Station departs every 15 minutes and is a half hour journey (cost is about £20 per person).

Coach transfers between London and the cruise ports can be arranged with your cruise line. However, if you prefer travelling independently there are regular rail connections between London and the cruise ports of **Dover** (see map page 130), **Southampton**, and **Harwich**. The train from London (Waterloo Station) to Southampton is 1.25 hours; from London (Victoria/London Bridge/Charing Cross Stations) to Dover is 1 hour and 40 minutes; and the trip from London (Liverpool Street Station) to Harwich is 1.5 hours. Visit BritRail.net for more information.

Car rental firms are located at the airports, and at Southampton and Dover cruise ports. For more information, visit Auto Europe (autoeurope.com; autoeurope.ca).

London

Greater London, with a population approaching 8 million, consists of the City of London (the historic and commercial core) and its surrounding boroughs (32 in total). The City of London is known simply as the City or the Square Mile because it is approximately one square mile in area.

Adjacent to 'the City' is the City of Westminster (a borough with city status), which is the seat of government containing the Houses of Parliament, Whitehall and Buckingham Palace. Westminster also encompasses most of the West End with its hotels, restaurants, shops, theatres and upscale residential areas.

Getting Around

London is a **walking** town. Much of the city core is a maze of narrow, winding backstreets and cobblestone lanes leading to hidden courtyards. A street map is useful for exploring London's West End and Square Mile on foot, and the pocket-sized Mini London A-to-Z Street Atlas provides excellent detail. The River Thames meanders through the heart of London, flowing past some of London's most famous landmarks, making it easy to maintain your bearings while walking along the Embankment.

Also pleasant for walking are the city's interconnecting parks – St. James's Park, Green Park and Hyde Park. The Mall (closed to vehicle traffic on Sundays) leads past St. James's Park and Green Park to Buckingham Palace. A variety of walking tours are offered by London Walks (walks. com).

There are, of course, alternatives to walking. Red double-decker **sightseeing buses** (operated by Big Bus Tours) follow two heritage routes and have boarding points near major landmarks and attractions throughout Central London. Commentary is provided, as are hop-on/hop-off privi-

Shore Excursions

LONDON

If you're ending your cruise in Southampton, Dover or Harwich, your cruise line likely will offer several shore excursions that can be combined with transfers to airports or into London if you are overnighting in the city. These excursions usually provide an overview of London, some with shopping in the West End and possibly an interior visit to Buckingham Palace. From Dover, the ship's shore excursions will likely offer Dover Castle (or other nearby castles such as Leeds and Walmer), Canterbury Cathedral, the medieval town of Rye and a selection of tours to London. From Southampton tours are offered to Windsor, Stonehenge, Salisbury and Winchester as well as various London tours. From Harwich, numerous tours to London are also available, as are visits to the university town of Cambridge. *Check your cruise line's website for details on your specific itinerary.*

Pedestrians take over the Mall in Central London on Sundays.

leges. You can purchase tickets beforehand online or through your travel agent. An all-day (24-hour) ticket is about £22 per adult. Several **river boat** firms service the Thames, providing both commuter service and narrated cruises for tourists. Fast river buses operate daily from Embankment pier and Waterloo (London Eye) pier, and river cruises are available between Westminster, Waterloo, Embankment, Tower and Greenwich piers, with longer trips available to Kew, Richmond and Hampton Court. River service also connects the Tate galleries, running between Millbank (Tate Britain) and Bankside (Tate Modern). Ticket information is posted at the piers, and Travelcard holders receive a discount.

The **Underground** (called the Tube) is an efficient way to get quickly from one point to another (www.thetube.com). Tickets can be bought at ticket windows

A Thames sightseeing boat passes the Tower of London.

inside the station. A flat-fee, all-day ticket is a good option, as are the various travel cards available through Rail Europe, including the Visitor Oyster Card (an electronic, refillable go card) and the London Travel Card, which provides unlimited travel on public transport (underground rail and buses). You can combine a London Travel Card with a London Pass, which provides single or multi-day access to dozens of London attractions and features fast-track entry past lineups at the popular venues. For more information on travelling around London by tube, rail, bus or riverboat, visit Transport for London (tfl. gov.uk).

If you're travelling with two or three others, getting around London by **taxi** is an affordable alternative to public transport. London's distinctive black taxi cabs can be hailed anywhere and their drivers know the city like the back of their hand. They undergo extensive training to acquire their knowledge, which entails study-

ing the Blue Book's 25,000 streets located within a six-mile radius of Charing Cross (the geographic centre of London). It takes a licensed cabbie several years to learn all of the streets and possible routes in Central London. To pass the licensing test, a successful candidate must be able to take a passenger to any destination requested without the aid of a map. Be sure to use the licensed taxis and not the unlicensed minicabs.

One approach to exploring London is to determine beforehand the attractions you want to visit that day, then take a cab, bus, river boat or the Tube to the point furthest from your hotel. After visiting the first attraction on your list, set off on foot in the general direction of your hotel. Walk to as many sites as you feel able, stopping along the way for refreshments, then hail a taxi back to your hotel (unless it's rush hour, when taking the Tube or walking are much faster).

Renting a car in London is not recommended. Traffic is heavy, fast-moving and driving is on the left. There are also numerous traffic circles (the word 'circus' is Latin for 'ring' and refers to a roundabout of converging streets, such as Piccadilly Circus). Should you decide to drive in London, also be aware of a £10 daily congestion charge levied on any private vehicle that drives through central London during peak business hours (7:00 a.m. to 6:00 p.m., Monday through Friday). Motorists' licence plate numbers are recorded by 800 cameras monitoring the 160-plus entry points to the Central Zone.

Public transport in London includes buses (top) and the Tube (above). A classic London taxi cab (below).

Where to Stay

London is one of the world's most expensive cities and hotel prices reflect this reality. Classic, five-star hotels in London are plentiful and are concentrated in Mayfair and St. James's. These include The Stafford (St. James's), The Connaught (Mayfair), Claridge's (Mayfair) and The Dorchester (Park Lane). The Grosvenor House, originally built as a private mansion for the Grosvenor family, is a five-star Marriott property on Park Lane. The Lanesborough is a St. Regis Hotel at Hyde Park Corner, and The Ritz is on Piccadilly overlooking Green Park.

Recently opened luxury hotels include the Corinthia Hotel in Whitehall and the Shangri-La in

The Morgan Hotel is a popular B&B hotel in Bloomsbury.

The Shard, on the south bank of the Thames near London Bridge.

Luxury boutique hotels include Dukes (St. James's Place) and Brown's, which opened in Mayfair in 1837. The family-owned Goring Hotel, near Buckingham Palace in the posh Belgravia district, is where Kate Middleton stayed with her family the night before her wedding to Prince William.

The Savoy, one of London's most illustrious hotels, is located on the Strand overlooking the Victoria Embankment and recently underwent a major renovation while retaining the interior's unique blend of Edwardian and art-deco decor.

Hazlitt's Hotel (Soho) is a four-star boutique hotel located in the heart of the theatre district. For families, Thistle Hotels are a good choice in the four-star category.

For three-star budget accommodation, good choices are the family-owned Morgan Hotel on Bloomsbury Street near the British Museum, or The Fielding Hotel near Covent Garden.

Mark Twain in the UK

Mark Twain caused quite a stir while staying at elegant Brown's in 1907 when he appeared in the hotel lobby one morning clad in a bathrobe and slippers. *The New York Times*, reporting on the incident, described how Twain startled staid Londoners as he walked out onto the street with his bare ankles showing and headed to the nearby Bath Club. Seemingly oblivious to the stares and gasps he was receiving, Twain later said, "I simply wanted to take a bath, and did the same thing I'd often done at the seaside. London is a sort of seaside town, isn't it?"

Dining

A traditional English breakfast consists of eggs, bacon or sausages and dry toast served with marmalade. Afternoon tea consists of finger sandwiches, warm scones and sweet pastries – all served, of course, with tea. The traditional British pub is the place to go for pub grub, such as the ploughman's plate of ham, cheeses and bread, washed down with a pint of lager or ale. If you want to eat well in London without blowing your budget, the city's gastro pubs serve fine food in a casual setting. Other options include fixed-price lunches and pre-theatre dinner menus.

When touring London, you can enjoy a convenient lunch onsite at many of the city's popular attractions. Restaurant choices include the New Armouries Restaurant at the Tower of London (lunch fare in a cafeteria-style setting); the Tate Modern's top-floor restaurant overlooking the Thames; The National Gallery's Oliver Peyton restaurant (serving classic British dishes) or its street-level café; the rooftop restaurant or the casual café at The National Portrait Gallery; and The Orangery restaurant beside Kensington Palace (serving lunch and traditional afternoon tea). The Wallace Collection's courtyard restaurant is another pleasant place for lunch or afternoon tea.

In fair weather, the outdoor cafés in Hyde Park are pleasant places to stop for refreshment. Shoppers can dine at one of the restaurants in Fortnum & Mason on Piccadilly or choose from the

(Above) A four-star Thistle Hotel. (Below) Casual diners enjoy an outdoor café in Hyde Park.

amazing assortment of restaurants and foodstands in Harrods department store.

Michelin-starred restaurants abound in London, with many overseen by celebrity chefs such as Gordon Ramsay who runs several London restaurants, including the Savoy Grill. Alain Ducasse at The Dorchester enjoys three stars for creative French cuisine. Fine dining in the English tradition is offered at Wiltons (est. 1742) in St. James's. **The Ivy**, near Leicester Square, is London's favourite theatre restaurant (reservations recommended). In Chelsea, **Tom's Kitchen** serves dishes by Tom Aikens in the relaxed setting of a converted pub.

Cecconi's in Mayfair serves some of the best Italian cuisine in London, but if you're looking for good Italian food at a more modest price, the Bella Italia has numerous locations in London, including one off St. Martin's Lane, just steps from The National Gallery. Also recommended is the family-owned **Taormina** in Bayswater, near Lancaster Gate tube station.

Bars, Pubs & Clubs

Several of London's famous watering holes are found in the luxury hotels of the city's Mayfair and St. James's districts. These include **Dukes Bar** at Dukes Hotel, which is famous for its martinis and is where author Ian Fleming, creator of James Bond, is said to have heard a bartender describe a martini as shaken, not stirred. Another swank bar in the upscale St. James's district is the **American Bar** at The Stafford (not to be confused with the American Bar in The Savoy).

Mayfair's famous establishments include the Champagne bar at **Scott's Restaurant & Bar** on Mount Street and **Donovan Bar** in Brown's Hotel. (Men should note that a jacket may be required at some of these establishments.)

For a more casual atmosphere, **The Only Running Footman** (on Charles Street near Berkeley Square) is a quintessential British pub/restaurant which is popular with locals and tourists. Also in Mayfair, on Mill Street, is the **Windmill** pub, famous locally for its steak and kidney pie. The **Anglesea Arms** in South Kensington is another gastro pub serving bar snacks and burgers.

Right beside Charing Cross train station on Northumberland is **The Sherlock Holmes** pub and restaurant, a favourite with locals since the 1960s. **Ye Olde Cheshire Cheese**, approached by a narrow alleyway (Wine Office Court) off Fleet Street, is one of London's oldest pubs and a great place to pause for a pint.

London's red-hot club scene attracts a young crowd of wealthy aristocrats and celebrities. One of the most popular is the Polynesian-themed **Mahiki Club** on Dover Street in Mayfair, which is run by a friend of Prince William.

Pubs are a big part of London's social scene.

Live Theatre

Charles Dickens called London a "magic lantern" – an apt description for the city's commercial theatre, which is second to none. The West End's famous theatre district (Theatreland) is housed in late Victorian buildings located in and around Leicester Square where long-running musicals include *The Phantom of the Opera, Chicago, Mamma Mia!* and *Les Misérables*.

To obtain discount and half-price tickets on the day of a performance, visit the TKTS booth in the clocktower building in the centre of Leicester Square (open daily from 10:00 a.m. to 7:00 p.m. except from 11:00 a.m. to 4:30 p.m. on Sundays). Tickets can only be bought only in person from the windows, and popular shows usually sell out early.

London is also famous for its non-commercial theatres, such as the National Theatre (South Bank), the Globe Theatre (Bankside) and the Old Vic (Lambeth), which stage classic and modern works by leading playwrights. The Royal Opera House, at Covent Garden, is where the Royal Ballet and Royal Opera perform.

Shopping

There are two main shopping areas in London's West End. One is centred on Oxford Street, Regent Street and Piccadilly Street in Mayfair; the other is in Knightsbridge, which is the location of Harrods department store and the high-end boutiques along Sloane Street.

Oxford Street is the major shopping street in London and considered the flagship location of numerous chain stores such as Marks & Spencer, H&M and Topshop. At the west end of Oxford Street is the famous Selfridges department store. Oxford Street intersects with Regent Street at Oxford Circus, and just south of this intersection is Hamleys, one of the world's largest toy stores. Other stores along Regent Street include Liberty, Burberry and Austin Reed.

Regent Street crosses Piccadilly Street at Piccadilly Circus – an enormous traffic circle filled with movie theatres. Just west of Piccadilly Circus on the south side of Piccadilly Street is Fortnum & Mason, founded in 1707 and famous for its gourmet food hampers. One block west, at the corner of Jermyn and Bury, is the exclusive clothier Turnbull

The famous Palace Theatre in London's West End is where Les Misérables played for 19 years.

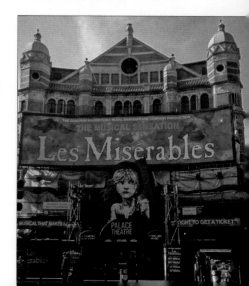

& Asser – whose famous clients have included Winston Churchill, Ronald Reagan and Prince Charles, who has bought shirts here since his youth.

The Piccadilly Arcade, lined with upscale shops, runs between Piccadilly and Jermyn, the latter connecting at its west end with St. James's Street, which is where London's most famous hat maker – Lock & Company – is located. The inventor of the bowler hat, this family-owned business was founded by James Lock in 1676 and has been at its current location (6 St. James Street) since 1765. Customers have included Oscar Wilde, Winston Churchill, Frank Sinatra and Johnny Depp. Also on St. James's Street (#71) is Truefitt & Hill – "Barbers to British Royalty since 1805" – which sells luxury grooming products for men.

Shopping in Piccadilly Arcade

On the north side of Piccadilly Street, opposite Piccadilly Arcade, is the Burlington Arcade – another covered pedestrian shopping street lined with upscale shops. Built in 1819, the arcade runs parallel with Burlington House (a mansion housing the Royal Academy of Arts).

North of Burlington Gardens, running parallel with Regent Street, is Savile Row – the 'golden mile of tailoring' where customized suits for gentlemen are made from selected cloths by British master tailors. Venerable firms include Huntsman (est. 1849) at 11 Savile Row, and Gieves & Hawkes, royal tailors since 1809. This prestigious house of bespoke tailoring is located at No. 1 Savile Row, a grand aristocratic home once occupied by the Royal Geographic Society, where gentlemanly explorers such as Dr. Livingstone would meet. The rooftop of the Apple building at 3 Savile Row is where the Beatles gave their final live performance in January 1969.

Immediately west of the Burlington Arcade is where Piccadilly Street intersects with Bond Street. Once a domain of exclusive art dealers and antique shops, Bond Street is now lined with fashion boutiques and fine jewellers. Sotheby's auction house has been located on Bond Street for over 100 years.

London's other shopping district is in Knightsbridge, where Harrods department store (on Brompton Road) is a famous landmark, lit each night by 11,000 energy-efficient light bulbs. One of the largest department stores in the world,

Harrods began in the mid-1800s as a small grocery shop operated by Charles Henry Harrod, whose son expanded the family business into a thriving retail operation.

Harrods was owned from 1985 to 2010 by Egyptian billionaire Mohamed Fayed, whose son Dodi died in 1997 alongside Diana, Princess of Wales, in a Paris car crash. Harrods, which has over 330 departments, contains more than 20 restaurants and is famous for its Food Hall.

Most London museums house gift shops offering an assortment of books, souvenirs and gifts, as do the Royal Collection shops on Buckingham Palace Road at The Queen's Gallery and Royal Mews.

Offering a completely different shopping experience are the weekend street markets at Portobello Road and Camden Lock where vintage clothing, jewellery, antiques and other items are sold.

Modern Art Galleries

London may be steeped in history and tradition, but its modern art scene is anything but bland. Controversy and contemporary art go hand in hand in London, where exhibits at local galleries often trigger a deluge of criticism – and public interest. Even the unveiling of the London Olympic Games 2012 emblem – a jigsaw-style design inspired by graffiti artists and reflecting youth culture – attracted controversy. The design was called hideous by critics, but defended as dynamic, funky and cutting-edge by its supporters.

One of the best places to view modern and contemporary art in London is the Tate Modern, which opened in 2000 in a refurbished power station overlooking the Thames. Tate Britain in Millbank also exhibits contemporary art, as does the Hayward Gallery, part of the Southbank Centre near Waterloo Bridge.

The Saatchi Gallery in Chelsea (housed in a refurbished army barracks on Kings Road near Sloane Square) is one of the largest contemporary art museums in the world, featuring exhibits that are often controversial.

Private galleries thrive in London. White Cube, which represents Damien Hirst, has two locations – at Mason's Yard (in a courtyard off Duke Street in St. James's) and on Bermondsey Street in Southwark. Other private venues include Laurent Delaye Gallery, which is housed above Huntsman at 11 Savile Row.

Henry Moore's 'Family Group' is part of the Tate Collection.

A Brief History of London

London began as a Roman fort called Londinium. Built on the north bank of the River Thames sometime before 61 AD, it was a strategic trading port of the Roman Empire, whose authorities constructed the first city walls (remnants of which still stand) following a rebellion led by the British queen Boadicea.

When the Roman legions withdrew from London in the 5th century, the city fell prey to warring Celts, Saxons and Danes. Then, in 886, the king of Wessex, Alfred the Great, gained control of London. He rebuilt the city's defences against the Danes, established a government, and organized a court school to revive learning among his subjects.

When William the Conqueror marched on the City of London, following his victory at the Bat-

17th century London map with the Tower on the far right side.

tle of Hastings in 1066, he was repelled at London Bridge. His troops then approached from a different direction, and London's rulers surrendered. As a reward, William granted the citizens of London a charter allowing them to retain some authority under Norman rule. However, to keep the Londoners subdued, William built three nearby castles, the most famous being the White Tower (the nucleus of the Tower of London) just east of the city wall.

London's powerful trade guilds established themselves during the Middle Ages, as did the Inns of Court – legal societies that controlled admission to the Bar (a term that originally referred to the rail enclosing the court judge). The reign of Elizabeth I (1558-1603) brought wealth, power and prestige to London, where Renaissance culture flowered and attained lasting prominence in the plays of William Shakespeare.

In 1665 the great plague claimed some 75,000 lives. Des-

perate Londoners fled the city to camp in Hyde Park in an effort to escape the Black Death. The following year the Great Fire swept through London, virtually destroying the city. During reconstruction, many of the city's new buildings (especially churches) were designed by Christopher Wren, the architect of St. Paul's Cathedral.

London grew tremendously during the 19th century, its surrounding villages transformed into fashionable districts of Georgian townhouses. During the Victorian era, London gained great prestige as the capital of the British Empire. A cultural and intellectual centre, London also began its tradition of attracting exiled foreigners.

Bombed heavily by German air raids in World War II, London remains one of the world's foremost financial, commercial and cultural centres. Immigrants from across Europe and from former British colonies are drawn to London's vibrant economy and tolerant atmosphere. Only the very wealthy can afford to live in Central London, where real estate prices are among the world's highest. But the national museums and art galleries are free, the Royal Parks are for all to enjoy, and the Changing of the Guard outside Buckingham Palace represents street entertainment at its ceremonial best.

Blue Plaque Buildings

Many famous people have lived in London, their former residences now marked by a commemorative plaque. Several plaque schemes are used in London, but the best-known is handled by English Heritage, which selects recipients   b   y strict criteria. Any famous person considered for a Blue Plaque must be dead for at least twenty years, must have made an outstanding contribution to human welfare, and be eminent in their field of endeavour as well as widely recognized.

Former London residents commemorated by a Blue Plaque include Samuel Johnson, who wrote the first definitive dictionary of the English language at 17 Gough Square in The City. His home is now a museum open to the public, and a statue of one his cats, named Hodge, stands in the courtyard outside. Other famous Blue Plaque homes that are now museums open to the public include Keats House Museum in Hampstead, Dickens House at 48 Doughty Street (Bloomsbury) and the 18th-century residence of George Frederic Handel at 25 Brook Street in Mayfair.

Notable Americans whose former London residences now carry a Blue Plaque include Mark Twain (23 Tedworth Square, Chelsea), John F. Kennedy (14 Prince's Gate, Knightsbridge) and Benjamin Franklin, who lived at 96 Craven Street, just off Trafalgar Square, in the late 1700s. The only surviving Franklin home in the world, it was restored and opened as a museum in 2006.

The awarding of Blue Plaques is a long-standing London tradition, initiated in 1867. Its current design was adopted in the 1930s.

Dr. Samuel Johnson's house.

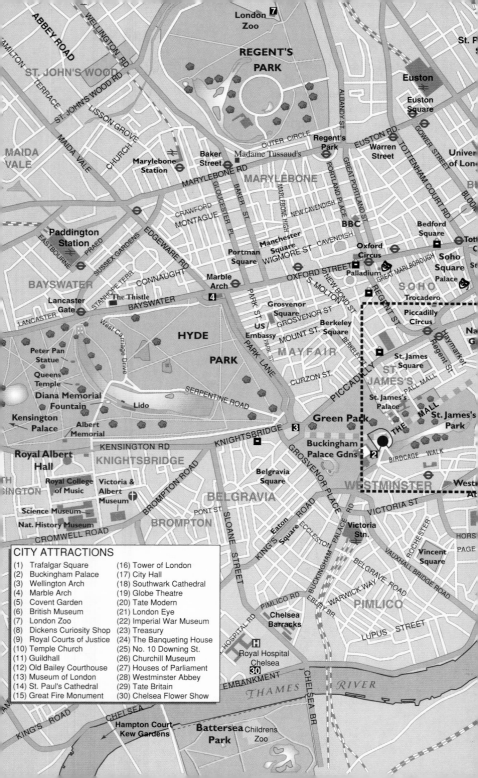

CITY ATTRACTIONS

(1) Trafalgar Square	(16) Tower of London
(2) Buckingham Palace	(17) City Hall
(3) Wellington Arch	(18) Southwark Cathedral
(4) Marble Arch	(19) Globe Theatre
(5) Covent Garden	(20) Tate Modern
(6) British Museum	(21) London Eye
(7) London Zoo	(22) Imperial War Museum
(8) Dickens Curiosity Shop	(23) Treasury
(9) Royal Courts of Justice	(24) The Banqueting House
(10) Temple Church	(25) No. 10 Downing St.
(11) Guildhall	(26) Churchill Museum
(12) Old Bailey Courthouse	(27) Houses of Parliament
(13) Museum of London	(28) Westminster Abbey
(14) St. Paul's Cathedral	(29) Tate Britain
(15) Great Fire Monument	(30) Chelsea Flower Show

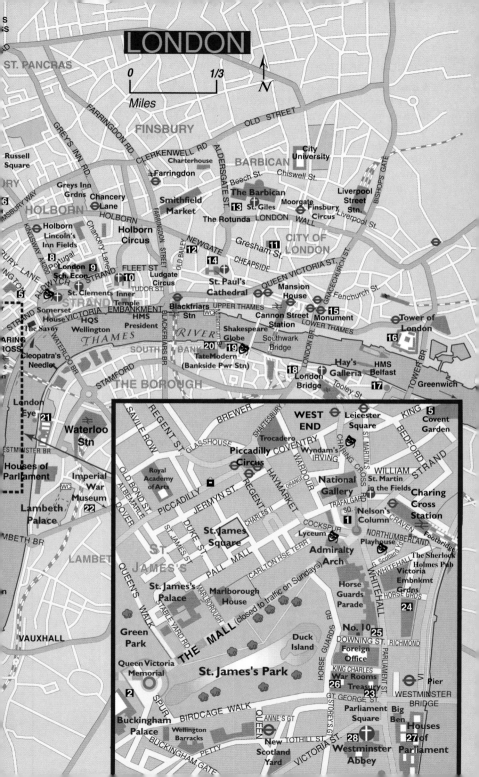

London Attractions

Charing Cross , named for the spot where King Edward I placed a cross in remembrance of his wife Eleanore of Castille, is considered the geographic centre of London. It marks an important midpoint, where the Strand (leading east to the City) intersects with Whitehall (leading south to Westminster). Charing Cross Underground Station is situated on the southeast side of fountain-filled **Trafalgar Square**, which is the symbolic heart of London and has become a traditional gathering place for public celebrations of historic events, including V-E Day in 1945 and London's winning bid in 2005 to host the 2012 Summer Olympics. The square was designed to commemorate Britain's decisive naval victory at the Battle of Trafalgar in 1805, with Nelson's Column erected in its centre to honour this national hero who commanded the British fleet. The National Gallery and National Portrait Gallery stand on the square's north side. To the east is St. Martin's-in-the Fields church, and on the west side of Trafalgar Square is Canada House, home to the Canadian High Commission in London.

The **National Gallery** houses one of the world's finest collections of Western European paintings, including Van Gogh's 'Sunflowers' and Turner's 'The

Nelson's Column (left) and the National Gallery (below) in Trafalgar Square.

Fighting Temeraire'. Works by Botticelli, Leonardo da Vinci, Raphael, Titian, Rubens, Rembrandt, Van Dyck, Goya, Constable, Monet and Cezanne are part of the gallery's permanent collection. An espresso bar, cafe and restaurant are located in the National Gallery, which is open daily from 10:00 a.m. to 6:00 p.m. (to 9:00 p.m. on Wednesdays).

The **National Portrait Gallery** houses portraits of famous figures in history – royalty, scientists, military leaders, artists, statesmen – from the Middle Ages to the present. It's open daily from 10:00 a.m. to 6:00 p.m. (until 9:00 p.m. on Fridays and Saturdays). The gallery's rooftop restaurant provides excellent views and the onsite cafe offers light meals.

West of Trafalgar Square

Leading southwest from Trafalgar Square, via Admiralty Arch, is **The Mall**. This park-lined avenue, which becomes a pedestrian-only mall on Sundays, leads directly to Buckingham Palace. **Admiralty Arch,** commissioned by Edward VII in memory of his mother Queen Victoria, is actually an office building that incorporates a three-arched passageway built adjacent to the Old Admiralty Building. A curious feature of this landmark is a protrusion resembling a human nose that is situated on the inside wall of the northernmost arch at a height of about seven feet (waist level for a rider on a horse). It symbolized Napoleon's nose and was to be rubbed by anyone riding through on horseback.

(Above) Admiralty Arch. (Below)
Trooping the Colour for the Queen.

Upon passing through Admiralty Arch into the Mall, you will come upon Horse Guards Road, which leads to the **Horse Guards Parade**. Once used for jousting tournaments by Henry VIII, this parade ground is now a venue for the daily **Changing of the Guard**, which takes place at 11:00 a.m. (10:00 a.m. on Sundays) beside the arch of Horse Guards Building. Also held here on the second Saturday in June is the annual Trooping the Colour, the official celebration of the monarch's birthday. This is a

Buckingham Palace and the Queen Victoria Memorial.

200-year-old military ceremony in which the 'colours' (flags) of the battalion are 'trooped' (carried) down the ranks. After inspecting the troops, the Queen rides in a carriage at the head of her guards back to Buckingham Palace where she and other members of the Royal Family gather on the balcony for a fly-past by the Royal Air Force.

Buckingham Palace 2 is the official London residence of Britain's sovereign and is one of London's most recognized buildings. Over the decades, millions of people from around the world have watched television footage of the Royal Family waving from the palace balcony during national celebrations while thousands of onlookers filled the Mall and the grounds surrounding the massive **Queen Victoria Memorial**, which stands in front of the palace gates. Smaller crowds also gather in this area to watch the **Changing of the Guard**, which takes place in the palace forecourt at 11:30 a.m. daily from May to July (on alternate dates the rest of the year).

When the Queen is in residence, the Royal Standard is flown above Buckingham Palace and four sentries are positioned at the front of the building. When the Queen is elsewhere, the Union Jack is flown and two sentries stand guard. (The Royal Standard is never flown at half mast, not even when a monarch dies, because the heir to the throne immediately becomes the new sovereign.)

Buckingham Palace was built in 1703 by the Duke of Buckingham. Purchased by George III in 1761, the palace was remodeled in 1825 by John Nash, with later additions including the great ballroom where state banquets are held. Queen Victoria was the first monarch to take up residence in Buckingham Palace, in 1837, moving her court here from St. James's Palace.

Many of Buckingham Palace's 775 rooms are used for official receptions, while the Queen and members of her family and staff occupy other parts of the palace. About 20 investitures take place each year in the palace ballroom. Recipients of a knighthood (or damehood, its female equivalent) include actors, scientists and industrialists who have made a significant contribution to national life. Non-British citizens are sometimes knighted, such as Bill Gates in 2005.

The **State Rooms** (open to visitors in August and September) are lavishly furnished and decorated with exquisite porcelain and paintings of the Royal Collection, including those by Rembrandt, Rubens and Vermeer. The **ticket office and entrance to the State Rooms** is off Buckingham Palace Road, which is where the Queen's Gallery and Royal Mews are also located. The **Queen's Gallery** contains changing exhibits from the Royal Collection of jewellery, paintings and furniture. The **Royal Mews** is a working stable which houses the horse-drawn carriages used for coronations, royal weddings, the opening of parliament and jubilee celebrations. The walled gardens behind Buckingham Palace are private, but the surrounding Royal Parks are all public. **St. James's Park** is the oldest and was a swampy meadow when acquired for hunting deer by Henry VIII, who commissioned the **Palace of St. James's**. Set within private gardens across the Mall from St. James's Park, the palace's original north gatehouse (built in the Tudor style of red brick with polygonal turrets) has survived. When fire destroyed Whitehall Palace in 1698, St. James's Palace became the monarch's principal London residence. Built around

(Above) The Tudor gatehouse at Palace of St. James's.
(Below) Wellington Arch.

(Above) The Italian Fountains in Hyde Park. (Below) Royal Albert Hall. (Opposite) Diana Memorial Fountain in Kensington Gardens.

four courtyards, the palace complex includes **Clarence House** – the official London residence of Prince Charles and the Duchess of Cornwall. Clarence House is open to the public during summer months, with visitors given a guided tour of the ground floor. The baby Prince George, son of Prince William and the Duchess of Cambridge, was christened at Chapel Royal in St. James's Palace, which is not open to the public and is where the coffin of Diana, Princess of Wales, lay in state in 1997.

Green Park, another former deer park, lies along the north side of Buckingham Palace's gardens and contains the Canada Memorial. Green Park connects with Hyde Park at Hyde Park Corner, site of the **Wellington Arch** 3. This victory arch, commemorating Britain's victories in the Napoleonic Wars, is crowned with a spectacular bronze sculpture depicting the angel of peace descending on a four-horsed chariot of war. Until 1992, the arch housed a small police station, but is now a museum. Visitors can enjoy sweeping views of London's Royal Parks from the balconies positioned below the bronze sculpture.

Marble Arch 4, designed in 1828 by John Nash and made of white Carrara marble, is based on the triumphal arch of Constantine in Rome. Originally erected on the Mall as a gateway to Buckingham Palace, it now stands at the northeast corner of Hyde Park, where Park Lane intersects with Oxford Street. This is also the location of Speakers' Corner, where the likes of Karl Marx and George Orwell have engaged in public speeches and debate, a Sunday afternoon tradition. Anyone can voice their opinion – and

be heckled – at Speakers' Corner.

Hyde Park is an expansive park containing a man-made lake called the Serpentine and miles of leafy pathways. The park's monuments include the **Albert Memorial**, which faces **Royal Albert Hall**. The **Diana Memorial Fountain,** designed by American landscape architect Kathryn Gustafson, lies at the west end of Hyde Park in **Kensington Gardens**. At the far end of Kensington Gardens is **Kensington Palace**, the former home of Diana, Princess of Wales. Part of the palace is open to the pubic, while the rest contains the private apartments of various Royal Family members, including Prince William and his family.

Exhibition Road leads south from Kensington Gardens to the **Victoria & Albert Museum** (exhibiting decorative art), **Science Museum** and **Natural History Museum** where the David Attenborough Studio is housed in the Darwin Centre.

Park Lane runs along the east side of Hyde Park and marks the western boundary of the exclusive **Mayfair** district, developed in the 17th and 18th centuries by the Grosvenor family, whose founder (Gros Veneur) came to England with William the Conqueror. The

American Embassy occupies the west side of **Grosvenor Square**, overlooking public gardens tended by London's Royal Parks.

Brook Street leads off the square's east side to the **Handel House Museum** (at 25 Brook Street) where the German composer lived in the mid-1700s. The rock musician Jimi Hendrix lived next door from 1968 to 1969.

Also in Mayfair is famous **Berkeley Square**, well-known from Vera Lyn's rendition of 'A Nightingale Sang in Berkeley Square.' Famous former residents include Winston Churchill who lived as a child at 48 Berkeley Square. Queen Elizabeth II was born on Bruton Street (which leads off Berkeley Square) when her parents were living at the London home of the Strathmores (the Queen Mother's family). A plaque at 17 Bruton Street commemorates the birthplace of the Queen, who moved as a young girl to Buckingham Palace when her father (George V) became king on the abdication of his brother (Edward VIII).

Mayfair's northern boundary is Oxford Street, a few blocks north of which is **The Wallace Collection** – a national museum of fine and decorative art. Housed in Hertford House at Manchester

Square, this acclaimed collection includes 18th-century French paintings, porcelain and furniture.

Mayfair's eastern boundary is **Regent Street**, lined with beaux-art architecture and designed in 1811 by John Nash as a ceremonial route from the regent's residence in St. James's Palace to Regent's Park. This street becomes Portland Place before reaching Regent's Park and leads past Broadcasting House, a 1930s art deco building which houses the BBC's headquarters.

North of Trafalgar Square

The opening scene of George Bernard Shaw's play *Pygmalion* (which inspired the musical *My Fair Lady*) takes place in **Covent Garden** 5, where Henry Higgins first meets Eliza Doolittle. The fruit, vegetable and flower market was moved in the mid-1970s to a new location, and the market building is now a shopping mall with cafes and a public square. Alfred Hitchcock was the son of a Covent Garden merchant, and supermodel Naomi Campbell was discovered by a model scout while strolling through Covent Garden at the age of 15.

London Transport Museum is located in Covent Garden Piazza and features interactive displays on London's Underground – the world's oldest underground network of railway tunnels, which opened in 1863 with steam-powered trains, followed by electric trains in 1890. The **Royal Opera House** is located at Covent Garden and is where the British ballerina Margo Fonteyn performed with Rudolf Nureyev in the 1960s.

Soho is a Bohemian district associated with rock music and counter-culture. Carnaby Street was a popular hangout during the 'Swinging Sixties' and is still a busy shopping street. Denmark Street, filled with music shops and recording studios, is where the Beatles, Rolling Stones and Jimi Hendrix all recorded music.

Bloomsbury is known for the many writers, including Virginia Woolf, who lived in this part of London in the 1930s. The Great Ormond Street Hospital, founded in 1852 to care for sick children, is also located in Bloomsbury and was granted the copyright to *Peter Pan* in 1927 by the playwright J. M. Barrie. Bloomsbury is best known as the location of the **British Museum** 6 – one of London's most famous attractions. Among its vast collections are such ancient treasures as the Rosetta Stone (engraved with Egyptian hieroglyphics) and the Elgin Marbles (taken from the Parthenon in Athens) as well as rare manuscripts, including

The Elgin Marbles are displayed at the British Museum.

Beowulf and *Magna Carta.*

The British Museum was established by the government in 1753 upon acquiring several private collections of priceless manuscripts and other antiquities. Its first location was Montagu House, but when larger quarters were needed, construction began on its current building in the 1820s. Britain's national library occupied its sprawling inner courtyard until the massive **British Library** near St. Pancras train station on Euston Road was completed in 1973. The Museum's transformed courtyard was unveiled in 2000 as the Queen Elizabeth II Great Court, its domed Reading Room restored to its Victorian splendour and newly added facilities including galleries, shops and a café and restaurant. (www.thebritishmuseum.ac.uk)

Regent's Park is a former hunting ground of King Henry VIII. This sprawling park covers 410 acres (166 hectares) and contains rose gardens as well as London's largest sports area with a pavilion and various pitches. Designed in 1811 by John Nash, Regent's Park is also where you'll find the **London Zoo** 7, which was once home to a famous bear named Winnie (short for Winnipeg). She was brought to England during the First World War as a mascot for a militia cavalry regiment of the Canadian army and was donated to the zoo by her owner, Lieut. Harry Colebourne, before he headed to France for active duty. Winnie entertained children and adults alike with her playful nature, prompting a little boy named Christopher Robin to name his stuffed teddy bear 'Winnie', and inspiring the boy's father, A. A. Milne, to write his children's classics about Winnie the Pooh.

At the northwest end of Regent's Park lies the posh residential district of St. John's where the **Abbey Road Studios** are located. The Beatles recorded most of their music here, including their Abbey Road album, its cover photograph featuring the four band members crossing Abbey Road.

East of Trafalgar Square

Leading east from Trafalgar Square into the City is the Strand, which traced the river bank before the **Victoria Embankment** was built in the 1860s to provide London with a modern sewage system. Points of interest along the Victoria Embankment include the **Battle of Britain War Monument** – a long, granite structure unveiled in 2005 by Prince Charles. Its design incorporates

The Battle of Britain war monument on the Embankment.

Cleopatra's Needle (above) and some nearby benches (below) on Victoria Embankment.

an existing smoke outlet once used for steam-powered underground trains. The monument honours the airmen who fought in this famous WWII battle and of whom Winston Churchill said, "Never in the field of human conflict was so much owed by so many to so few."

Another landmark along Victoria Embankment is **Cleopatra's Needle** – an ancient Egyptian obelisk cut from red granite which was quarried at Aswan on the Nile River in about 1450 BC. It was presented by the Egyptian government to the United Kingdom as a diplomatic gift in 1819 and was erected on the Victoria Embankment in September 1878.

The Savoy, Britain's first luxury hotel, opened in 1899 on the Strand, overlooking a sweep of the River Thames – a view painted by Claude Monet while staying in a fifth-floor suite. Bob Dylan filmed *Subterranean Homesick Blues* in a nearby alley while staying at the Savoy in 1965.

Somerset House stands on the south side of the Strand, just east of Waterloo Bridge. The original structure was replaced in the late 1700s with a neoclassical building (its Victorian wings later added). Built to house the Admiralty, Somerset House is now home to the Courtauld Gallery's important collection of old master and impressionist art.

The Old Curiosity Shop 🎱 on Portsmouth Street was built in 1567 of old ships' timber and is believed to be the inspiration for Charles Dickens's classic novel of the same name. On the north side of the Strand, just outside the

entrance to the City, is the **Royal Courts of Justice** ▣, an imposing Victorian Gothic building. In the vicinity of the Royal Courts of Justice are the four **Inns of Court** – Gray's Inn, Lincoln's Inn, Inner Temple and Middle Temple. All barristers in England belong to one of these law societies, and each inn is a complex of buildings, which includes offices, libraries, dining facilities, accommodation and a church or chapel. The famous Order of Knights Templar established an English seat in London in the 12th century, building the **Temple** hall, library and church ▣ – the latter a private chapel for lawyers of the two Temples. A round Norman church, it was restored following severe fire damage during the Blitz and gained a high profile when featured in Dan Brown's novel *The Da Vinci Code*.

The City, London's historic core and location of the London Stock Exchange, Lloyds of London and the Bank of England, is entered from the west at Temple Bar – a stone monument standing in the middle of the road where the Strand becomes Fleet Street. Places of interest include ▣ **Guildhall**, constructed in the 1400s when the Lord Mayor rivalled the monarch for influence and held court here with the City's wealthy merchants. Its high-ceilinged great hall is still used for glittering banquets.

(Top) The Old Curiosity Shop. (Middle) Lincoln's Inn. (Bottom) Temple church.

The **Old Bailey** 🔢 criminal court (well known to fans of John Mortimer's *Rumpole of the Old Bailey*) is located on Old Bailey Road. The **Museum of London** 🔢, which contains prehistoric, Roman and medieval galleries, is located a few blocks north of St. Paul's Cathedral, along St. Martins-le-Grand.

St. Paul's Cathedral 🔢, one of England's finest churches, stands at the head of Ludgate Hill where a Roman temple once stood. When the great fire of London (1666) damaged the church at this site, Christopher Wren was commissioned to design a new one. He laid the first foundation block in 1675, and 35 years later his baroque masterpiece was completed.

The dome, one of the largest in the world, is magnificent. Its interior is decorated with paintings of biblical scenes and is ringed by the Whispering Gallery, which can be reached by climbing up 163 stone steps. Another 119 steps will get you to the Stone

(Above) Approaching St. Paul's from the Millennium Bridge and (below) the domed interior.

Gallery, on the outside of the dome, and 152 steps further up is the Golden Gallery with panoramic views across London.

In the basement of the cathedral is a crypt containing the tombs of Admiral Lord Nelson, the Duke of Wellington, Sir Christopher Wren, Florence Nightingale and Sir Henry Moore. (A cafeteria, gift shop and toilets are also located on this lower level.)

Although royal weddings are traditionally held in Westminster Abbey, the wedding of Prince Charles and Lady Diana Spencer was held at St. Paul's in 1981 because the cathedral was large enough to accommodate all of the invited guests. Admission is charged to St. Paul's Cathedral.

The **Monument 15** is east of St. Paul's, near the north end of London Bridge. A stone column over 200 feet tall (311 stairs to the top), it stands near the spot where the Great Fire of London started in a baker's shop on Pudding Lane.

The **Tower of London 16**, one of London's most famous landmarks, was built as a medieval

(Above) The White Tower.
(Below) Tower Green.

(Above) Royal regalia on display in the White Tower's Great Hall. (Below) St. John's Chapel.

fortress and royal castle. Most people think of it first and foremost as a prison for queens and courtiers, princes and priests, many of whom spent their final days within the Tower's walls awaiting execution. Declared a World Heritage site in 1988, the Tower of London draws visitors by the millions, who come to view the **Crown Jewels** on display in the Waterloo Barracks or to pause beside **Tower Green** and ponder the final minutes of the lives of Anne Boleyn, Katherine Howard and Lady Jane Grey before they were beheaded.

The Tower was built to assert royal authority over London and, in times of unrest, to provide safe haven for a monarch escaping an angry mob. There were no dungeons in the Tower, and prisoners – most of whom were from the upper classes – were treated according to their social rank. When Anne Boleyn was brought to the Tower to await execution, she was taken to the same lodging she had slept in while awaiting her coronation. The Tower was a busy place during the reign of Henry VIII, who ordered the beheading of two queens, a lord chancellor, an archbishop and numerous others who challenged his kingship.

Ghosts are said to inhabit the Tower of London, but the 35 Yeoman Warders who work and live with their families within the Tower walls (about 150 residents in total) aren't too bothered. Those with flats in the Beauchamp Tower, overlooking Tower Green, don't mind that their 'village green' used to have a scaffold on it, or that their local church – the

Chapel Royal of St Peter ad Vincula – is the burial place of three English queens and two Roman Catholic saints (Thomas More and John Fisher). The Yeoman Warders have a local pub like any other community and after school the resident children can be heard playing outside.

A menagerie of animals once lived within the Tower grounds, but today there are only six **ravens** who sleep in cages outside the White Tower but who roam freely during the day. It was Charles II who decreed there must always be six ravens living at the Tower or the Kingdom of England would fall. To prevent the ravens from flying away, their feathers are trimmed.

The **White Tower** is the original Tower building, its construction begun by William the Conqueror in about 1070 (the walls were painted white in 1240 to make the citadel more imposing). **St John's Chapel** (one of England's most complete examples of early Anglo-Norman ecclesiastical architecture) occupies the White Tower's first floor, as does a **Great Hall** now used to display 16th-century armour and weaponry, including equipment made for Henry VIII.

In 1674, the skeletons of two boys (aged about 10 and 12 years) were found hidden under a staircase leading to the Chapel of St. John. These presumably were the remains of Edward IV's two young sons, who were ordered to the Tower in 1483 by their uncle upon their father's death. When the two princes mysteriously disappeared and their uncle was

(Above) Waterloo Barracks.
(Below) Tower Bridge.

crowned Richard III, it was widely believed that he had ordered the boys murdered.

Admission is charged at the Tower of London, and tickets can be bought in advance online (365tickets.com).

Tower Bridge, constructed in the late 1800s, crosses the Thames opposite the Tower of London. It was designed as a combination suspension and bascule (moveable) bridge so that large vessels can access the port facilities in the Pool of London, which lies between the Tower of London and London Bridge. The bridge's high-level walkway is part of the Tower Bridge Exhibition, housed in the bridge's twin towers.

The south bank of the Thames opposite the City is where the Globe Theatre and Tate Modern are located. A riverside pedestrian promenade leads from Tower Bridge past Greater London's new **City Hall** **17** (a modern glass structure shaped like a beehive) and the permanently moored **HMS** *Belfast*, a WWII Royal Navy cruiser which is maintained by the Imperial War Museum and serves as London's Floating Naval Museum. Nearby is **Hay's Galleria**, a converted wharf now housing shops and a riverside pub. Nearby, located next to London Bridge Station, is **The Shard** – a skyscraper designed by Renzo Piano which contains offices, the

(Top) Millenium Bridge.
(Middle) London's City Hall.
(Bottom) Anchor Pub, Bankside.

Shangri-La hotel and a viewing gallery on its top floors.

London Bridge marks the eastern edge of **Bankside**, once a seedy area of dockyards, taverns and brothels. Attractions here include **Southwark Cathedral** **18**, the oldest Gothic church in London, its main structure built between 1220 and 1420. William Shakespeare's actor brother was buried here in 1607. Moored in a nearby quay is a replica of Francis Drake's warship the *Golden Hinde*. Close by is the historic **Anchor Pub** where Samuel Pepys watched the Great Fire of London burning across the river in 1666 and where Dr. Johnson was a regular with a room reserved here in which to write.

West of Southwark Bridge is the **Shakespeare Globe Museum & Theatre** **19**. This open-air theatre is a reconstruction of the round-shaped Elizabethan theatre where Shakespeare's plays were first performed. The original theatre burned down in 1613 when a theatrical cannon misfired during a performance of *Henry VIII* and set

Shakespeare Globe Theatre

THE ENGLISH LANGUAGE

Not marble, nor the gilded monuments
Of princes, shall outlive this powerful rhyme.
William Shakespeare
England's greatest gift to the world is its language. Spoken by a quarter of the world's population and scattered across every continent, English is the first truly global language. Its vocabulary consists of about 500,000 words, plus a further half million technical and scientific terms. By comparison, the German vocabulary has about 185,000 words and French has fewer than 100,000. English is the predominant language of international business, politics and science. It is the official voice of air and sea travel, and the official language of the Olympic Games.

When the Anglo-Saxons of northern Europe first landed in the British Isles in AD 450, they spoke an obscure sub-branch of the Germanic family of languages. Over time, English absorbed words from nearly every language, including Celtic, German, Scandinavian, Dutch, Latin and French.

English is a practical language. Unlike other European languages, English nouns do not require an article to determine their gender. English is also flexible – many words can be used as either a noun or a verb. But English is also frustratingly inconsistent in spelling and pronunciation. Yet, because English has "borrowed" words from almost every other language (80 per cent of its vocabulary is foreign-born), its richness and diversity have provided the tools with which the great writers of English literature have excelled.

(Top) Tate Modern. (Above and below) BA's London Eye.

the thatch roof ablaze. No one was hurt, but one man had to douse his burning breeches with a bottle of ale. In Shakespeare's time, Bankside was a cesspool of taverns, bawdy-houses, gambling joints and bear-baiting rings, with church sermons warning about the evils of the theatre. Sam Wanamaker, an American actor and filmmaker, campaigned for years to have the new Globe built within a few hundred yards of its original site and work finally began in 1987. Ten years later, Queen Elizabeth II arrived by royal barge to officially open the Globe Theatre. In 2014 the Sam Wanamaker Playhouse opened and Shakespeare's plays (along with tours) are now staged year-round at the Globe.

West of the Globe Theatre, is the **20** **Tate Modern** – a public art gallery featuring international modern and contemporary art, including works by Picasso, Matisse and Dali. Housed in a converted power station, Tate Modern opened in 2000. Its massive Turbine Hall is five storeys high and a restaurant is located on the top floor overlooking the Thames where the **Millennium Bridge** – a footbridge that opened in 2000 – crosses the river to St. Paul's Cathedral.

The **London Eye** **21** has become a London icon since its completion in 2000. This gigantic, cantilevered wheel holds 32 passenger-observation capsules from which you can enjoy fabulous views of London. It moves very slowly, allowing time to identify and photograph famous landmarks, such as the Houses of Parliament and Buckingham Palace. Tickets can be booked in advance online and the ride lasts about thirty minutes.

The **Imperial War Museum**  22 on Lambeth Road is housed in a former psychiatric hospital called Bedlam. The museum's six floors house a vast treasury of galleries, displays and collections that catalogue modern-day conflicts, from World War I to the present. In addition to hundreds of war paintings, archival photographs and private letters, large exhibits include the command tank of Field Marshall Montgomery.

South of Trafalgar Square

Whitehall, which leads south from Trafalgar Square, is lined with government buildings, including the **Treasury** 23, with its rooftop providing a vantage for Prime Minister Churchill to watch enemy bombers attacking London during World War II. Whitehall was once a wide road that led to the Palace of Whitehall, a Tudor palace that was destroyed by fire in 1698. The **Banqueting House** 24, an addition to the palace designed by Inigo Jones in 1622, survived the fire and is today open for public viewing. The two-storey banqueting hall within the house is a splendid example of the Italianate Renaissance style studied by Jones in Italy, with its bays of windows, Ionic pilasters and a ceiling painted by Rubens.

Charles I was executed here, outside a first-floor window, from which he stepped onto a scaffold.

Sidestreets leading off Whitehall include **Scotland Yard**, the former site of a 12th-century palace used by visiting Scottish kings and where the Criminal Investigation headquarters of the London Metropolitan Police was located before relocating to New Scotland Yard on the Victoria Embankment in 1890.

Downing Street 25 is another Whitehall side street, where Number 10 is the residence and office of the Prime Minister of the United Kingdom. Originally three houses, they were joined together in 1732 to create a building large enough to accommodate the headquarters of Her Majesty's Government, including offices, meeting rooms and dining rooms, in addition to the private living quarters of the Prime Minister

Churchill waves the victory sign outside No. 10 Downing Street.

and his family. The public is no longer allowed access to Downing Street, which is blocked at each end with iron gates (installed in the 1980s) and retractable electronic barriers (installed in the 1990s).

During World War II, German air raids forced Prime Minister Winston Churchill and his government to seek shelter underground. A bunker located under King Charles Street (one block south of Downing Street) was used and some of these rooms have been preserved as a museum called the **Churchill Museum** and **Cabinet War Rooms** 26. Here visitors can view the map room, cabinet meeting room and Churchill's office-bedroom containing the desk and BBC micro-

phones with which he made his world broadcasts. The trans-Atlantic telephone room (a converted broom closet) is where Churchill placed his top-security phone calls to President Roosevelt. A cable connected Churchill's phone to a large computer-sized scrambler (developed by American Bell Telephone Laboratories) located in the basement of Selfridges department store on Oxford Street. Partially enciphered messages from Churchill's phone were fully enciphered by the scrambler and sent by radio waves to the President in Washington.

South of Westminster Bridge, overlooking the River Thames, is one of London's most famous landmarks – the **Palace of Westminster** 27, built in the mid-1800s to house the British Houses

Palace of Westminster

of Parliament. This famous neo-Gothic palace took 30 years to build at a cost of over £2 million (£1.3 million over budget) and took its toll on the architect Charles Barry and his assistant August Welby Pugin, both of whom literally worked themselves to death overseeing every detail. Neither lived to see their creation completed, but they left behind a national monument recognized the world over as a symbol of democracy and home to one of the most ancient of parliamentary monarchies. The immense complex contains nearly 1,200 rooms, 100 staircases and over two miles of passages.

The medieval palace that once occupied this site was a royal residence for several centuries, until a fire in 1512 prompted Henry VIII to move to nearby White-hall Palace, leaving the Palace of Westminster to become, over time, a parliamentary building. A devastating fire destroyed most of the Palace in 1834, and the current structure – still called Westminster Palace – now stands on this site.

Westminster Palace's north tower – the Clock Tower – was renamed the Elizabeth Tower in 2012 in honour of Queen Elizabeth II and contains the huge bell nicknamed **Big Ben**. The palace's west side is where the medieval **Westminster Hall** has stood since 1099, its magnificent hammerbeam roof rebuilt in the 1300s. Westminster Hall was used for royal feasts, coronation banquets and notable state trials (Charles I was condemned to death here). The hall survived the 1834 fire (which destroyed the rest of the palace) and the 1941 bombing that devastated the Commons Chamber, and is used for major public ceremonies and the lying in state of monarchs, consorts and, occasionally, distinguished statesmen such as Sir Winston Churchill.

St. Stephens Entrance – the public entrance to the Palace of Westminster – is at the southern end of Westminster Hall. The House of Commons occupies the north part of the palace and the House of Lords is in the south part. Both visitor galleries are open to the public when the Houses are in session. Overseas visitors can queue outside St. Stephen's Entrance to obtain entry (only UK residents can obtain free tickets in advance to ensure entrance). Tours are held during the Summer Opening (early August to early October) and tickets can be bought in advance online or on the day at the Ticket Office (located next to the Jewel Tower). Visit www.parliament.uk for more information.

Across the street from the Houses of Parliament is **Westminster Abbey 28**, where nearly

FREE ADMISSION SITES

National Museums and Art Galleries:
British Museum (Bloomsbury)
Museum of London (Barbican)
National Gallery and National Portrait Gallery (Trafalgar Square)
Natural History Museum and Science Museum (South Kensington)
Tate Britain (Millbank)
Tate Modern (Bankside)
Victoria & Albert Museum (Knightsbridge)
Wallace Collection (Marylebone)
Admission is free to all of these venues.

every English king and queen has been crowned since the 11th century, including Queen Elizabeth II's coronation in 1953. A magnificent Gothic structure with tiered arches, fan vaulting and rich carving, Westminster Abbey is also a national shrine, containing the tombs of 18 monarchs, including half-sisters Queen Elizabeth I and Queen Mary I. Distinguished subjects are also buried in the Abbey, and Poets' Corner contains the tombs of Chaucer, Browning, Tennyson and other great poets. Royal weddings and funerals are held in the Abbey, which dates to the 13th century when construction began to replace the site's original Benedictine abbey. Next door to the Abbey is the medieval church of **St. Margaret's**, first built in the late 11th century by Benedictine monks and today the parish church for the Houses of Parliament. Winston Churchill and Clementine Hozier were married in this church in 1908.

South of Westminster, overlooking the Thames at Millbank, is the **Tate Britain** 29, founded in 1897 by sugar magnate Sir Henry Tate, who owned the patent for making sugar cubes and quietly donated much of his personal fortune to charitable causes, including construction of the Tate Gallery. Historic and contemporary art is exhibited at the Tate Britain, including works by Turner, Gainsborough, Constable, James McNeill Whistler and Henry Moore.

Upriver from Millbank is **Chelsea** – an upscale district of exclusive residential squares which was an enclave of 19th-century artists and the heart of the Pre-Raphaelite movement. Famous former residents include Oscar Wilde (34 Tite Street), James Abbott McNeill Whistler (96 Cheyne Walk) and Mark Twain (23 Tedworth Square). The famous **Chelsea Flower Show** 30, held each May by the Royal Horticultural Society on the grounds of the Royal Hospital (a retirement and nursing home for military veterans), is always attended by the Queen. During the 'Swinging Sixties,' members of the Beatles and the Rolling Stones lived on King's Road, which intersects with Sloane Street at fashionable Sloane Square.

Westminster Abbey

Chelsea Bridge, a self-anchored suspension bridge, crosses from Chelsea to Battersea Park on the south bank of the River Thames. During the Queen's Diamond Jubilee celebrations in 2012, crowds thronged here to watch Her Majesty's royal barge and accompanying flotilla of boats sail down the River Thames.

Hampton Court Palace lies upriver from London and can be reached by train from Waterloo Station or by riverboat from Westminster Pier. Originally built as a country home for Cardinal Wolsey, Hampton Court became Henry VIII's favourite residence and much of this Tudor palace has survived, including the Great Hall, Chapel Royal and Haunted Gallery. Baroque updates to the palace were made by Christopher Wren. The palace grounds run down to the River Thames where visitors can enjoy picnics amid the fountains and gardens.

Kew Palace and the famous **Kew Gardens** are located along the River Thames in Richmond and can be reached by riverboat from Westminster Pier. One of the world's leading botanic gardens,

Kew is a UNESCO World Heritage Site containing extensive gardens and greenhouses. Kew Palace, a red-brick mansion built in 1631, was the family home of George III (the 'mad' king) who lived here with Queen Charlotte and some of their 15 children.

Greenwich, located six miles downriver of the Tower and accessible by river boat, is a World Heritage Site and home to the **National Maritime Museum** and the tea clipper *Cutty Sark*. Greenwich Mean Time was (until 1954) based on observations at Greenwich's Royal Observatory. Greenwich is the birthplace of Henry VIII and Elizabeth I, and a Tudor palace once stood on the site of the Old Royal Naval College – a baroque masterpiece designed by Christopher Wren. Nearby, on the Greenwich Peninsula, is the O2 arena and Emirates Air Line cable car spanning the River Thames between North Greenwich and the Royal Docks in Newham. A new cruise terminal is slated to open in 2016 at Greenwich's Enderby Wharf.

National Maritime Museum

Exploring England

Passengers beginning or ending their cruise in England should consider spending not only a few days in London, but also touring the south of England by train or rental car to see places such as **Bath** (famous for its Roman baths), **Stratford-upon-Avon** (birthplace of William Shakespeare), **Oxford** (the steepled university town and locale of the *Inspector Morse* mysteries) and **Blenheim Palace** – a masterpiece of English baroque architecture and the birthplace of Winston Churchill. Situated beside the medieval town of **Woodstock**, Blenheim Palace stands on the site of a former royal palace and was built for John Churchill, Duke of Marlborough, as a reward from the Crown for his military victory at Blenheim in Bavaria. The palace, set in miles of landscaped park, is a World Heritage Site.

Places of interest near the port of **Southampton** include **Winchester** (12 miles away), with its famous Gothic cathedral. Further afield (34 miles distant) is **Stonehenge** (see page 42), for which tickets can be pre-booked online;

visitors are taken to the site via a short shuttle ride from the new welcome centre). The naval port of **Portsmouth** (25 miles west of Southampton) is located on Portsea Island and is a base port for small cruise ships. Soaring above the city's revitalized waterfront at Gunwharf Quays is the Spinnaker Tower, providing breathtaking views for miles in every direction. Charles Dickens was born in Portsmouth (his family's modest house now a museum) but the city's main attraction is the Historic Dockyard, where visitors can step aboard Nelson's flagship *Victory* and view a Tudor-era warship at the Mary Rose Museum.

(Opposite, top to bottom) HMS Victory; a Portsmouth street; Blenheim Palace. (This page, top to bottom) Stonehenge; Woodstock; Dover Castle.

Should your cruise depart from **Dover**, it's worth spending an extra day or two in the Kentish countryside visiting a few castles, gardens and magnificent Canterbury Cathedral. Right in Dover, overlooking the port, is **Dover Castle** – atop the famous white cliffs of Dover Naturally cleaned by rainfall (which also erodes the white-coloured chalk) these cliffs are managed by the National Trust and a visitor centre at Langdon Cliffs provides information about the cliff-top hiking trails.

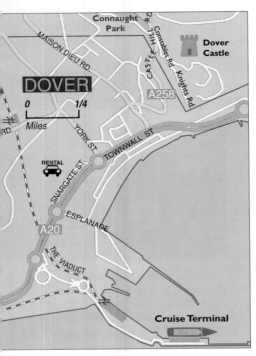

Standing guard atop the white cliffs is **Dover Castle**. No fortress in England has a longer history than Dover Castle, its initial construction begun by William the Conqueror in 1066. Overlooking the shortest sea crossing to France, the castle was designed to defend England from invasion. Hidden beneath Dover Castle is a labyrinth of dark, medieval tunnels, used as recently as World War II when the castle was a military headquarters with wartime personnel working and sleeping underground. A chain of fortresses was built along this coast during Henry VIII's reign, and these include nearby **Deal Castle** (one of the finest Tudor artillery castles in England) and **Walmer Castle and Gardens**, linked to Deal by a beachfront cycle path. All of these castles are managed

Canterbury Cathedral (below) and (opposite) its vast interior.

by English Heritage and are open daily, April to October.

Also close to Dover (about 15 miles north) is the cathedral town of Canterbury. Remains of its medieval walls still stand, within which is a warren of winding streets that lead to **Canterbury Cathedral** – a magnificent structure built over several centuries, starting in 1070. The cathedral stands on the site where an abbey was built by St. Augustine in 597 when he arrived from Rome to convert England to Christianity. In 1170, several of King Henry II's knights entered the cathedral and murdered Thomas Becket, whose shocking martyrdom made Canterbury famous throughout Europe as a place of pilgrimage. A stone slab in the northwestern transept marks the exact spot of St. Thomas's

(Right) The manor house at Goodnestone Park Gardens.

slaying. The marble chair in which archbishops are enthroned stands in the east chapel. The cathedral's long and storied history is reflected in various architectural styles, including the splendid nave, which was rebuilt from 1377 to 1405 in the Perpendicular Gothic style.

Five miles from Canterbury is **Goodnestone Park Gardens**, fifteen acres of resplendent gardens showcasing a stately manor home built in 1704. Jane Austen's brother married a daughter of the

estate's third baronet, and the famous author was a regular visitor who found inspiration here for her novel *Pride & Prejudice*.

Also located in Kent is **Leeds Castle**, famous for its fairytale setting on an islet in a lake, and furnished with medieval tapestries and treasures. Another Kent castle, located in Edenbridge, is **Hever Castle** – where Anne Boleyn spent her childhood. The castle had fallen into disrepair when purchased in 1903 by William Waldorf Astor, who tapped into his vast fortune to restore the castle and gardens to their former splendour. He also built a replica Tudor village of half-timbered cottages that was once part of the castle complex. A few miles from Hever Castle is **Chartwell** – the country estate of Sir Winston Churchill. Managed by the National Trust, this family home is where Churchill drew inspiration from the surrounding hillside gardens.

Close to Heathrow Airport is the town of Windsor, its narrow winding streets overshadowed by fortress-like **Windsor Castle** – the largest and oldest occupied castle in the world. Built by William the Conqueror, with additions and renovations carried out by successive royal rulers, Windsor

Castle remains one of the monarch's chief residences. The Queen spends most weekends at Windsor Castle, where 300 full-time staff (200 of which are resident) keep things running smoothly. A national monument, Windsor Castle's sumptuous State Apartments are open to the public (admission is charged).

Other attractions within the castle complex include Queen Mary's doll house and the splendid 14th-century **St. George's Chapel** – one of the finest examples of Gothic architecture in England – which contains the tombs of ten sovereigns, including King Henry VIII and his third wife Jane Seymour. Changing the Guard takes place outside the Castle at 11:00 a.m. daily (except Sundays) from April to July, and on alternate days the rest of the year. The grounds of Windsor Castle cover 26 acres and also contain **Frogmore House** with its nearby mausoleum where Queen Victoria and Prince Albert are buried.

To visit Windsor Castle from London, take the train from Paddington Station to the Windsor Royal Shopping Pavilion, which is a short walk to the castle.

Leeds Castle in Kent

Weddings in Windsor

The local town hall seems an unlikely place for the heir to the British throne to tie the knot, but Windsor's Guildhall (completed by Christopher Wren) is where Prince Charles married Camilla Parker-Bowles in a civil ceremony in April 2005. They had planned their betrothal for St. George's Chapel in Windsor Castle until legal experts determined that such a move would open this venue to anyone else who wanted to do likewise. Later that same year another high-profile ceremony took place at Windsor's Guildhall when Sir Elton John arrived with his partner David Furnish for their same-sex civil partnership ceremony. In 2013, the Queen gave her royal assent to a bill legalizing same-sex marriages in England and Wales.

For more information on land tours of England, see the Pre- and Post-Cruise section in Part I.

(Top and right) Inviting side-streets near Windsor Castle. (Below) The Long Walk in Windsor Great Park leads to Windsor Castle.

Ports of Call

Dartmouth, Devon

The rural county of Devon is known for its seaside resorts and quaint villages that dot the rolling hillsides. The port of Dartmouth, its natural harbour lined with shops, is best known as the home of the **Britannia Royal Naval College**, which is where a teenaged Princess Elizabeth first met a young naval officer named Philip Mountbatten when she visited the college with her parents in 1939. Many a famous mariner has been born in Devon, namely Francis Drake, Walter Raleigh and Francis Chichester, while the seaside town of **Torquay** (about 10 miles from Dartmouth) was the birthplace of Agatha Christie and is where Oscar Wilde wrote *A Woman of No Importance*. Sketches for Monty Python's *Flying Circus* were filmed in and around Torquay, which became John Cleese's inspiration for

Britannia Royal Naval College overlooks Dartmouth harbour.

Fawlty Towers. The moors of **Dartmoor National Park**, lying inland from Dartmouth, draw hikers and nature lovers, its stark scenery providing the fictional setting for Sir Arthur Conan Doyle's *The Hound of the Baskervilles*.

Falmouth, Cornwall

The windswept Cornish coast consists of craggy headlands and beach-lined coves where pirates once roamed. Whitewashed fishermen's cottages hug the harbours' hillsides, as they have done for centuries, while the stone ruins of **Tintagel Castle**, set atop a rocky, cliff-edged coastline, silently mark the ancient birthplace of the legendary King Arthur. Nearby is the fishing village of **Port Isaac** (which doubles as Port Wenn in the television series *Doc Martin*) where visitors can enjoy sweeping views from a hilltop car park before walking down into the village's narrow winding streets. **Bodmin Moor** lies inland and is where the novelist Daphne Du Maurier got lost in the mist while staying at Jamaica Inn.

Falmouth was once a major trading port, and the author Joseph Conrad spent nine months here in 1882 while serving as second mate aboard a cargo ship that had pulled in for repairs. Cruise visitors to Falmouth can visit the new **Tate Gallery** in the coastal town of **St. Ives**, an artists' enclave since Victorian times, and also visit **St. Michael's Mount** – a rocky islet in Mount's Bay upon which was built a medieval castle and priory – connected to shore at low tide by a natural causeway. Another Cornwall attraction is the **Eden Project** – a giant greenhouse that opened in 2001 in St. Austell, its series of translucent domes rising from the bottom of an abandoned clay quarry and containing 80,000 plants from around the world.

Liverpool

Situated near the mouth of the Mersey River, Liverpool was Britain's most important seaport at the height of the British Empire. Its busy docks stretched for more than seven miles, and grand Georgian and Victorian buildings were erected to house the headquarters of shipping firms and insurance companies. But the 20th century was not kind to Liverpool, which was heavily bombed during World War II. The advent of container shipping in the 1970s made many of Liverpool's docks obsolete, ushering in three decades of decline to the Merseyside port. The economic tide has since turned, with the city's revitalized waterfront of historic buildings earning it World Heritage Site designation by UNESCO in 2004.

Liverpool has always been a city of song and in the late 1950s the Liverpudlian sea shanties gave way to the Merseybeat era of youth culture and homegrown rock bands, the most famous being **The Beatles**. Sites associated with this legendary group include the houses in which Paul McCartney and John Lennon grew up (both restored as museums managed by English Heritage) and the reconstructed Cavern Club (where the group was

Liverpool's historic Pier Head

discovered by Brian Epstein). The Casbah Coffee Club, located in the basement of the home of original Beatles drummer Pete Best, has been granted protected heritage status.

The Beatles Story museum is located at historic **Albert Dock**, and a second museum which covers their solo careers – **The Beatles Story Pier Head** – is at the Mersey Ferries Terminal building. Two-hour Magical Mystery Tours begin at Albert Dock and finish at the Cavern Club.

Albert Dock is also where you will find the **Merseyside Maritime Museum** and **International Slavery Museum**, as well as the **Tate Liverpool**, its exhibits of international modern and contemporary art housed in a 19th-century brick-and-stone waterfront warehouse.

Pier Head is the location of three historic buildings nicknamed the 'Three Graces' – the Royal Liver Building, the Cunard Building and the Port of Liverpool Building – and cruise ships dock in the city centre near these landmarks. Liverpool's main **shopping** area is centred on Church Street and Paradise Street, where the Liverpool One shopping complex is located.

Liverpool shore excursions include walking and driving tours of the city and out-of-town motorcoach trips to the **Lake District** where the poet William Wordsworth lived at Dove Cottage near Lake Windermere.

(Above) A John Lennon statue.
(Below) Liverpool's Albert Dock.

Newcastle upon Tyne

This port city, famous for its coal-shipping industry, was founded in 1080 when the Normans built a "new castle" here. Parts of the city walls and towers remain, and the city's medieval monuments include the Cathedral of St. Nicholas, Trinity Almshouse and the Royal Grammar School. Newcastle is a gateway to numerous historic sites, including **Hadrian's Wall** and Lindisfarne – one of the earliest Christian monasteries in the British Isles. **Durham Cathedral**, set on a promontory high above the River Wear, is one of England's finest examples of Norman architecture. This famous cathedral, along with Durham Castle, comprise a UNESCO World Heritage Site that can be visited on a shore excursion from Newcastle. Also offered is a full-day tour to the historic city of **York**, which is home to the largest Gothic cathedral in England. Construction of York Minster – a stunning sight of flying buttresses and soaring spires – began in the 13th century, when the House of York was a powerful royal dynasty.

Wales

Politically united with England since the reign of the Welsh-born Tudor king Henry VII, Wales nonetheless has a distinct cultural identity. For centuries the region's Celtic-speaking Welsh clans resisted English rule and were eventually placated by introducing the royal custom of investing the English monarch's eldest son with the title Prince of Wales.

Wales is famous for its castles and choirs, with Welsh-born singers including Shirley Bassey and Tom Jones. Welsh actors include Richard Burton and Catherine Zeta Jones, but the artist most closely associated with Wales is Dylan Thomas, author of *A Child's Christmas in Wales*, who is considered one of the 20th century's greatest poets. Born in Swansea, he lived his final years in the estuary village of **Laugharne**, which was his inspiration for the fictional town of

(Above) Newcastle's historic city centre. (Below) St. Davids Cathedral in Wales.

Llareggub ('bugger all' spelled backwards) in his famous radio play *Under Milk Wood*.

Welsh ports of call include **Cardiff**, the capital of Wales and once a major coal-shipping port. The city's historic castle was first built in 1090, and the **St. Fagans** open-air museum encompasses some forty buildings, including a Celtic village where exhibits include a hand-carved wooden lovespoon dating from 1667 (young men would traditionally give an intricately designed

lovespoon to their prospective brides). Mermaid Quay on Cardiff's waterfront is a good place to buy Welsh lovespoons and freshly baked Welshcakes. Also worth sampling is the three-cheese Welsh Rarebit served at Madame Fromage café in the Royal Arcade (the city's oldest covered Victorian street). Cardiff's visitor centre is located beside the Wales Millennium Centre, which overlooks Roald Dahl Plass – a plaza named for the Cardiff-born writer whose parents were Norwegian.

The port of **Holyhead**, situated on Holy Island (which is connected by bridge to Isle of Anglesey), was once a major port for Royal Navy packet ships running between Wales and Ireland. His-

(Top) Laugharne Castle.
(Middle) Dylan Thomas's house in Laugharne.
(Below) Pembroke Castle.

toric attractions in the area include **Beaumaris Castle** (a World Heritage Site) and Plas Newydd (an 18th-century manor house and gardens.) Birds and other wildlife can be viewed along the Anglesey Coastal Path. Welsh is still spoken throughout Wales and is reflected in place names, the longest of which is Llanfairpwllgwyngyllgogerychwyrndrobwllllantysiliogogogoch – which means 'St. Mary's Church in the hollow of the white hazel near to the rapid whirlpool of St. Tysilio of the red cave.'

A stop at the port of Milford Haven in Pembrokeshire offers the opportunity to visit Pembroke Castle, built in 1093 and the birthplace of the Tudor king Henry VII. Other historic attractions include the 12th-century St. David's Cathedral, built on the site of the original church of St. David (patron saint of Wales). Also featured on local excursions is a visit to Lower Town Fisgard (where an adaptation of 'Under Milk Wood' was filmed) and a stop at the picturesque village of Laugharne, the final home of this great Welsh poet.

Channel Islands

When the writer Victor Hugo was banished from France for opposing Napoleon III, he retreated to the small island of **Guernsey**. There he remained for fifteen years, writing *Les Miserables*. Hugo seemed in no hurry to return to France, but in some ways he was already there. Guernsey lies just 30 miles off the coast of Normandy and, along with the other Channel Islands, became

a possession of the British crown when William the Conqueror (Duke of Normandy) conquered England in 1066. Most of Normandy was restored to France in 1450 during the Hundred Years War, but not the Channel Islands, which have remained a British dependency ever since. They are the last remnants of the Duchy of Normandy, and the tiny island of **Sark** (reached by ferry boat from Guernsey) is a fiefdom whose hereditary lord owes allegiance directly to the British crown.

The Channel Islands were once geographically connected to continental Europe, before rising sea levels in about 6000 BC transformed these promontories into islands. Settled by Neolithic farmers, the islands are still used for agriculture – including the famous Jersey and Guernsey cows – although tourism and banking are now major industries, the latter benefiting from generous tax laws. The rivalry between Guernsey and **Jersey** (the other major Channel Island) is reflected in the nicknames they have given one

St. Peter Port, Guernsey

another – donkey (if you're from Guernsey) and toad (if you're from Jersey). Guernsey currently receives the lion's share of visiting cruise ships, which anchor outside St. Peter Port and tender their passengers ashore.

Guernsey, only 25 square miles (40 square km) in size, is a bailiwick divided into parishes. The capital of **St. Peter Port** (called Town by the locals) is where about a quarter of the island's 65,000 residents live. The island feels quite British to most foreigners but it does reveal slight differences. For example, the telephone booths and post boxes are identical to their British counterparts but are painted blue instead of red. Residents predominantly speak English, although French is also an official language, and some speak Guernesiais (a mixture of

(Below) Church of St. Peter.
(Opposite) A fortification built during the German occupation.

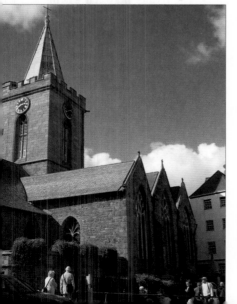

English and French). Driving is on the left, and rental cars are available, but the island is a maze of small lanes with a complicated one-way system. The Guernsey pound is at par with the British pound. Shoppers should look for the traditional Guernsey sweater, knitted with specially spun wool and tight stitches to create a durable garment worn by local fishermen since the 16th century.

Attractions located right in St. Peter Port include **Hauteville House** – the former residence of Victor Hugo and now a museum. The 14-century **Church of St. Peter** is in the heart of Town, which is also home to the **Elizabeth College** for boys, founded in 1563 by Queen Elizabeth I, its main building constructed in 1826. The 13th-century **Castle Cornet**, standing on an islet overlooking the harbour, was built to protect Guernsey from repeated attacks during the Middle Ages by French pirates and naval ships. Full-scale invasion finally came in June 1940, when German troops landed on Guernsey (and Jersey) and remained there for the duration of World War II. Schoolchildren had already been evacuated to Britain to live with relatives or strangers, but smaller children stayed behind with their mothers and fathers. Many residents came close to starving during the German occupation, which ended in May 1945. Fortifications from that era remain, including a bunker built under a low hill which contains a maze of concrete tunnels. Now called the **Occupation Museum**, its underground chambers include a wartime hospital.

A driving tour of the island usually includes a stop at the Occupation Museum and at Little Chapel – a miniature church made with pebbles and shells in 1913 by a monk from Nantes who belonged to a religious order founded by Jean-Baptiste de la Salle that was devoted to teaching. The island itself consists of steep hills and narrow country lanes leading past stone-built farmhouses. The west coast is lined with broad sandy bays and the south coast consists of rocky cliffs with secluded beaches lying at their bases. Two-hour guided bicycle tours of the island are available, as are walking tours of St. Peter Port.

Other excursions include the 45-minute ferry boat ride to the island of **Sark**, which consists of two islets connected by an isthmus and is just two square miles in size. A tractor bus transports ferry passengers from the jetty up Harbour Hill to the village of La Maseline from which the island can be toured by horse-drawn carriage or by bicycle. You can reach the even smaller island of **Herm** (less than one square mile/1.6 square km) by ferry boat from St. Peter Port for a walking tour. Rigid Inflatable boat rides take visitors to the **Humps**

off Herm Island; these islets are a nature reserve protecting seabird nesting colonies. Several species of whales are often sighted in local waters, as are bottlenose dolphins and harbour porpoises.

Jersey, the largest of the Channel Islands, is only 15 miles from the Normandy coast. Its capital and main port is **St. Helier**, where small cruise ships dock at Albert Terminal. Large ships anchor in St. Aubin's Bay and tender their passengers ashore. The town's parish church dates back to the 14th century, and protecting the harbour on an adjacent island (connected to the main island at low tide) is Elizabeth Castle, built in the late 1500s. The island's sub-tropical climate and pleasing scenery make it an appealing vacation resort.

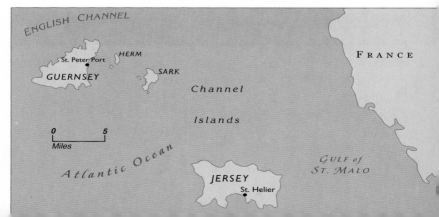

SCOTLAND

Scotland is small in size, but large in stature. Not only has it given the world the games of golf and curling, Scotland is home to tartans, scotch whisky and the poet Robbie Burns, whose composition 'Auld Lang Syne' is sung by millions of revellers on New Year's Eve. You don't even have to go to Scotland to experience Scottish culture, for there are dozens of clan associations in the United States, Canada and other parts of the English-speaking world whose members are proud of their Scottish heritage and celebrate such traditions as wearing kilts and playing bagpipes.

The Scottish comedian Danny Bhoy has described bagpipes as "the missing link between noise and sound," but anyone who has heard a pipe band play a thunderous rendition of 'Scotland the Brave' would have to concede there's a deeply stirring sound to this ancient instrument, its mournful wail once a call to battle in the lonely glens of the Scottish Highlands.

Today people flock to local Highland Games to enjoy the pipe bands, the Highland dancing and athletic events such as the hammer throw and caber toss. The sight of burly men in kilts heaving tree trunks end over end into the air makes it easy to envis-

age the fierce farmer-warriors, called Picts, who first inhabited Scotland back in prehistoric times. According to legend, the dreaded Picts smeared themselves with blue dye and were covered in tattoos. To maintain order among these tribes, the Romans built Hadrian's Wall in the 2nd century. This complex of forts stretched across a wilderness of nearly 80 miles from coast to coast and marked the northernmost frontier of the Roman Empire.

The Scottish clans, ruled by chieftains, slowly formed a kingdom under one leader, only to become a fiefdom of England in 1174. The Scots rose in revolt under the leadership of William

A Scottish pipe band on parade.

'The Battle of Culloden' (1746)
by David Morier.

Wallace, followed by Robert the Bruce, and regained their independence. But Scotland was plagued by repeated attacks from the English and by internal power struggles. When the Reformation arrived in the person of John Knox, founder of Scottish Presbyterianism, the country became split between pro-French (Catholic) and pro-English (Protestant) factions.

It seemed peace and unity would at last prevail when James VI of Scotland, son of Mary Queen of Scots, ascended the English throne in 1603 upon the death of Elizabeth I, thus uniting England and Scotland under one crown. Dissent continued, however, as successive Stuart kings tried to impose their Catholicism on England and Scotland, and were eventually exiled to France. Their supporters in Scotland, the Jacobites, were opposed to the constitutional union of England and Scotland in 1707, and tried

to destroy it. Their final and most famous revolt ended in disaster at the Battle of Culloden in 1746, where they were crushed by English forces.

The Jacobite rebels were led by Bonnie Prince Charlie, born in Rome and 25 years old when he landed in Scotland to regain the British throne for his father James (the Old Pretender). Charles worked his charm on the Highland chiefs, who led their clans onto Culloden Moor to face the might of a government-trained army. In the aftermath of the battle, the rebels were treated as traitors, not prisoners of war, and hundreds were summarily executed. As for Charles, who had fled the battlefield, Flora Macdonald helped him (disguised as her maid) to escape to Isle of Skye where a French ship picked him up and returned him to Europe. There he spent the rest of his life as a broken drunkard.

Peace descended on Scotland, which became intellectually vibrant, producing the likes of philosopher David Hume and economist Adam Smith. The inventor James Watt (for whom electrical wattage is named) devised improvements to the steam engine and coined the term horsepower. As a member of the thriving British Empire, Scotland prospered economically. To meet the growing demand for Scottish wool, more efficient farming methods were introduced and thousands of sheep herders in the Highlands were dispossessed of their grazing land. These Highland Clearances resulted in a mass migration of Scots to Canada and the United States in the 18th and 19th centuries.

The independence movement never completely disappeared in Scotland, which retains its own legal and education systems within the United Kingdom. Scotland was granted limited self-government in 1998 and now has its own parliament, but separation from the United Kingdom was rejected by a majority of voters in a referendum held in September 2014. And so the uneasy alliance continues, as it has for centuries, between Scotland and England.

Scotland at a Glance

Mainland Scotland is divided geographically into two basic regions: the hilly southern Lowlands where Edinburgh and Glasgow are located, and the mountainous northern Highlands. Isle of Skye and the Inner and Outer Hebrides lie off Scotland's northwest coast, and the Orkney Islands and Shetland Islands lie off its northeast tip. The population of Scotland is about 5 million and its land area is 30,414 square miles (78,772 km).

The country's **currency** is the pound sterling. Scottish Standard English is the official language and is spoken by nearly everyone; Scots dialects are also spoken throughout the country and a small minority also speak Scottish Gaelic. Some distinctly Scottish words include: *loch* (a lake or nearly landlocked arm of the sea); *firth* (a broad arm of the sea); *glen* (a secluded, narrow valley); *kirk* (church) and *Hogmanay* (New Year's Eve).

Shore Excursions
SCOTLAND

Scotland's scenic landscapes of heather-covered hills, misty lochs and hilltop castles are featured on a variety of shore excursions.

Edinburgh city tours typically focus on the famous Royal Mile and Edinburgh Castle. If your ship is overnighting in the city, the famous Royal Edinburgh Military Tattoo, with massed pipes and drums, is held at Edinburgh Castle in August and may be offered by your cruise line.

Edinburgh's out-of-town excursions include a scenic drive to Stirling Castle or a full-day visit to the medieval town of St. Andrews for a chance to play a portion of its famous golf course. Some cruise lines offer a day trip to Roslin to visit Rosslyn Chapel.

Glasgow excursions feature city highlights and scenic drives to Loch Loman and Stirling Castle. **Invergordon** tours take in Loch Ness, Culloden Moor and the scotch distilleries of the Spey River valley. Balmoral Castle is highlighted on excursions from **Aberdeen**, while the main attraction of a port stop in **Scrabster** is the Castle of Mey.

If you're exploring independently, rental cars are available at the port of Leith and in Edinburgh, near Waverley Train Station.

Shopping

Scotland is famous for its scotch whisky, especially the Highland single malts (see page 150), and for its lamb's wool sweaters, which are extremely soft and densely woven. Look for cable knit sweaters, most notably those made with Shetland wool, which is naturally insulating and water resistant. Tartans remain popular, with kilts, scarves, ties – even turbans and scull caps – available in some 7,000 registered patterns. If you have Scottish roots, you may want to purchase something in your ancestral clan's unique design, available in most tartan shops. Fine kilts are tailor made and require yards of wool cloth to accommodate the garment's pleats. A man's kilt opens on the right and should fall at mid-knee. The sporran, which hangs in front of the groin, serves as a pouch since most kilts are pocketless. Kilt hose (knee-high woollen socks with garters) complete the look. A decorative sheathed dagger is tucked into the right sock (or left sock if you're left handed) – a traditional gesture of friendliness that symbolizes a man's revealing his weapon when invited into someone's home.

Ports of Call

Edinburgh

Several ports service Edinburgh, including **Leith**, which is located three miles from the city centre on the south shore of the Firth of Forth. Ships docking at Leith use the Ocean Terminal Complex, where the Royal Yacht *Britannia* (decommissioned in 1997) is permanently berthed as a tourist attraction. From here you can make easy connections to downtown Edinburgh by rail, bus, taxi or ship's shuttle bus (take buses 22 or 35 from Ocean Terminal for the 15-minute ride into town.) Leith can only handle ships up to 55,000 tons, so the larger ships either anchor at **South Queensferry**, located 10 miles west of central Edinburgh, or dock at the port of **Rosyth** on the north side of the Forth, from which it's 30 to 45 minutes by shuttle bus to downtown Edinburgh. At **South Queensferry**, taxis and buses depart from the tender pier; the train can be caught at nearby Dalmeny, located a half mile uphill from the pier. The train trip is about 15 to 20 minutes and gets you right into Waverley Train Station. Most cruise lines will offer a free or inexpensive shuttle to Edinburgh from any of the above ports.

Edinburgh (pop. 500,000) is the cultural and administrative capital of Scotland. The city is also a publishing centre with a strong literary heritage which earned it UNESCO's first City of Literature designation in 2004. Famous writers associated with Edinburgh

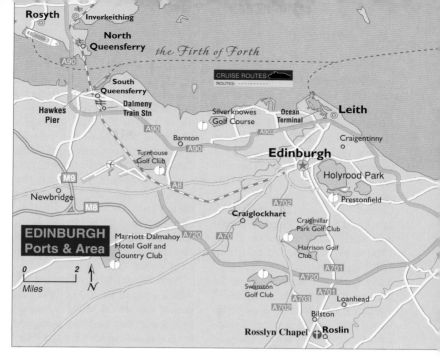

A Scotsman greets visitors to South Queensferry beside Forth Bridge – a cantilever rail bridge built in 1890.

include James Boswell, Sir Walter Scott, Robert Louis Stevenson, Sir Arthur Conan Doyle and J.K. Rowling, who completed *Harry Potter and the Deathly Hallows* in a room of the Balmoral Hotel on Princes Street. Fans of Ian Rankin's detective 'Rebus' can soak up the atmosphere at the **Oxford Bar** in New Town. *The Scotsman* newspaper, before moving to new premises on Holyrood Road, occupied for nearly a century an imperious Victorian building (now the five-star **Scotsman Hotel**) which stands beside North Bridge, in between the Royal Mile and **Princes Street** – the latter being Edinburgh's main **shopping** area, along with **George Street**'s designer stores and fashionable bars in the vicinity.

Edinburgh's famous **Royal Mile** runs through the heart of **Old Town** – a World Heritage Site of cobbled lanes and courtyards containing historic buildings which date back to the 16th and 17th centuries. Edinburgh Castle stands at one end of the Royal Mile, and the **Palace of Holyroodhouse** **1** (the Queen's official residence in Scotland) is located at the other end. The palace occupies the site of a 12th-century abbey, and its original Chapel Royal contains the tombs of several Scottish kings. The palace itself was begun in about 1500 but was destroyed by fire in 1650 and rebuilt by Charles II. Mary Queen of Scots survived an attempted coup while living here.

Places of interest along the Royal Mile and its warren of side-streets and alleyways include **Mary King's Close** **2**, a subterranean street that was built over in the 1700s and is said to be haunted. Opposite is the **High Kirk of Edinburgh (St. Giles)** **3**, easily recognized by its Scottish crown steeple, where **John Knox** preached in the 1500s. (**Knox's house** **4** is just a few blocks to the east.) The floor of St. Giles's Chapel of the Thistle is tiled with a rare granite quarried on Ailsa Craig Island in the Firth of Clyde, which supplies most of the world's granite used for curling rocks. Incidentally, the sport of curling began in medieval Scotland and was first played on frozen ponds with flat-bottomed river stones.

New Scottish Parliament **5**, which opened in 2004 at the east end of the Royal Mile, is housed in a modernist building designed by Catalan architect Enrico Marrales. One of its decorative motifs is based on 'The Skating Minister' by Sir Henry Raeburn, which portrays Reverend Robert Walker, clad in black, skating on Dud-

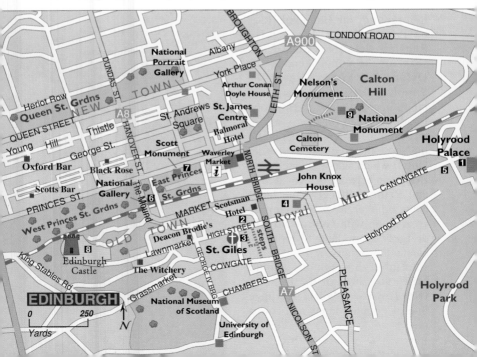

dingston Loch. This iconic painting hangs in the **National Gallery of Scotland** 6, which is located on The Mound next to the grounds of Edinburgh Castle. An imposing neo-classical building, the National Gallery houses one of Britain's finest art collections, including important works by Tintoretto, Titian, Rembrandt, Gainsborough and Turner. Nearby is a celebrated landmark of Edinburgh, the **Walter Scott Monument** 7.

Edinburgh Castle 8 is the city's most dominant landmark, built atop Castle Rock where it looms above the city skyline. This mighty fortress is surrounded on three sides by rocky cliffs, making it nearly impregnable, and its approach from the town is a long sloping forecourt, the scene of the Edinburgh Military Tattoo, which is held each August and showcases regimental pipe bands. The castle complex contains the Royal Pal-

(Above) Edinburgh Castle overlooks the city of Edinburgh and its famous Royal Mile (below).

ace, the 16th-century Great Hall and St. Margaret's Chapel, which dates from the early 12th century.

Calton Hill provides an excellent view of the city and on clear days you can see Leith and across the Forth to Inverkeithing. Calton Hill can be accessed by stairs located opposite Calton Cemetery. A statue of Abraham Lincoln, erected in memory of Scottish Americans who died in the American Civil War, is at Calton Cemetery.

Outlying attractions include **Rosslyn Chapel** (of *Da Vinci Code* fame) and the **Royal & Ancient Golf Club of St. Andrews** where the Old Course is the favourite of the game's greatest players, including Jack Nicklaus, who played his last round of professional golf here in 2005. (Golf originated in 12th-century Scotland with shepherds knocking stones into rabbit holes.) The public Old Course is closed on Sundays to let the grass recover. On some Sundays, the links are opened as a park for the towns-people to enjoy. The grounds over-look beach-lined St. Andrews Bay, where the iconic running scene in the 1981 film *Chariots of Fire* was filmed. Steeped in history, the medieval town of St. Andrews is small and friendly, with a universi-ty campus founded in 1413. Prince William met his future wife, Kate Middleton, when both were stu-dents here.

Another out-of-town attraction is dramatic **Stirling Castle**, which sits atop a lofty crag. Beautifully restored, this castle is where Mary Queen of Scots and other Scottish monarchs were crowned.

Scotch Whisky

Scotland has produced whisky commercially since the 16th cen-tury, when the art of making scotch passed from monks to landowners. Thus began an industry that became a mainstay of Scotland's economy. Scotch whisky was originally used as a tonic or medicine, and was called *aqua vitae* ('water of life').

For scotch afficionados, a visit to a distillery is a must. Scotch is made from the fermented grain mash of malted (partially germinated) barley and unmalted (grain) barley. Single malt and vatted (pure) malt whiskies use only malted barley while blends will use a mixture of malt and grain whiskies. The spirit from the stills is matured in oak casks previously used to mature bourbon, sherry, port or dessert wine – this lingering aroma lending a subtle taste and colour to the scotch which is specific to the type of cask used. The 'age' of a whisky is the time between distillation and bottling.

Single malt whisky is from a single distillery and usually contains whisky from many casks and different years, which enables the master blender to achieve a taste typical of the distillery. Cask-strength whisky is bottled direct-ly from the cask, undiluted. Usually, this is a showcase product brought to a very high quality by specialists.

Glasgow

Inveraray Castle near Glasgow

Glasgow (pop. 600,000) lies along the banks of the River Clyde and is Scotland's leading seaport and shipbuilding centre. Ships dock at Greenock Ocean Terminal, located 25 miles from Glasgow in a wide stretch of the scenic Firth of Clyde. Glasgow's revitalization in recent decades has transformed what was once a gritty, industrial city into a dynamic cultural centre. Points of interest include the city's 13th-century cathedral, the Kelvingrove Museum and Art Gallery, and the Hunterian Museum and Art Gallery (Scotland's oldest museum) located on the main campus of Glasgow University.

The art nouveau architect Charles Rennie Mackintosh designed numerous civic and private buildings in Glasgow, most notably the Glasgow School of Art. Modern architecture in Glasgow includes the Clyde Auditorium (dubbed The Armadillo) and the Riverside Museum, built on a former shipyard site at Pointhouse Quay and housing collections of the Glasgow Museum of Transport. The Burrell Museum, in a park setting on the city's south side, houses a famous art collection bequeathed by shipping magnate Sir Alexander Burrell.

Outlying attractions include **Inveraray Castle** (seat of the Duke of Argyll, Chief of Clan Campbell), Glengoyne Distillery and the national park at **Loch Lomond** – the largest freshwater loch in Scotland. Dotted with wooded islands at its southern end, Loch Lomond is overlooked at its northern end by Ben Lomond, a mountain rising over 3,000 feet (900 m). A cave at Loch Lomond was once used as a refuge by Robert the Bruce before he was crowned king of Scotland in 1306.

Scottish Highlands & Isles

Invergordon, situated near the entrance to Cromarty Firth, is the busiest port of the Highlands and is a half-hour drive to Inverness, capital of the Highlands with a population of 55,000. The best way to take in the area's numerous attractions is via organized

Urquhart Castle ruins on the shores of Loch Ness.

shore excursions, which include a visit to the historic battlefield at **Culloden Moor**, as well as a tour of the scotch-producing **Spey River valley**, home to the Glenlivet and Glenfiddich distilleries. **Loch Ness** is another popular excursion and is known worldwide for a legendary sea monster living in its depths (which reach 700 feet/213 meters). Newspapers began reporting sightings in 1933, at about the same time a circus started visiting the nearby town of Inverness. Circus trainers would sometimes lead their elephants down to the loch for a drink of water and a swim. An elephant swimming in the water could easily be mistaken for a sea monster with two humps (the top of its back and head) and an upraised trunk appearing above the surface. A variety of **castles** can be visited on excursions from Invergordon, namely Dunrobin Castle, Cawdor Castle and Urquhart Castle ruins.

Aberdeen, on Scotland's east coast, is the centre of Scotland's oil industry (supplied by North Sea oil wells) and is the port of access to **Balmoral Castle**, the Queen's 50,000-acre (20,234 hectare) summer retreat where she spends her annual summer holiday. Queen Victoria, who loved all things Scottish, purchased the Balmoral Estate in

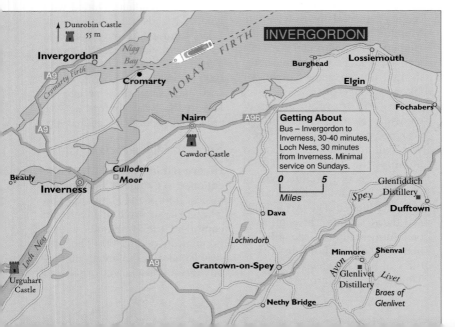

INVERGORDON

Dunrobin Castle
55 m

Invergordon

Nigg Bay

Cromarty

MORAY FIRTH

Cromarty Firth

Burghead

Lossiemouth

Elgin

Fochabers

Nairn

A96

Cawdor Castle

Getting About
Bus – Invergordon to Inverness, 30-40 minutes, Loch Ness, 30 minutes from Inverness. Minimal service on Sundays.

Beauly

Inverness

Culloden Moor

Glenfiddich Distillery

Spey

Dufftown

0   5
Miles

Dava

Lochindorb

Minmore   Shenval

Grantown-on-Spey

Glenlivet Distillery

Avon   Livet

Braes of Glenlivet

Urquhart Castle

Loch Ness

Nethy Bridge

1852 and commissioned the existing castle. The Estate grounds, gardens and the Castle Ballroom are open annually to visitors from early April to the end of July.

Scrabster is located at the northern tip of mainland Scotland, its most popular area attraction being the **Royal Castle and Gardens of Mey**, which was the Queen Mother's holiday home for more than 50 years. (The Queen Mother spent her childhood years at Glamis Castle, her family's ancestral home near Dundee.)

The **Orkney and Shetland Islands** stretch northward from Scotland's northern tip into the Norwegian Sea. These remote islands were originally settled by Picts, then invaded by Vikings in the 8th century. They remained Norse possessions until 1472, when they were given to the Scottish crown in trust for the undelivered dowry of Margaret of Norway who had married James III in 1469. Scandinavian traces remain in the people and their culture, and attractions for cruise visitors include the islands' numerous neolithic sites

Only 16 of the 70 Orkney islands are inhabited, and **Kirkwell** is the main port, located on the principal island, called the Mainland (a corruption of the Old Norse name of Meginland). This island's concentration of ancient relics – Stone Age villages, a borch (prehistoric fort), burial chambers and standing stones – was granted World Heritage Site status by UNESCO in 1999.

Lerwick is the principal town of the Shetland Islands, where visitors can visit Pictish forts and

(Top) Dunrobin Castle, seat of the Clan Sutherland, and (above) Castle of Mey.

a Bronze Age village. These rugged, windswept islands are also home to several unique breeds of small-statured animals, including the Shetland pony and the Shetland sheepdog.

IRELAND

The green and rolling hills of Ireland are as timeless as the harp music of Turlough O'Carolan, whose travels on horseback took him from town to town performing his lyrical tunes for appreciative patrons. The winding bridle paths of the early 18th century are now narrow country roads navigable by car but still bordered by stone fences, upon which working sheepdogs regularly clamber to look around as if in search of something. It could be they just want a better view of the grazing sheep and whitewashed cottages.

The pastoral beauty of the Emerald Isle long ago inspired its early poets, whose intense love of nature created a folklore of Celtic magic and mysticism. But equally impressive to most visitors is the warm welcome of the Irish people, who must surely rank among the world's friendliest.

Irish hospitality harks back to the days when heroes wandered the world disguised as common men and all strangers were received graciously, for you could never be sure just who that was sitting at your table. Ancient myths and legends were preserved orally in the stories of the Druids – pagan priests who enjoyed a privileged position as official poets to the tribal chiefs. When St. Patrick introduced Christianity to Ireland in the 5th century, he too was a gifted writer who possessed an unusually winning personality.

One of the most successful missionaries in history, St. Patrick was born in Britain to affluent parents of Roman citizenship.

Dunmore East, near Waterford.

A page from the Book of Kells.

Captured at the age of 16 by Irish marauders, he was enslaved as a herdsman for six years before escaping to continental Europe. There he entered a monastery and, following a vision that called him to return to Ireland, he spent years studying to become a missionary. A quarter of a century later, he returned to convert the Irish – tribe by tribe – until nearly all of Ireland was Christian. But pagan traditions lived on in the imagination of the Irish poets, whose verse – composed in Gaelic Irish – was admired for its melodic richness and harmonious combinations of sounds. The Irish use of rhyme was adopted into Latin and eventually spread throughout Europe as Ireland's unique Celtic Christianity produced brilliant scholars and attracted foreign stu-

dents to its monastic schools. Up until the 8th century, Ireland was a centre of learning while much of Europe was plunged into turmoil following the collapse of the Western Roman Empire.

Irish artistry thrived in medieval Ireland, including the creation of beautifully illuminated manuscripts and epic poems of romance and heroism. This golden age of Irish literature was revisited in the late 19th century when the country's struggle for self-government inspired a cultural movement called the Irish Literary Renaissance, led by William Butler Yeats. Considered Ireland's greatest lyric poet, Yeats was fascinated by Celtic mythology. When he accepted the Nobel Prize for Literature in 1923, he did so as "a representative of Irish literature" and his inspired poetry was described by the Nobel committee as expressing the spirit of an entire nation.

The Troubles

Ireland's period of sectarian violence known as the Troubles began in the 1960s, but its seeds were sown in the 12th century when England's King Henry II established an overlordship in Ireland, marking the start of an Anglo-Irish struggle that would last for nearly 800 years. When England imposed Protestantism on a largely Catholic Ireland in the 16th century, Irish rebellions were brutally put down by Henry VIII, Elizabeth I and Oliver Cromwell, who crushed an uprising in 1649 and confiscated Irish lands, giving these to absentee English landlords.

In 1800 Ireland was politically united with England under the Act of Union, but Irish agitation continued. Then, one of the worst natural disasters in history struck when a five-year blight ruined the country's potato crop, the staple food of the Irish population. The Great Potato Famine lasted from 1845-49, during which time hundreds of thousands of Irish died, and 1.6 million eventually emigrated to the United States.

Irish nationalism became increasingly militant with the founding of Sinn Fein in 1905. Outlawed by the British government, Sinn Fein went underground and waged guerrilla warfare. Ireland was partitioned in 1920, its northernmost province of Ulster remaining part of the United Kingdom and thenceforth called Northern Ireland. The Irish Free State was established by treaty with Great Britain in 1922 but not fully accepted by the Irish, who wanted total independence and whose cause was pursued by the Irish Republican Army. The Republic of Ireland finally attained independence in 1949, but the troubles in Northern Ireland were far from over.

Unlike the rest of Ireland, which is overwhelmingly Irish Catholic, Ulster was populated with Scottish and English Protestant settlers who retained strong ties to Britain. Following World War II, a new generation of educated Catholics in Northern Ireland refused to accept the status quo, but hard-line Protestants refused to make concessions.

A vicious cycle of sectarian bloodletting engulfed Northern Ireland until British Prime Minister Tony Blair brokered a tentative peace deal in 1998. A power-sharing agreement between the two sides was struck in 2007, with Queen Elizabeth making a symbolic visit to Ireland in 2011. This was followed in 2014 with the first state visit to Britain in nearly a century by an Irish president. In a speech to the British Parliament, President Michael Higgens declared the two nations had attained "a closeness and warmth that once seemed unachievable."

Meanwhile, American presidents continue to receive a warm welcome in Ireland, with Barack Obama telling a cheering crowd at Dublin's College Green in 2011 that he had come to Ireland in search of his name's missing apostrophe.

Famine memorial in Dublin

Shore Excursions

IRELAND

In addition to tours covering city highlights at each Irish port of call, out-of-town driving excursions take visitors through the scenic countryside see famous castles, monasteries and magnificent country estates, as well as the region's natural landmarks. At **Dublin** these include a tour of the Wicklow Hills and a visit to Glendalough to view the ruins of a 6th-century monastery (an all-day tour). A four-hour tour to Malahide Castle provides a close look at an early Norman castle, built in the 12th century, and views of the scenic coastline north of Dublin. **Belfast**'s outlying attractions include the Giant's Causeway and places associated with St. Patrick.

Cork provides access to Blarney Castle and village, as well as tours to the fishing port of Kinsale, the walled town of Youghal, and the scenic lakes and mountains of Killarney National Park viewed from the lovely grounds of Victorian-era Muckross House. Of interest to passengers of Irish descent is the Cobh Heritage Centre which offers a unique genealogy search service. Blarney Castle can be visited on a ship's shore excursion or by booking a seat with ECoach (www.ecoach.ie); their 8-hour tour includes Kinsale and picks up right at the dock at 8:00 am.

Shore excursions in **Waterford** include guided walking tours of the town's historic monuments, including two cathedrals. Driving tours take you to see Lismore Castle (the town was founded in the 7th century), the Rock of Cashel and magnificent Kilkenny Castle, built in 1192. This massive castle is well maintained and with beautiful grounds. Also offered by some cruise lines is an all-day tour to the JFK Arboretum – a plant and forest collection on 623 acres surrounding the summit of Slieve Coillte.

A walking tour of **Dunmore East** has much to recommend it with a picturesque harbour and historic Hook Lighthouse at the eastern entrance.

Most ports have car rentals either in or near the city or at the airport. Driving is on the left in Ireland.

Visit your cruise line's website for specific information on shore excursions and costs. Local tour options include those offered by Dublin-based Excursions Ireland (excursionsireland.com)..

Kilkenny Castle

Shopping

Shopping items to look for in Ireland include traditional Aran sweaters made with merino wool (extremely soft and warm) in patterns reflecting the fishing culture of the Aran Islands, such as cable stitch and basket weave. Irish linens are excellent buys as are Donegal tweed sweaters and caps. Traditional Irish jewellery features the Celtic knot (symbolizing infinity) and the heart knot, which represents everlasting love when combined with the Celtic knot.

(Left) The Celtic heart knot

Ireland at a Glance

The Republic of Ireland (pop. 4.6 million) occupies five-sixths of the island of Ireland, and Northern Ireland (pop. 1.8 million) occupies the remaining one-sixth. Dublin (with a half million population) is the capital of the Republic of Ireland. Belfast is the capital of Northern Ireland.

The Republic of Ireland joined the European Union in 1973 and the country's unit of **currency** is the euro. The British pound is Northern Ireland's currency.

Irish Gaelic (taught in the schools) is Ireland's first official language, but English (the country's second official language) is predominant throughout most of Ireland. Irish Gaelic is spoken in parts of the western seaboard and appears on road signs. Driving is on the left.

Irish pubs have long been the heart of the country's social life and musicians often gather for a lively session over a few pints of Guinness.

Ports of Call

Dublin

Dublin began as a Viking settlement called Dubh Linn ('dark pool') – named for the small lake that formed where the River Poddle flowed into the River Liffey. When King John ordered construction of Dublin Castle, its moat was filled with water from the River Poddle. This tributary now flows through a brick tunnel lying beneath city streets, with Dublin Castle's gardens lying above the site of the dark pool.

The River Liffey runs through the middle of Dublin and is spanned by numerous bridges. Large cruise ships berth at Alexandra Quay, which is about 2 miles (3.2 km) from the city centre and small ships dock along the River Liffey at North Wall Quay. **Getting to town** from the cruise port can be done by taxi (10 euros), your ship's shuttle or by catching Bus #53. Hop-on Hop-Off buses operate in Dublin, starting on O'Connell Street. The port is an industrial area, but once you're outside the gates, it's a pleasant 45-minute walk along the River Liffy into town. Attractions along the way include an O2 amphitheatre, Samuel Beckett Bridge and Jeanie Johnston Tall Ship and Famine Museum at Custom House Quay. Dublin's outlying suburbs include the seaside community of Killiney where **Bono, The Edge, Enya** and other celebrities have gated homes.

A young boy and his dog inside an Irish country pub.

City Attractions 👁

The attractions in Dublin are numerous and most lie close to the River Liffey, within walking distance of one another. They include the **12th-century Christ Church Cathedral 1** (the city's earliest church) and its rival cathedral – **St. Patrick's 2**, which was begun in 1191 by Dublin's first Anglo-Norman archbishop on a site near a well at which St. Patrick is said to have performed baptisms. Both cathedrals became property of the Church of Ireland during the English Reformation, and during Oliver Cromwell's conquest of Ireland he stabled his horses in St. Patrick's nave to show his Puritan disrespect for the Anglican religion (which was associated with Royalists). Today St. Patrick's is Ireland's national cathedral and Christchurch Cathedral is the seat of the Church of Ireland's arch-bishop. Dublin's Roman Catholic cathedral is St. Mary's on Marlborough Street.

Dublin Castle 3 was the residence of the lord lieutenants of Ireland until 1922, after which it has housed government offices. Beside it is Dublin's **City Hall**, housed in the 18th-century Royal Exchange.

Nearby is the famous **Temple Bar** area **4** – the city's cultural quarter – which is a medieval maze of cobblestoned alleys and narrow streets lined with pubs, shops and art galleries. Fishamble Street is where the first performance of Handel's *Messiah* was held in 1742, and a tavern on Eustace Street is where the Society of the United Irishmen was formed at a meeting in 1791. The historic Clarence Hotel on Wellington Quay, overlooking the River Liffey, is home to the beautiful art deco Octagon Bar.

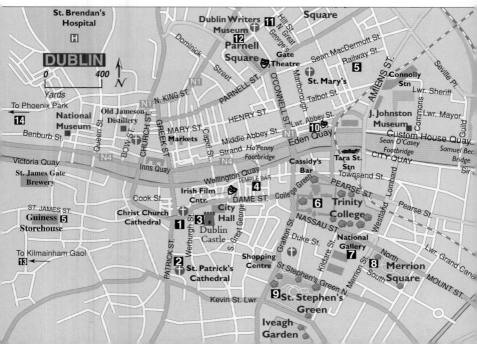

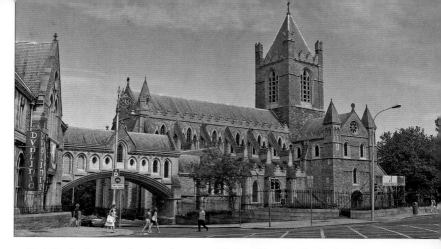

Dublin is famous for its abundance of convivial **pubs**, many of them concentrated in the Temple Bar area, while less touristy pubs include Mulligan's on Poolbeg Street (mentioned in one of the *Dubliners* stories). The Davy Byrnes (on Duke Street off Grafton) was frequented by James Joyce and is one of Dublin's most storied pubs, as is O'Donoghue's on Merrion Row, where the Dub-

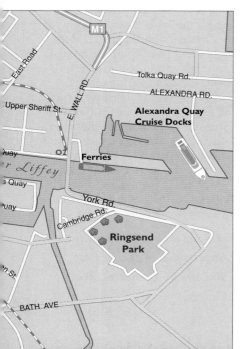

Christ Church Cathedral is Dublin's oldest church.

liners folk band formed. Cassidy's Bar at 27 Westmoreland (near College Green) is run by cousins of Bill Clinton, who dropped by while visiting Dublin in 1995 during his peace trip to Northern Ireland. The Bull & Castle on Christchurch Square serves good pub food, and for take-out fish and chips, try Burdock's on Werburgh Street near Dublin Castle.

Not to be missed is the **Guinness Storehouse** 5 – a former fermentation plant transformed into a seven-storey visitor centre featuring a museum (tickets available online), restaurant and circular rooftop bar with views over central Dublin. Founded in 1759 by Arthur Guinness, the Guinness Brewing Company occupied dozens of grey-brick warehouses in the cobblestoned St. James's Gate area.

Across College Green from Temple Bar are the grounds of **Trinity College** 6, founded in 1591, where the Book of Kells is on display in the library. This 8th-century manuscript of the Latin

Gospels is considered the finest example of Celtic illumination. Famous Trinity alumni include Oscar Wilde, Oliver Goldsmith and Jonathan Swift, who is buried in the nave of St. Patrick's Cathedral where he was dean from 1713 to 1745.

Close to Trinity College are several National Museums and the **National Gallery 7** (housing a collection of old masters), which faces onto **Merrion Square 8**. This fine Georgian square is associated with Oscar Wilde (who lived at No. 1 Merrion Square), W. B. Yeats (who lived at No. 82) and Daniel O'Connell, Ireland's Catholic emancipator, who lived at No. 58.

St. Stephen's Green 9 is an ancient commons which developed over time into a city park with a small lake, formal garden and bandstand. The Shelbourne Hotel opened in 1824 on the north side of St. Stephen's Green and is where the Irish Constitution was drafted and signed in 1922. Members of Ireland's parliament and judiciary frequent the hotel's lounge, called the Horseshoe Bar.

Leading off the northwest corner of St. Stephen's Green is **Grafton Street** – a pedestrian shopping street, busy with buskers and other street entertainers. Grafton eventually joins with Westmoreland, which leads over the O'Connell Bridge to the north side of the River Liffey. The next bridge over

(Top to bottom) Oliver St. John Gogarty pub in Temple Bar; St. Patrick's Cathedral; Trinity College.

(to the west) is the **Ha'penny Bridge** – a pedestrian bridge built of cast-iron in 1816.

O'Connell Street is Dublin's main thoroughfare, its paved central median featuring statues and monuments to various Irish political leaders. This broad boulevard has been the scene of many public celebrations and demonstrations over the years (the Post Office was seized by Irish republicans during the 1916 Easter Rising) and is the main route of the annual St. Patrick's Day Parade.

Attractions near O'Connell Street include the **Abbey Theatre** **10** (Ireland's National Theatre, founded by Yeats), the **James Joyce Centre** **11** (devoted to the life and work of Joyce; housed in a Georgian townhouse on N. Great George's Street) and the **Dublin Writers Museum** **12** at No. 18 Parnell Square.

Dublin is a literary city, its homegrown talent including the playwrights Samuel Beckett and George Bernard Shaw, and the novelist James Joyce, who spent most of his adult life abroad but whose novels are set in Dublin. *Ulysses*, one of the great works of world literature, recreates the events of a single June day in Dublin in 1904. This day is celebrated each June 16 as Bloomsday (for the protagonist Leopold Bloom) with Dubliners dressing up as characters in the book.

Outlying Dublin attractions include **Kilmainham Gaol** **13**, now a museum, where Irish leaders of the 1916 Easter Rising were held and executed. **Phoenix Park** **14**, home to the Dublin Zoo.

Waterford

Founded by Vikings in 914, the coastal town of Waterford (pop. 50,000) is as scenic as it is historic. Three verdant river valleys flow into the fjord-like harbour where large cruise ships anchor and tender their passengers ashore at the seaside village of **Dunmore East**. The small ships proceed upriver to Waterford quay.

The historic village of Dunmore East, where settlement dates back to the Iron Age, is worth spending time in. Hook Head Lighthouse – a 13th-century Norman structure – marks the eastern entrance to Waterford

Large ships anchor at Dunmore East (Waterford's harbour).

(Above) Waterford's cathedral.
(Below) Dunmore East street.

Harbour and today houses a visitor centre, gift shop and café. The 16th-century Duncannon Fort – situated on a rocky promontory – is now home to a maritime museum, café and craft shops. There are plenty of harbourfront pubs and restaurants in Dunmore East, including The Spinnaker Bar and The Strand Inn.

Getting to **Waterford** from Dunmore East requires either taking a taxi, a cruise line tour or catching the Suirway bus which picks up at the Harbour House and at all bus stops on the Dunmore Road (www.suirway).

The famous crystal factory in Waterford is no longer in operation but the town remains an appealing destination with its narrow streets lined with quaint houses and shops, and its historic cathedral. It is a compact city and has been described as the Salzberg of Ireland. Nearby is a challenging golf course at Waterford Castle.

Stunning scenery around Waterford includes the Nore Valley and spectacular Vee Pass and Golden Vale in the Comeragh Mountains.

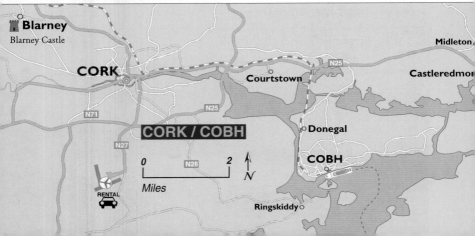

Ballycotton Bay, County Cork

Cork

Situated near the mouth of the River Lee, Cork is the major city of southern Ireland, where scenic County Cork is edged with sandy bays and seaside villages. The cruise liners dock at **Cobh** (meaning 'cove' in Irish) right beside the Heritage Centre, which offers a unique genealogy search service for people of Irish descent. Hundreds of thousands of Irish emigrants heading to America boarded ships in Cobh, which was the last port of call for RMS *Titanic* before it headed across the Atlantic on its doomed voyage. Cobh is about ten miles (16 km) from Cork and regular rail service connects Cobh with Cork. A train station is located just above the Heritage Centre in Cobh.

Cork began as a monastic settlement founded in the 7th century by the monk Fin Barre, and was walled by the Danes in the 9th century. Much of its medieval architecture was destroyed during the guerilla warfare of the 1920s when Cork was set afire by pro-British paramilitaries. The blaze, which destroyed much of the city's core, originated on **St. Patrick's Street**, which is today part of Cork's shopping district, as are pedestrian-only **Paul Street** and the covered English Market – a food market constructed in Victorian times. Cork's most famous landmark is the 19th-century St. Fin Barre Cathedral, built of Cork limestone in the French Gothic style.

Cork's inviting **pubs** include Mutton Lane Inn, located on a narrow alleyway off St. Patrick's Street, near the English Market. Another recommended pub is The Bierhaus on Popes Quay with its selection of over 200 beers. A good restaurant choice is Bodega, housed in historic Coal Quay's old St. Peter's Market building on Cornmarket Street, where a Saturday Food Market is held. Suggested pubs in Cobh include the Clifton Bar on Midleton Street (just north of Cobh Cathedral) and the Rob Roy on Pearse Square.

Within easy driving distance of Cork are several major attractions, including the romantic ruins

(Top) Old Head of Kinsale
(Above) Muckross Estate

of **Blarney Castle**, its medieval battlements containing the famous Blarney Stone. Placed in an almost inaccessible position near the top of the castle's thick stone walls, the Blarney Stone is said to bestow the powers of eloquence on anyone who kisses it. The village of Blarney is known for its hand-loomed tweed and is a good place to shop for Irish goods at the Blarney Woolen Mill Shop.

The seaside resort of **Kinsale**, 16 miles (25 km) south of Cork City, is a medieval harbour town of winding streets lined with gourmet restaurants and art galleries housed in 18th-century buildings. The defeat of two Irish earls by English forces at the Battle of Kinsale in 1601 brought an end to the old Gaelic aristocracy as their members were forced to abandon their lands and seek exile in Europe, their departure from Ireland called the Flight of the Earls. Another historic event associated with Kinsale is the sinking of the *Lusitania* in May of 1915 when a German U-boat torpedoed the Cunard liner off Old Head of Kinsale; 1,198 of the ship's 1,959 civilian passengers perished in this wartime tragedy.

Further afield, in County Kerry, is the beautiful scenery of **Killarney National Park**. Originating with the 1932 donation of **Muckross Estate** near Killarney, this park features beautiful lakes, woodlands and mountain peaks.

Belfast

Now that the Troubles have ended in Northern Ireland, the capital of Belfast is rebuilding its neighbourhoods and welcoming cruise passengers to its historic harbour. Here the great shipyards of Harland and Wolff have built some of the world's largest ocean liners, including the *Titanic*. In 2012, a museum commemorating this famous, ill-fated ocean liner opened on Queen's Island. Called **Titanic Belfast**, the attraction consists of a massive building housing nine galleries that tell the story of the ship – from its construction, launch and maiden voyage, to its tragic sinking and eventual salvaging of the wreck.

Other Belfast landmarks include **City Hall** (built in the Baroque Revival style and completed in 1906) and the modern Waterfront Hall – a concert hall and exhibition centre with bars and a restaurant. The city's cultural quarter – called Cathedral Quarter – is a former warehouse district centred on **St. Anne's Cathedral** and dotted with atmospheric bars, such as The John Hewitt (a local favourite). The Crown Liquor Saloon is Belfast's most celebrated bar with its wooden snugs and stained glass, located on Great Victoria Street. Other city attractions include the Victorian architecture of the covered St. George's Market on May Street.

Out-of-town tours offered in Belfast include a drive north of the city to the **Giant's Causeway**, where basalt columns descend from a cliff's edge into the sea. Designated a World Heritage Site, these remarkable landforms were created by volcanic upheaval but, according to ancient legend, a giant named Finn McCool fell in love with a lady giant in Scotland and built this causeway to bring her across the channel in grand style. Other attractions in this area include Bushmills Distillery and **Carrick-a-Rede Rope Bridge**, a suspension bridge made of wire rope and Douglas fir, which spans a deep chasm to connect the mainland with tiny Carrick Island. The current bridge is much safer than earlier ones, yet there are still instances of visitors having to be removed by boat from the island because they can't face walking back across the swaying bridge.

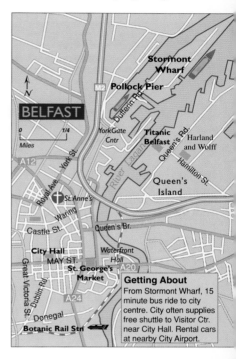

Getting About
From Stormont Wharf, 15 minute bus ride to city centre. City often supplies free shuttle to Visitor Ctr. near City Hall. Rental cars at nearby City Airport.

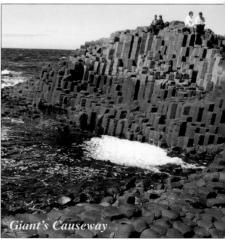

Giant's Causeway

Western Europe

France, Belgium and the Netherlands comprise the western seaboard
of continental Europe, their coastal cities facing the English Channel
and North Sea. France's Normandy ports of Cherbourg and Le Havre
provide access to Paris and to the D-Day landing beaches of World
War II. Zeebrugge is the Belgian port providing access to Brugge,
Ghent, Antwerp, Brussels and Ypres. The major cruise ports in the
Netherlands are Amsterdam and Rotterdam.

These nations were part of Charlemagne's great medieval empire before it was divided into three smaller kingdoms. For centuries the resultant West Frankish kingdom (France) fought the East Frankish kingdom (Germany) for control of the Netherlands and Belgium, which were called the Low Countries in reference to their low-lying river deltas. Today this flat, windmill-dotted countryside is laced with canal-side bicycle paths and the region's historic merchant cities are noted for their medieval squares and gabled guild houses.

FRANCE

French culture has been widely admired since the 13th century, when the other courts of Europe adopted its language, poetry and manners. Today it's the food, the wine and the *joie de vivre* that many of us admire about the French. In a nation where dining is an art form, and where the arts are for all to enjoy, the many aspects of gracious living fall into fascinating perspective. Politics are important, but so is lunch. And for the average visitor to France, figuring out the lunch menu could well be easier than understanding the many departments, districts, cantons and communes of French government.

France has had a centralized administration since the Revolution of 1789, yet each region has retained its own distinct character. This diversity harks back to the Middle Ages, when provinces were ruled by dukes and counts, and feudal power was held by nobles, guilds and the clergy.

France was first settled by Greek and Phoenician traders, then conquered by Julius Caesar in 58 BC. For five centuries Gaul, as the Romans called it, was under Rome's rule. Then, in 486 AD, the Franks – a Germanic tribe – routed the last Roman emperor of Gaul and the region soon lay in ruins. The only remnant of Roman civilization was the church, which also faced ruination when Saracens invaded in the 8th century.

The Carolingian dynasty, led by Pepin the Short, rescued the region, and his son Charlemagne (Charles the Great) became a legendary figure. Crowned Emperor of the West on Christmas Day in the year 800, Charlemagne was immortalized in medieval poems as the champion of Christendom. A great leader and administrator, he ushered in an intellectual renaissance and promoted the rebirth of learning and the arts.

Studying the lunch menu in Paris's Latin Quarter.

Crowds along the Champs Elysées celebrate the liberation of Paris.

A thousand years later Napoleon Bonaparte drew on Charlemagne's example when forging his empire, and his liberal reforms lay the groundwork for modern-day France. The nation's most recent military hero was Charles de Gaulle, who organized the Free French forces during World War II and became the first president of France's Fifth Republic. General de Gaulle is regarded by the French as one of their greatest citizens of all time, while icons of French culture include the writer Victor Hugo, the impressionist painter Claude Monet and the cabaret singer Edith Piaf. July 14 is Bastille Day, a national holiday celebrated with parades and fireworks. (For information on the French Revolution, see page 52 in Part I.)

A Few French Facts

The population of France is 65 million, and Roman Catholicism is the major religion. Paris is the capital and the country is governed by an elected president, who appoints a premier responsible to the National Assembly. France is an industrial nation and major economic power, yet more than half of its land area is still used for agriculture. Tourism is also a major industry, with France receiving more international tourists than any other country in the world. The official language is, naturally, French, although some English is spoken in most tourist areas. When entering a shop, be sure to greet the proprietor before you start browsing, or you will be considered rude. It's also polite to say goodbye when leaving. Useful words in French are: *bonjour* (hello), *au revoir* (good-

The Wines of France

French wines, the best of which set the standard for the rest of the world, are identified by regions, called *appellations*. These vary in size from single small vineyards to large districts. The French tradition of familiarizing oneself with the appellations and, more importantly, the best growers and merchants within each appellation, can be a daunting task for wine drinkers who rely on identifying the variety of grape (varietal) when choosing a wine. Generally speaking, the Cabernet Sauvignon and Merlot grapes feature predominantly in red Bordeaux wines, and the Sauvignon Blanc and Semillon grapes are most often used for making white Bordeaux. A red Burgundy is made with the Pinot Noir grape and a white Burgundy is made with the Chardonnay grape. Bordeaux wines come in high-shouldered bottles whereas Burgundy bottles have sloping shoulders.

A Bordeaux bottle (on the left) and a Burgundy bottle.

bye) and, when asking for assistance, *pardonez mois* (pardon me), *parlez vous Anglais?* (do you speak English?) and *merci* (thank you). When ordering in a restaurant, begin with *s'il vous plait* (if you please) and ask for your cheque when finished.

France uses the 24-hour clock: 0:00 to 11:59 is AM and 12:00 to 23:59 is PM (12:00 = noon, 24:00 = midnight). France's country code is 33 when telephoning internationally. **The unit of currency is the euro**.

Ports of Call

The two main French ports of call on a Northern Europe cruise are Cherbourg and Le Havre. These Normandy ports provide access to the D-Day landing beaches and historic towns such as Honfleur and Rouen. Le Havre also serves as a port of access to Paris, which is a three-hour drive or a two-hour train ride each way.

Le Havre is a large commercial port at the mouth of the river Seine. Destroyed during World

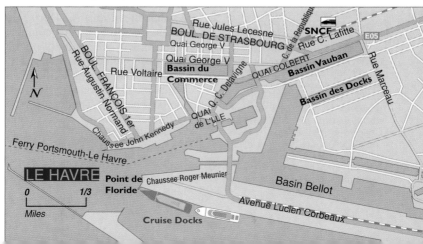

Cherbourg's cathedral

Shore Excursions

France

Cruise line excursions to **Paris** are by motorcoach and they include panoramic drives of the city, sightseeing cruises on the River Seine, walking tours of Montmartre, a visit to the Louvre, or a ship's shuttle (with a central drop-off and pick-up spot) for passengers wanting to tour Paris on their own.

For independent travellers, rail is the best way to get to **Paris** from Le Havre. The station is just a few minutes away by taxi and the trip is about two hours. You arrive at Gare Saint Lazare, which is close to the city centre. Trains from Le Havre run every hour (check raileurope.com for current schedules). Taxis or the metro are excellent choices for getting around quickly in Paris.

Organized excursions are also available to Versailles Palace and Monet's Giverny home and garden. Normandy shore excursions usually include Honfleur, Rouen and the D-Day beaches, with some tours going as far south as the famous abbey atop Mont-Saint-Michel. Check your cruise line's website for details on shore excursions available with your cruise.

(For brief descriptions of Normandy attractions, please turn to the end of this chapter.)

War II, the city (pop. 185,000) was rebuilt in the modernist style, for which it has been classified a World Heritage Site. The cruise ships dock at Florida Pier where a Cruise Welcome Centre provides a full range of services and visitor information. Car rentals are available for self-drive tours of the Normandy countryside or you can hire a taxi at the cruise dock for a tour of the area. Walking from the port into town is restricted and the cruise lines usually offer a shuttle bus between the port and the train station, where there are regular departures for Paris (Gare Saint Lazare). Most cruise lines also offer a coach shuttle to Paris, dropping passengers off at a central location with pick-ups in the same spot four or five hours later for the return trip to Le Havre. ATMs and currency exchange kiosks are plentiful in Le Havre and Paris.

Cherbourg (pop. 42,000) is a naval base and industrial seaport overlooking the English Channel. Its new cruise terminal (Gare Maritime Transatlantique) opened in 2006 next to the Cité de la Mer, a maritime museum, both of which are housed in the refurbished remains of a 1930s Art Deco ship terminal and train station complex where great ocean liners of the past once called. The cruise terminal is a short walk to the town centre of cobblestoned streets near the boat harbour. The train station is further afield on Avenue Francois-Miller; the train ride from Cherbourg to Paris-Saint-Lazare is three hours. Cars can be rented in town (reserve ahead online) and taxis are plentiful.

Paris

Paris, the City of Light, is one of the world's most beautiful cities. Stately tree-lined avenues lead to monumental squares from which winding medieval streets fan out in all directions. At night, a sparkling blanket of lights adorns the city, especially when viewed from atop Montmartre Hill, and the River Seine becomes a shimmering ribbon that winds through the heart of the city. Once a grubby town of crowded, filthy streets, Paris was remodelled in the mid-1800s when many of its narrow streets were torn down to make way for wide avenues lined with handsome neo-classical buildings, their heights limited by building codes to create a unified roofline. Street lighting was also introduced, enhancing the riverside walks and tree-lined boulevards.

With a population of 10 million, Paris is France's economic engine and one of the world's leading business centres. The skyscrapers of the city's business district are strategically located apart from the historic core, where the elegant 19th-century atmosphere has been preserved, making the city centre an inviting place for walking and soaking up the sights and sounds.

Getting Around

Paris is divided into sections called *arrondissements*, which are numbered 1 to 20 in a circular pattern. Each of these neighbourhoods is worth exploring, but if your time is limited, focus on the must-see sights located near the River Seine, which flows through the heart of the city centre and divides it into the Right Bank (north side) and Left Bank (south side). Île de la Cité lies in the middle of the river and contains the Cathedral of Notre Dame de Paris. Famous attractions on the Right Bank include the Louvre, Place de la Concorde, Champs Elysées and Arc de Triomphe. Famous Left Bank attractions include the Eiffel Tower, Latin Quarter, La Sorbonne, Pantheon and Luxembourg Gardens.

The Paris skyline at night

(Top to bottom) Cluny La Sorbonne metro station; sightseeing boat on the Seine; the new Shakespeare & Company bookstore on Rue de la Bucherie.

A convenient and pleasant way to obtain an overview of the city's highlights is by taking a one-hour **river cruise** on a glass-covered tour boat. There are also on-and-off boat tours that depart from numerous quays along the Seine between the Eiffel Tower and the Cathedral of Notre Dame. Red double-decker sightseeing buses also offer on-and-off tours. The Paris Metro is an efficient way to quickly get from point to point.

Walking is the best way to truly experience the charm and variety of the Parisian neighbourhoods, where you can pause for refreshment at a sidewalk café or relax on a park bench with a picnic lunch. On Sundays, designated roads – including those along both sides of the Seine – are car free. Sturdy touring bicycles can be rented from public bicycle racks using a credit card.

NOTE: Mornings are the best time to visit the interior of the **Eiffel Tower** (when the elevator lineups are their shortest) and **Notre Dame Cathedral**, when the morning sunlight floods through the stained-glass windows. Expect long lineups at the Louvre, especially to view the *Mona Lisa*. The **Paris Museum Pass** provides fast-track entry to these major attractions. Museums in Paris generally close one day a week (usually Monday or Tuesday).

Shopping

Paris is famous for its designer stores and boutiques, and the most glamorous of these are found along the Champs-Élysées and Rue de Faubourg Saint-Honoré, the latter being the epicentre of Parisian fashion with stores showcasing major international designers such as Dior, Valentino and Chanel. Place Vendome is the location of flagship stores of Cartier, Chanel and Piaget. The arcaded Rue de Rivoli, which runs alongside the Louvre, is another fashionable shopping street.

Several department stores are located on Haussman, including the opulent, glass-domed Galeries Lafayette – a collection of designer shops with a food court on the bottom level and a rooftop café. The Bon Marché is another well-known department store, located on the Left Bank on Rue de Sèvres, about a half mile west of St. Sulpice Church.

Outdoor markets are located throughout Paris, each neighbourhood containing a warren of pedestrian streets that wind their way through open-air markets selling everything from fresh fruits and vegetables to bargain-priced clothing and antiques. The Marché aus Fleurs (flower market) on Île de la Cité is one of the oldest markets in Paris.

Note: Some shops are closed on Sundays.

Dining

Dining in France is pure pleasure. Whether a simple continental breakfast or a five-course dinner accompanied by fine wines, the meal will be expertly prepared and presented. Restaurants usually offer a *plat du jour* (menu of the day) featuring two or three courses at a set price, which is

The Latin Quarter is famous for its sidewalk cafés and food stands.

less expensive than ordering *a la carte*. Most restaurants include a 15% service charge in their prices. Cafés, bistros and brasseries traditionally serve beverages accompanied by light fare. Typical opening times for lunch are noon to 2:30 pm and dinner is generally served from 7:30 pm to 11:00 pm. Many restaurants are closed on Sundays and some shut down for the month of August.

Hemingway called Paris a moveable feast. The city's famous café culture held a special appeal

The cafés at Saint-Germain des Pres attracted famous writers of the 1920s, including Ernest Hemingway.

for writers in the 1920s when the Lost Generation of expatriates descended on Paris. The city's cafés are where Parisians meet friends, people watch or sit and read undisturbed. A young Hemingway spent hours in various Left Bank cafés working at his craft, including La Coupole on Boulevard du Montparnasse and Café Les Deux Magots on Rue St-Benoit, one of three famous cafés at Saint-Germain des Prés. The art deco Café de Flore is next door and around the corner on Boulevard Saint-Germain is Brasserie Lipp, where generous portions of Alsatian cuisine are served. These three cafés with their outdoor terraces have long been a focal point for intellectuals and artists, attracting such luminaries as Picasso, F. Scott Fitzgerald and Jean-Paul Sartre. Another iconic café in the Saint-Germain area is La Palette on Rue de Seine. The shop windows and food displays along nearby Rue Bonaparte are a feast for the eyes.

There is a huge and diverse selection of restaurants and sidewalk cafés throughout Paris, and most of the city's major attractions, such as the Eiffel Tower, the Louvre, Centre Pompideau and Musée D'Orsay, offer on-site dining. The domed rooftop café at Galeries Lafayette offers great views over Paris, and the terrace at Le Rostand (6 Place Edmond Rostand) overlooks Jardin du Luxembourg. Some of the city's best restaurants are found in or near the train stations. Le Train Bleu in Gare Lyon serves lunch and dinner in an opulent Belle Epoque setting.

For a more modest dining experience, sample one of many bistros serving French home-style cooking. Rue Mouffetard, in the Latin Quarter, is a cobblestone street lined with tiny bars, bistros and food markets where Julia Child shopped for ingredients in her gourmet feasts.

City Attractions

The **Eiffel Tower** ■ was designed by the architectural engineer Gustave Eiffel (who also designed the internal structure of the Statue of Liberty) and was erected at the entrance to the Paris World's Fair of 1889. Its bold revolutionary design symbolized the triumph of science and engineering, but it so dominated the Paris skyline (as it does to this day) that it provoked a storm of protest among leading intellectuals.

However, the public soon accepted this monument to modern technology because, for a small sum, anyone could ride the elevators to the top of the tower for sweeping views of Paris that were previously seen only by the privileged few able to afford a hot-air balloon ride. Thus, the Eiffel Tower, which served no practical purpose, was quickly adopted as an iconic symbol of Paris.

One of the world's most popular tourist attractions, the Eiffel Tower is more than 300 metres high, constructed of iron and illuminated at night by projected light beams and 20,000 sparkling light bulbs that have been installed by mountain climbers. The tower has received more than 200 million visitors (it took 94 years to reach the 100-million-visitors mark, but just 19 more years to double that). The tower's first and second floors are reached by lifts or by stairs (704 steps to the second floor). From the second floor, another set of lifts take visitors to the top for panoramic views of Paris. For more information, visit www.tour-eiffel.fr/en.html.

The Eiffel Tower is Paris's most famous landmark.

Stretching southeastward from the Eiffel Tower is **Parc du Champs de Mars** – a large, public green space originally used for military drills. Also near the Eiffel Tower, directly upstream, is a footbridge called **Passerelle Debilly**, which leads across the river to the **Palais de Tokyo** ■ on the Right Bank. Built for the 1900 World's Fair, this bridge became a secret meeting spot for East German spies during the Cold War. The Palais de Tokyo is a contemporary art museum.

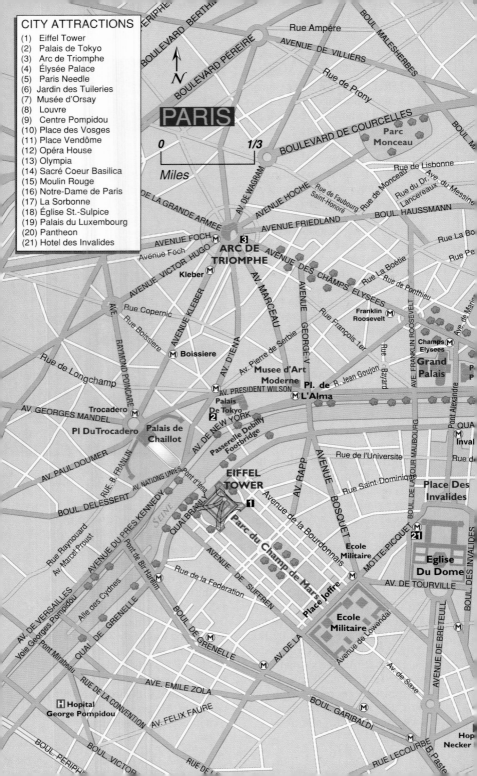

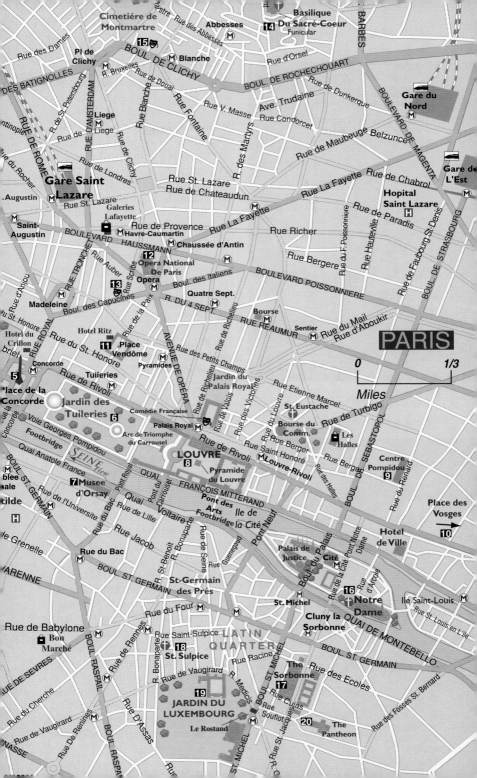

Arc de Triomphe (above) and Pont Alexandre III (below).

Directly east of Palais de Tokyo is **Place de L'Alma** where several main avenues converge. The tunnel that runs beneath Place de L'Alma is where Princess Diana was killed in August 1997 when her speeding limousine, pursued by paparazzi, crashed into a pillar. Avenue Marceau leads north to the **Place de L'Étoile**, formed by the intersection of 12 radiating avenues at the centre of which stands the massive **Arc de Triomphe** ▣. Honouring those who fought for France, the arch stands 162 feet (50 m) high – a climb of 40 stairs to the top for great views of Paris. To reach the arch's entrance, do not cross the traffic circle but take the pedestrian tunnel on the Avenue de le Grande Armee side of the circle. The principal sculptural group flanking the arch is *La Marseillaise* by Francois Rude. The body of an unknown French soldier was interred beneath the arch in 1920 and a perpetual flame was lighted.

France's most celebrated avenue, the tree-lined **Champs Elysées** leads directly from the Arc de Triomphe to the Place de la Concorde. Exclusive shops line its length, and numerous side streets lead off this spacious avenue, including Avenue de Marigny, which runs past the opulent **Élysée Palace** ▣ (official residence of the French President) to **Rue Du Faubourg Saint-Honoré**. This exclusive shopping street, although narrow and nondescript compared to Champs Elysées, is one of the world's most luxurious, with nearly every major global fashion house located here, as well as the Paris offices of Vogue magazine and the American, British and Canadian embassies. Leading in the opposite direction off Champs Élysées is **Avenue Winston Churchill**, which runs between the **Grand Palais** (a glass-roofed exhibition hall) and the **Petit Palais** (the city's Fine Arts Museum) before connecting with **Pont Alexandre III** – an arch bridge ornately decorated with Art Nouveau lamps and sculptures. It was named for the Russian czar who concluded the Franco-Russia alliance of 1892.

(Above right) Champs Elysées viewed from Place de la Concorde. (Right) Tuileries Gardens. (Below) The Louvre.

Place de la Concorde marks the eastern end of the Champs Élysées and contains the **5** **Paris Needle** – an ancient obelisk from the temple of Luxor which was presented to France by the Egyptian government in 1826. This red-granite column, flanked by fountains, stands near the spot where Louis XVI and Marie Antoinette were guillotined in 1793. Stretching eastward from Place de la Concorde to the Louvre is the lovely **Jardin des Tuileries** **6** (Tuileries Garden). Tuileries Palace once stood at its

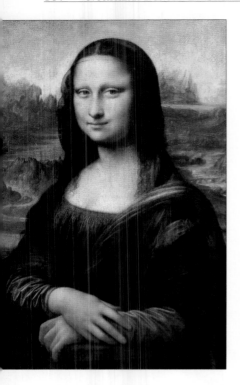

The famous de Vinci painting of
'Mona Lisa' is at the Louvre.

eastern end, which is where Louis XVI and Marie Antoinette were held under house arrest in Tuileries Palace, which was burned by insurrectionists in 1871, its ruins later demolished. A pedestrian footbridge (Passerelle Solferino) links Tuileries Garden with the Left Bank's **Musée d'Orsay 7**. This fine art museum is housed in a former railway station and contains the world's largest collection of Impressionist masterpieces, with works by Monet, Renoir, Gauguin and Van Gogh.

The **8 Louvre** is one of the world's largest and most important art museums, its series of galleries stretching for almost a mile. It began as a medieval fortress and served as a royal palace before the French court moved to Versailles. Over time, new buildings were added to the sprawling site, the most recent additions being the glass pyramid erected in the 1980s at the museum entrance and, in 1993, the Carrousel du Louvre shopping mall, which leads to the main reception area under the pyramid. Famous works of art housed in the Louvre include the *Mona Lisa*, the *Nike* and the *Venus of Milo*, as well as a vast collection of ancient Egyptian antiquities. The Louvre is open 9:00 am to 6:00 pm every day, except Tuesday when it remains closed.

Pont des Arts is a pedestrian bridge linking the Louvre to the Institute of France on the Left Bank. With its delicate ironwork arches and beautiful views of the Seine, this celebrated bridge was rebuilt after being rammed by a barge in 1979.

Rue de Rivoli runs eastward from the Louvre to **Hotel de Ville** (8) (City Hall) which was rebuilt in the 1870s after the Paris Commune set fire to this 16th-century French Renaissance building. A few blocks north of Rue de Rivoli is the **Centre Pompidou 9** (designed by Renzo Piano and Richard Rogers) which opened in 1977 to house the National Museum of Modern Art.

Continuing east on Rue de Rivoli, you will eventually arrive at **Place des Vosges 10** – the oldest planned square in Paris. This elegant quadrangle of symmetrical two-storey townhouses was built in the early 1600s as Place Royale and, although royalty did not live here, the French aristocracy did. Famous former residents include Cardinal Richelieu and Victor Hugo, whose home is now a museum. A central fountain and lawns occupy the spacious courtyard where duels were once fought, and the arcaded townhouses now contain restaurants and shops.

Other Right Bank attractions include **Place Vendôme 11**, where the Hotel Ritz opened its doors in 1898 after César Ritz converted a private residence into a luxury hotel. Coco Chanel lived at the Ritz off and on for thirty years, including during the Nazi occupation of Paris, and she died there in her private suite in 1971 at the age of 87. The bar off the hotel's lobby was a favourite haunt of Ernest Hemingway.

(Top to bottom) Place des Vosges; Opéra House; Moulin Rouge.

The city's famous **12 Opéra House**, designed by Charles Garnier in the Beaux-Arts style, stands at the convergence of several main avenues north of Place Vendôme. Completed in 1867, the Opéra typified the new, modernized Paris with its opulent façade of arches, columns and a profusion of sculpture and ornamentation brilliantly combined for theatrical effect. Nearby on Boulevard des Capucines is the **Olympia 13**, the oldest music hall in Paris and the venue at which Edith Piaf achieved great fame in the 1950s, followed by Jacques Brel in the 1960s.

The bohemian **Montmartre** district stretches up the hillside to **Sacré Coeur Basilica 14**, where the view overlooking the city

(Above and below) Notre-Dame's exterior and interior.

from its steps is spectacular. Montmartre was once an enclave of famous artists, including Renoir, Toulouse-Latrec, Picasso and Van Gogh, and the Montmartre Cemetery, which occupies an old quarry, contains the graves of some of the world's finest creative talents, including Nijinsky, Berlioz, Degas and Truffaut. The famous cabaret **Moulin Rouge** **15** (Red Windmill) is nearby on Boulevard De Clichy.

Pont Neuf, the city's oldest bridge, connects the Right Bank to **Îsle de la Cité** – home to **Notre-Dame de Paris** **16** (Our Lady of Paris). This early Gothic cathedral, known the world over for its flying buttresses and majestic nave of stained-glass windows, was built between the late 12th century and the early 14th century. Visitors can climb to the top of the north bell tower (ticket purchase required) and, from the rampart connecting the north and south bell towers, come face to face with the stone gargoyles of Notre-Dame. The great bell, made famous by Quasimodo in Victor Hugo's novel *The Hunchback of Notre Dame*, is in the south bell tower and reached by a wooden staircase.

Also on Îsle de la Cité is the **Conciergerie** (a prison-turned-museum associated with the Reign of Terror) and the **Palais de Justice**. A pedestrian bridge connects to the smaller **Île St. Louis** where you will find elegant 17th-century apartment buildings, restaurants and sidewalk cafés.

The Left Bank's Latin Quarter, situated around **La Sorbonne** **17** (University of Paris), is famous for its bookstores and cafés associated with legendary writers of the 1920s (see Dining section). Ernest Hemingway lived at 6 rue Ferou, near **18** **Église St.-Sulpice** (a large neo-classical church featured in Dan Brown's *The Da Vinci Code*) and he was a frequent visitor to **Shakespeare & Company**, a bookstore once located on Rue de l'Odéon where the American expatriate Silvia Beach published James Joyce's *Ulysses* (banned elsewhere) in 1922. Shakespeare & Company shut down during the Nazi era and a new bookstore of the same name is on Rue de la Bucherie.

Palais du Luxembourg **19** (housing the French Senate) overlooks the expansive **Jardin du Luxembourg** – a public park featuring lawns, fountains and a pond where children sail toy boats, as well as a playground, puppet theatre and vintage carousel.

Nearby is the **Pantheon** **20** – a monumental domed church (its façade modelled on the Pantheon in Rome) which serves as the mausoleum of France's most honoured citizens and contains the remains of Voltaire, Rousseau and Victor Hugo, among others. Napoleon's tomb lies beneath the **Dome des Invalides**, part of an architectural complex containing the **Hotel des Invalides** **21** – a 17th-century war veterans hospital that is now a military museum. Across the street from Les Invalides is the Musee Rodin, dedicated to the works of the French sculptor.

(Above) Luxembourg Palace
(Below) Interior of the Pantheon

Attractions outside of Paris include the **Palace of Fontainebleau**, a royal chateau favoured by Napoleon (reached by train in 45 minutes from Gare de Lyon) and the **Palace of Versailles** (a half hour outside Paris by train from Gare Saint Lazare) where Louis XIV (the Sun King) converted his father's hunting lodge into a magnificent palace set on 2,000 acres of grounds filled with landscaped gardens and dozens of fountains.

Chartres, 50 miles southwest of Paris (1-1/4 hours by train from Gare Montparnasse) is an ancient town famous for its Cathedral of Notre Dame, built in the 12th and 13th centuries, and widely considered to be the finest Gothic cathedral in the world. Outstanding features include its two spires, magnificent stained glass windows and superb sculpture. Henry IV was crowned king of France here in 1594.

Allied armies landed at several beaches along Normandy.

Normandy Attractions

The rolling farmland and picturesque fishing ports of Normandy were an inspiration to the French Impressionist painters of the late 19th century, led by Claude Monet. His famous works include a group of paintings of the Gothic cathedral in **Rouen** – the medieval capital of Normandy where half-timbered buildings line the narrow streets and Joan of Arc was burned in the market square in 1431. Monet's celebrated series of water lilies was painted at his home in the riverside village of **Giverny**.

The Norman fishing port of **Honfleur**, much of its medieval architecture preserved, was a focal point of the Impressionist art movement and its cobbled streets are lined with galleries and sidewalk cafés. The idyllic atmosphere of this seaside town was shattered during World War II when the nearby beaches became a landing site of the Allied inva-

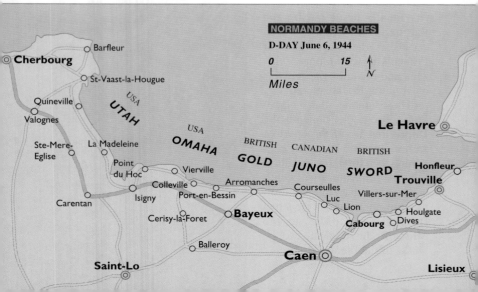

sion of Europe in June 1944. Known as **Operation Overlord**, the assault began in the early hours of June 6 when British and American airborne forces landed behind German coastal fortifications. They were followed at daybreak by a flotilla of transports, warships and small craft from which thousands of Allied soldiers swarmed ashore. British and Canadian forces landed on Gold, Juno and Sword beaches, while US forces landed on Utah and Omaha – the latter beach the scene of the fiercest fighting. This battle is vividly portrayed in Steven Spielburg's film *Saving Private Ryan*, and the Normandy American Cemetery, containing the graves of over 9,000 American soldiers, is set on a clifftop plateau overlooking **Omaha Beach**. A Visitor Centre provides insight to this momentous battle, as does the War Memorial in **Caen**, a town that endured widespread destruction during WWII. Caen's medieval fortress was built by William the Conqueror and now houses a Museum of Fine Arts. The town's Abbaye-aux-Hommes is where William the Conqueror was buried in 1087. Following his death, Normandy was fought over by various French and English kings until it was permanently restored to France in 1450.

The fortified Benedictine monastery on **Mont-Saint-Michel**, a rocky tidal isle just off the coast of Normandy, came under frequent assault by the English during the Hundred Years War (1337 – 1453) but was never captured. Today it's a major tourist attraction with its imposing Gothic architecture and dramatic setting.

Brittany lies west of Normandy and ports of call along this scenic coast include St. Malo, Brest and Lorient. Regional attractions include Pont-Aven with its numerous art galleries, and Carnac – site of more than 3,000 prehistoric standing stones.

D-day at Omaha Beach

BELGIUM

Considered the cross-roads of Western Europe, Belgium is densely populated and crisscrossed with an extensive network of railroads and canals. The country's central location has been both a blessing and a curse, for it was turned into a battlefield when invaded by Germany in both World Wars, and prior to that was the site of the Battle of Waterloo, which marked the end of the Napoleonic Wars.

Belgium was originally a Roman province of ancient Gaul, its people called Belgae. Conquered by the Franks in the 5th century, the region – known as Flanders – was part of the great Carolingian dynasty until the death of Charlemagne in 814, after which the region became a French fiefdom ruled by powerful counts.

Their authority was eventually challenged by the merchant cities of Brugge, Ghent and Ypres, which prospered in the 13th century as producers of luxury textiles, their finished cloth – made exclusively of the finest English wool – finding a market all over Europe. Belgium's traditional industries of lace making (in Brugge) and diamond cutting (in Antwerp) still thrive, and its beautifully preserved medieval towns are major draws for tourists.

The medieval cloth workers hall in Ypres.

Belgium At a Glance

Small in size, Belgium has a population of 11 million and consists of three partially autonomous regions – Flanders in the north, Wallonia in the south and Brussels, with a population exceeding one million, in the centre. Wallonia contains the country's mining areas and heavy industries; Flanders is the location of the country's textile, shipping and farming industries.

Famous for its fine chocolate, Belgium has also given the world the Brussel sprout, the Belgian horse (a large breed of draft horse) and the Belgian sheepdog.

The people of Flanders speak Flemish (the Belgian variant of Dutch) while Wallonians speak French. Brussels, the capital, is officially bilingual (French and Flemish). Regional tensions often dominate Belgium's political scene.

The nation's form of government is a parliamentary democracy under a constitutional monarchy dating to 1831, when Leopold I was installed as king after Belgium declared its independence from the United Kingdom of the Netherlands.

Officially neutral during both world wars, but defiant in the face of German occupation, Belgium has long been a proponent of European cooperation and unity, and its capital Brussels serves as the headquarters of the European Union.

Belgium's unit of currency is the euro. The country calling code is +32. July 21 is National Day.

Shopping & Dining

Old World artisanship still thrives in Belgium where popular shopping items for visitors include fine linens, Belgian tapestries (wall hangings, cushions, table mats) and delicate lacework items such as christening gowns and wedding veils. Famous for its gourmet chocolate, Belgium is where the praline – a chocolate shell (*couverteur*) filled with nougats or creams – was invented by a chocolatier in 1912.

Cafés serve a wide variety of Belgian beers, and local cuisine features Flemish *carbonnade* (beef stewed in beer), *frites* (French fries), mussels in a white-wine sauce and Belgian waffles topped with whipped cream.

Getting Around

Zeebrugge is the port of access for Belgium's historic sites and cities. The cruise ships dock in the western outer port, at the Leopold II dam or the adjacent Albert II dock for smaller ships. Getting to Brugge by cab or by the ship's shuttle can be pricey and the train is a good alternative. Zeebrugge-Dorp (village) and Zeebrugge-Strand (open only in summer) are the nearby train stations – both about 1-1/4 miles (2 km) from the pier but along a busy industrial port area, so walking this stretch is not pleasant. There is usually a shuttle bus available at quay-side to the nearby town of Blankenberge where

A student band performs in traditional Belgian attire.

Shore Excursions

Belgium

Brugge is the most sought-after destination for passengers arriving at Zeebrugge and a variety of excursions is offered to this beautifully preserved medieval city, including guided walking tours. Shuttles to Brugge for passengers exploring the city on their own are usually available, starting at about $60 per person. A taxi ride from the cruise port to Brugge's city centre takes about 30 minutes and costs about 45 euros each way. (See Getting Around for train info.) Bicycling tours of the Brugge countryside are also offered.

Excursions to **Ghent** feature medieval city landmarks, such as the thousand-year-old Castle of the Counts, and often include a stop at a chocolatier to learn the fine art of Belgian chocolate making. The WWI battlefields and memorials in and around **Ypres** can be visited on half-day or full-day excursions, while full-day tours of **Antwerp** give insight to the world's diamond capital. **Brussels** tours include a stroll through Grand Place – a beautiful central square of medieval buildings and outdoor cafés. Some cruise lines also offer a visit to famous **Waterloo**, the location of Napoleon's last major land battle in June of 1815.

rail service to Brugge is more frequent. Efficient train service (www.b-rail.be) connects from Blankenberge with all parts of Belgium. Travelling between Brugge, Ghent and Antwerp on local trains takes between half an hour to an hour. Distances to various cities from Zeebrugge: Brugge (9 miles/15 km); Ghent (31 miles/50 km); Antwerp or Brussels (63 miles/100 km). Most railway stations rent bicycles, which is a popular way for locals to get around (bike lanes are marked in red). However, walking is a good way to sightsee in Brugge and Ghent, where the attractions are concentrated in a compact area of narrow streets. Canal boat tours provide excellent overviews in both cities.

Brugge

Founded in the 9th century on an inlet of the North Sea, Brugge (spelled *Bruges* in French) became a major port of the Hanseatic League and a bustling centre of trade,

commerce and wool processing. Powerful and prosperous, Brugge was also the cradle of Flemish art in the 14th and 15th centuries, its churches and museums housing works by Jan van Eyck and Gerard David. Brugge lost its lucrative maritime trade to Antwerp after its harbour filled with silt, but it remained a centre of commerce and humanism. Erasmus called Brugge "the new Athens" and Sir Thomas More wrote *Utopia* while in Brugge on a trade mission in 1515.

Today, Brugge a UNESCO World Heritage Site and is considered one of the best-preserved medieval cities in Europe. Many of its brick Gothic buildings were restored in the 19th century when a colony of English aristocrats took an interest in the city's artistic heritage. Much of Brugge would likely have been destroyed by retreating German forces during World War II if not for the actions of the 4th Canadian Armoured Division, whose soldiers surrounded the city in September 1944. The commanding officer of the 22nd Manitoba Dragoons, who entered Brugge to meet with the German commanding officer, agreed to let the German soldiers evacuate unharmed if first they disarmed all the explosives they had wired to the bridges and buildings. A pair of bronze bison statues flanking one end of Canada Bridge

A canal boat in Brugge

were installed to commemorate the liberation of Brugge.

Brugge's notable buildings include the 13th-century **Market Hall**  with its famous belfry, which featured prominently in the movie *In Bruges*. Its narrow steep staircase of 366 steps (accessible by entry fee) leads to an observation deck at the top. In nearby Burg Square stands the 14th-century **City Hall 2** and the **Chapel of the Precious (Holy) Blood 3**, begun in the 12th century.

The **Church of Notre Dame 4**, begun in the 13th century, contains the tombs of Charles the Bold (ruler of the Low Countries) and his daughter Mary of Burgundy. Its brick spire is one of the tallest of its kind and the church's altarpiece enshrines a marble sculpture by Michelangelo called *Madonna of Bruges*, which was acquired by a local family of wealthy cloth merchants and donated to the church. Twice this treasure was looted, first by French revolutionaries in the 1790s and again by Nazi Germans in 1944, and has been protected by bullet-proof glass since 1972.

(Top to bottom) A painting of Brugge given to a Canadian soldier in 1944 by a grateful resident who had been in hiding from the Gestapo. Market Hall's famous belfry. Michelangelo's Madonna in Church of Our Lady.

Behind the church is the **5** **Gruuthuse Museum**, a former palace now housing a collection of 16th- and 17th-century tapestries. The nearby **6** **Groeninge Museum** houses paintings by Flemish masters.

Ghent

Founded by a French missionary in 630 AD at the confluence of the Leie and Scheldt rivers, Ghent is packed with churches, museums and sidewalk cafés. Canal boats take visitors past many of the small city's medieval monuments, including the 12th-century Gravensteen fortress (known as the Castle of the Counts), which stands in a bend of the river with a view over the old town. Groot Leeshuis was the city's meat house during the Middle Ages and this cavernous building now houses a food market selling Belgian specialties.

St. Michielsbrug (St. Michael's Bridge) provides the best vantage for viewing the towers of St. Niklaaskerk (St. Nicholas church), Belfort and St. Baafskathedraal, which contains Van Eyck's altar painting *Adoration of the Mystic Lamb*. Shops and cafés are found in the

Ghent's canalside architecture

harbour area, including Patershol (north of the Gravensteen), which is one of the oldest parts of the city. Attractions lying south of the historic core include Vooruit (a monumental concert hall built in 1912) and S.M.A.K. (a contemporary art museum).

Ypres

The town of Ypres (called *Ieper* in Flemish) rivalled medieval Brugge and Ghent as the centre of Flanders' flourishing cloth industry. Today it's remembered as the scene of three great battles fought during World War I as German forces attempted to advance toward the Channel ports of Dunkirk and Calais. The famous poem 'In Flanders Fields' commemorates the thousands of British and Canadian soldiers killed at Ypres, and it was written by Lieutenant Colonel John McCrae, a physician serving with the Canadian Expeditionary Force at Ypres. The town was completely destroyed during the war and later rebuilt, its restored buildings including a 13th-century cloth workers hall and the Gothic Cathedral of St. Martin.

Grand Place in Brussels

Outside the town walls there lie some forty military cemeteries, where "poppies blow, between the crosses, row on row."

Brussels

The capital of Belgium and the European Union, Brussels was a medieval commercial centre on the trade route from Brugge and Ghent to the Rhineland. It became the seat of the dukes of Burgundy in 1430 and a city of art and culture. Grand Place is the city's beautiful central square of medieval buildings and outdoor cafés. This massive square, described as "a rich theatre" by Victor Hugo, is surrounded by Gothic buildings such as the 13th-century Maison du Roi or Broodhuis (meeting place of the old States-General of the Netherlands), the 15th-century City Hall, and a number of rebuilt Gothic guildhalls. Nearby is the famous Mannekin-Pis, a statue sculpted in 1619 of a small boy urinating. Another famous landmark in Brussels is the Atomium, a gigantic model of an iron molecule built for the 1958 World Fair in Brussels. The Waterloo battlefield is 10 miles south of the city.

Antwerp

Antwerp, the gem-trading capital of the world, is located 60 miles (97 km) up the Scheldt River from the North Sea. The cruise terminal is located in the heart of the city where the river quays – constructed in the 19th century to prevent flooding – have been reinvented in the 21st century to reconnect the historic waterfront with the cobble streets of the old town.

The great Flemish painters Rubens and Van Dyck resided in Antwerp and their works adorn the city's churches and museums. Splendid buildings include the Gothic Cathedral of Notre Dame overlooking Groenplaats (Green Square), the churches of St. Paul and St. James (the latter containing the tomb of Rubens), and Rubens's house, which is now a museum. The Renaissance-style city hall stands in the central square, called Grote Markt (Market Place), which is lined with guild halls.

The modern Museum ann de Stroom (Museum on the Stream) focuses on Antwerp's history, and the new Red Star Line Museum tells the story of the two million emigrants who embarked here on their voyages to America and a new life.

NETHERLANDS

The genius of the Dutch is how they transformed a flood-prone coastal lowland into one of the world's most prosperous seafaring nations. When the Dutch East India Company, founded in 1602, was granted a monopoly to colonize Indonesia – the 'Spice Islands'– the profit generated from the risky but lucrative spice trade brought fabulous riches to the Netherlands.

The Netherlands eventually owned half of the world's merchant fleet and the 17th century became its Golden Age of prosperity and colonial expansion. Amsterdam grew into a centre of international trade, its affluent merchants building themselves impressive canal houses and filling them with paintings by Dutch masters.

The Netherlands also opened its doors to religious refugees, notably Spanish and Portuguese Jews and French Huguenots. These newcomers contributed greatly to Holland's prosperity and to this day tolerance remains a pillar of Dutch society, where liberal attitudes prevail.

Netherlands at a Glance

Although densely populated with nearly 17 million inhabitants, the Netherlands maintains a high standard of living. Industries include petroleum refining and food processing, and the country's large natural gas reserves supply more than half of its energy needs. Agricultural exports include flower bulbs and cheeses from Gouda and Edam.

Amsterdam is one of the world's major financial centres and Rotterdam is one of the world's busiest ports. Lying at the mouths of three major rivers interconnected by artificial waterways, the Netherlands is also linked with the canal systems of Belgium and Germany.

Dutch windmills such as this one at Kinderdijk were once used to pump water from canals.

The Dutch system of government is a constitutional monarchy. Queen Beatrix was the nation's ceremonial chief of state from 1980 to 2013, when she abdicated in favour of her son Willem-Alexander, who became the first Dutch king since 1890. His birthday, April 27, is a national holiday called King's Day. Amsterdam is the nation's capital, and The Hague is the seat of government.

The red band of the tricolour Dutch flag used to be orange, reflecting the colours of William I, Prince of Orange, who led the Dutch Revolt against Spanish sovereignty in the 16th century when Holland's northern provinces united and declared their independence from Spain. Because the orange band tended to fade over time, the colour was eventually changed to red.

Dutch is spoken throughout the Netherlands, with a small minority speaking Frisian. The country calling code is +31.

The euro is the unit of currency used in the Netherlands.

Amsterdam

Located on the Amstel River where a sluice dam was first built in about 1240, Amsterdam is laid out in a concentric pattern of canals that are flanked by streets and crossed by hundreds of bridges, their stone arches outlined with lights at night. Patrician homes built on wooden piles along the canals have been converted over time into offices, museums, restaurants and hotels. Many of these multi-storied townhouses are so narrow that moving furniture up and down their steep staircases is impossible, so large pieces are swung out an upstairs window on a pulley attached to a beam extending from the gabled roof.

Getting Around

Amsterdam is connected with the North Sea by the North Sea Canal, which opened in 1876, and is transited by cruise ships that travel from the sea locks at the seaside town of IJmuiden to the Amsterdam Cruise Terminal – a distance of 15.5 miles (25 km).

Tulipomania

The Dutch landscape – flat, swampy and monotonous – is not naturally scenic. Its beauty derives from man-made improvements, such as winding canals lined with gabled houses, or cultivated fields punctuated with windmills, so it's no wonder the Dutch people embraced tulips with such a passion when these bulbs were first imported from Turkey in the 17th century. Tulipomania swept across the Netherlands, with wild speculation driving up the price of tulips to such a level that a single bulb could fetch several thousand dollars. The government eventually intervened, but Holland remains the centre of tulip culture, its flower-growing region of Haarlem blanketed each spring in fields of bright-coloured tulips.

Semper Augustus, left, was the most expensive tulip sold during Holland's tulip mania.

More dike power

As early as 1200 the Dutch began reclaiming land from the sea by digging canals and building dikes along their coastline to hold back the sea. The English word 'dike' derives from the Dutch 'dijk' and the modern form of dikes appeared in Holland in the 17th century, with the construction of overflow and lateral diversion channels. Early pumping systems were powered by windmills. When the Netherlands was invaded by Louis XIV in 1672, the Dutch defended their territory by piercing their dikes and flooding the land to create a watery barrier between themselves and the invading French army. By the 20th century, dikes lying directly on the sea were being repeatedly raised, reinforced and built with slopes designed to reduce the energy of the incoming sea and minimize wave erosion. Today about 30 percent of the Netherlands lies below sea level.

Some ships dock at IJmuiden's Felison Cruise Terminal (which opened in 2012). Passengers travelling between Felison Terminal and Amsterdam or the airport can utilize cruise line shuttles, taxis or the public bus/train system. Amsterdam's cruise terminal is adjacent to the historic city centre and provides a variety of services, including shops and tourist information. Passengers can reach the nearby city attractions by foot, public transport or touring boat, and a tram car travels from the passenger terminal to the city centre. Most of the large tourboat companies are located around Central Station (a five-minute walk from the cruise terminal) and offer a variety of tours of the city's canals and main attractions. The Canal Bus offers hop-on/hop-off sightseeing cruises and a day pass costs 18 euros. An IAmsterdam Card can be purchased at tourist

(Below) Gabled townhouses line the canals of Amsterdam.

(Top to bottom) Central Station; a sightseeing canal boat; an Amsterdam tram car.

information offices; the card offers unlimited travel on trams (the most efficient way to get around) and discounts for canal cruises, museums and other attractions (www.iamsterdam.com).

Amsterdam is a city of 800,000 people and 600,000 bicycles, the trill of their bells alerting pedestrians who wander into the dedicated cycling lanes. Many of the streets are closed to cars and used only by buses, trams and taxis. Sturdy black bicycles, popular with the locals, can be rented at Central Station, Leidseplein and Dam Square. The daily rate is about 8 euros, and locks are included.

Amsterdam Airport Schiphol is connected by rail to Amsterdam's main train station (Central Station); travel time is 15 to 20 minutes and a one-way ticket is about 4 euros. A taxi ride from the airport to central Amsterdam is about 30 minutes and will cost about 45 euros. Connexxion operates shuttle vans to a wide selection of downtown Amsterdam Hotels; the one-way fare is about 15 euros. Most major hotels provide a complimentary shuttle.

Where to Stay

Luxury hotels in Amsterdam include the **Hotel Pulitzer** (once owned by a member of the famous newspaper publishing family) which occupies a block of restored 17th-century canal houses on Prinsengracht in the fashionable Jordaan district. **InterContinental Amstel Amsterdam**, the city's first grand hotel, was built in 1867 on the banks of the Amstel River.

Shore Excursions – Netherlands

Amsterdam shore excursions offer an array of city sightseeing tours that include cruises in glass-topped canal boats, visits to art museums and guided walking tours. Amsterdam's three must-see museums – Rijksmuseum, Van Gogh Museum and Anne Frank House – are featured in various excursions. Driving tours of the Dutch countryside take in windmill villages and fishing harbours. Places visited include the villages of Edam, Marken and Volendam, and the town of Delft where the famous hand-painted porcelain is produced. In spring, the dazzling display of tulips at the ornamental gardens of Keukenhof (in the flower-growing Haarlem region) is usually featured. Check your cruise line's website for detail on specific excursions. *(Photo, right) Cheese runners in Gouda.*

Royalty and rock stars have stayed at this palatial hotel and its Restaurant La Rive serves French-Mediterranean cuisine for which its has received a Michelin star.

Boutique hotels include the 117-room **Lloyd Hotel**, built by the Lloyd shipping company in the 1920s and situated in the revitalized East Docklands area. The **Hotel Piet Hein** is a contemporary boutique hotel located in the museum district near Vondel Park and the luxury shops along PC Hoofstraat. The canal-side **Ambassade Hotel** is a four-star boutique hotel located in The Nine Streets district, as is the cozy, family-run **Amsterdam Hotel Wiechmann**.

The charming 26-room **Canal House Hotel** on Keizersgracht features a breakfast room overlooking the back garden. A traditional Dutch breakfast spread consists of toast sprinkled with chocolate flakes, and crisp bread served with cheeses and ham.

Dining

Brown cafés, so named for their traditional dark-wood interiors that have deepened in tone over the centuries, are popular places to enjoy casual meals of soup and sandwiches, local cheeses and sausages, and a variety of Dutch beers, including Heineken and Amstel, or a shot of chilled jen-

Canal House Hotel

ever (a juniper-flavoured liqueur known as Dutch gin). **Cafe Karpershoek** in the Bellevue Hotel is one of the oldest brown cafés in Amsterdam; this former sailors inn was built in 1606 when Martelaarsgracht (Martyrs Canal) was part of the harbourfront. The canal has since been filled in but the Cafe Karpershoek, frequented

by locals and tourists, has retained its authentic atmosphere, with sand still sprinkled on the wooden floor to make cleaning easier (a traditional Dutch method).

Other popular brown cafes include **Café de Druif** near the Maritime Museum, and **Café 't Smalle** at Egelantiersgracht 12 in the Jordaan area. The nearby **Café Papeneiland** (at 2 Prinsengracht) is housed in a beautiful gabled property dating to 1642 and is famous for its homebaked apple pie, a caramelly version thick with cinnamon-scented apple.

Numerous cafés and restaurants are clustered around **Leidseplein**, which is a lively square filled with cafés, restaurants, theatres and outdoor entertainment. Chocolate lovers will want to sample the handcrafted chocolates sold by renowned chocolatier **Puccini Bomboni** at Singel 184 or at Staalstraat 17.

Shopping

Amsterdam is the place to browse for artwork, antiques and, if your budget allows, diamonds. Nieuwedijk is a major pedestrian shopping street leading from Central Station to Dam Square, location of De Bijenkorf (Amsterdam's largest department store). Behind the Royal Palace is Magna Plaza – a shopping mall featuring designer clothes and fashion accessories in an elegant 19th-century building. Continuing south from Dam

(Top to bottom) Flower market; souvenir wooden shoes; hand-painted Delft porcelain.

Square is the pedestrian shopping street Kalverstraat, which ends at the Floating Flower Market on Singel Canal where bulbs ready for export can be purchased. One of the prettiest places to shop is The Nine Streets district where the cobblestone streets are lined with designer boutiques, art galleries and cafés that straddle the 17th-century canals from the Singel to the Prinsengracht, about a five-minute walk from Dam Square.

Art galleries are located throughout the city and bookstores are concentrated around Spuiplein. An array of antique shops line Niewe Spiegelstraat, which runs between the Flower Market and the Rijksmuseum. Fashion boutiques are found along the Leidestraat (which leads to Leidseplein) and exclusive fashion shops are concentrated on PC Hoofstraat near the Rijksmuseum.

Amsterdam has been a diamond centre for more than 400 years, and you can witness the art of diamond cutting and polishing on a guided tour at Gassan Diamonds (on Nieuwe Uilenburgerstraat, near Waterlooplein). Amsterdam Diamond Centre, which carries an extensive collection of loose polished diamonds as well as jewellery and watches, is located opposite the Royal Palace on Dam Square. The Waterlooplein Flea Market is situated in between the Opera House and Rembrandt's House. The city's sex shops are located in the Red Light District.

Amsterdam's Canal District is a UNESCO World Heritage Site.

City Attractions

Amsterdam is a city packed with museums, and several are located in the immediate vicinity of the cruise port, such as the **NEMO Science Museum 1** and the **Netherlands Maritime Museum 2**. The area immediately opposite the port is the city's Red Light District, better known for its window displays of prostitutes than for **Oude Kerk 3** (**Old Church**), which is Amsterdam's oldest monument, built in 1334. A parish church in the time of Rembrandt, whose first wife was buried here in 1642, the Oude Kerk is now a venue for exhibitions and concerts. Nearby is **Amstelkring Museum 4** (**Our Lord in the Attic Museum**), a clandestine Catholic church built on the upper floor of a canal house during the Reformation when open worship by Catholics was outlawed in Amsterdam.

Other museums in the Red Light District are the **Sex Museum 5**, **Erotic Museum 6** and **Hash, Marijuana and Hemp Museum 7**. In recent years the city has been buying up

bordellos and converting them into residential housing and designer showcases as part of a cultural revitalization project, and many of the area's cannabis cafes are closing down and being replaced by restaurants, shops and boutiques.

Dam Square is the location of **Nieuwe Kerk (New Church)** **8**, which was first built in the 15th century when the Oude Kerk became too small for the growing population of Amsterdam. Nieuwe Kerk, which was rebuilt in the Gothic style following a fire in 1645, is where royal weddings and investiture ceremonies are held. **Dam Palace** **9**, built in

the 17th century, was formerly city hall but became a royal palace in 1808 when the Kingdom of the Netherlands was briefly ruled by Louis Bonaparte, a brother of Napoleon. King Louis couldn't decide which city should be the capital of his kingdom, but the constitution of 1814 made Amsterdam the capital.

A few blocks south of Dam Square are the **10** **Amsterdam History Museum**, housed in a collection of buildings that served as a 16th-century orphanage, and **11** **Begijnenhof**, a garden courtyard entered off Spui along a narrow, vaulted passageway. This quiet courtyard contains a medi-

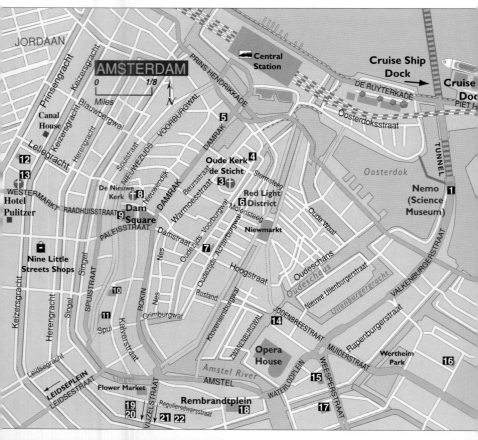

eval church and is surrounded by old houses once occupied by Béguine nuns (including No. 34, the oldest house in Amsterdam).

The **Anne Frank House** 12 is where a teenaged Jewish girl hid during World War II with her family and four other Jews in a concealed annex within the warehouse of her father's office building. Aided by their non-Jewish friends who secretly brought them food and other essentials, the Franks spent two years in hiding before they were discovered by the SS and hauled off to concentration camps where only the father survived. The two Dutch men who had helped the Frank family were imprisoned by the Nazis but the two female helpers were released after questioning and, upon returning to the ransacked annex, they found Anne's diaries, notebooks and papers strewn across the floor, which they hurriedly retrieved and later returned to her father Otto after the war. First published in Amsterdam in 1947, *Anne Frank, The Diary of a Young Girl* was eventually translated into 67 languages and adapted for a Pulitzer-winning play and a screenplay starring Shelley Winters. Anne Frank's candid diary has been read by millions of people and continues to touch the modern reader with its poignant portrayal of youthful optimism and courage in

(Top) Dam Palace and Nieuwe Kerk. (Above) Anne Frank.

the face of evil. During the Nazi occupation of the Netherlands, 24,000 of the country's 140,000 Jews went into hiding, aided by their fellow Dutch citizens, and of those 8,000 were discovered.

A block away from the Anne Frank House is **Westerkerk (West Church)** 13, built between 1602 and 1631 in the Dutch Renaissance style, its tower topped with a copy of the crown of Hapsburg emperor Maximilian I.

Rembrandt House Museum 14 has preserved the famous painter's three-storey house in which he painted many of his masterpieces. Rembrandt van Rijn, a miller's son, was the greatest of the Dutch masters and he received valuable art training when he moved from his birthplace of Leiden to Amsterdam in 1624 to spend time in the studio of Pieter Lastman. Rembrandt's portrait paintings were soon in demand, making him a wealthy man, and he was able to buy an impressive house for himself and his well-connected wife. Following her death, Rembrandt's finances became strained and he was forced to move into more modest quarters.

Rijksmuseum (above) and (below) Rembrandt's 'Night Watch'

Other museums in the vicinity are the **15 Jewish Historical Museum**, **16 Dutch Resistance Museum** and **17 Hermitage Amsterdam Museum**, a satellite of St. Petersburg's Hermitage. On the other side of the Amstel is the **Willet-Holthuysen Museum 18**, which is a fully furnished canal house bequeathed to the city in 1895 by its last owner.

Museumplein (Museum Square) is where Amsterdam's three major art museums are located, including the world-famous **Rijksmuseum (National Museum) 19** which houses an outstanding collection of Dutch paintings and drawings from the Golden Age, its selection of masterworks including *Night Watch* by Rembrandt and *The Kitchen Maid* by Vermeer.

The **Van Gogh Museum 20** is housed in a modern building and contains the world's largest collection of Van Gogh paintings and drawings, including *The Potato Eaters*, *Bedroom in Arles* and one of the *Sunflower* paintings. **Stedelijk Museum 21** is Amsterdam's museum of modern and contemporary art, housed in a recently refurbished 1895 building with a new extension. Nearby is **Vondel Park 22**, a large urban park containing green expanses, bicycle trails and a film museum.

Rotterdam

Situated on the Maas River, Rotterdam is the industrial centre of the Netherlands and one of the busiest ports in the world. Its historic centre was completely destroyed by German bombardment in May 1940, with St.

Laurens Kerk (Grote Kerk) the only building left standing amid the rubble. The post-war rebuilding and ongoing construction have made Rotterdam a showcase of modernist architecture.

The cruise ships dock in the revitalized docklands area of the city at Holland America Quay. The quay's historic terminal building, which has been completely renovated, is an historic landmark of the thousands of emigrants who left Europe for the United States of America. Overlooking the quay is the Hotel New York, which once housed the original head office of Holland America Line. Towering nearby is the World Port Center, a high-tech design by Sir Norman Foster. Further along the harbourfront is the striking KPN Telecom Tower (designed by Rezo Piano) and the spectacular Erasmus Bridge, supported by a 445-foot pylon and nicknamed the Swan.

It's a short walk across this modern suspension bridge to downtown Rotterdam, or you can take the water taxi service (about 3 euros each way). The city's excellent museums include the Natural History Museum and the Maritime Museum, in front of which stands a statue called 'Destroyed City' which commemorates the WWII bombing of Rotterdam. The city's main art museum is Boijmans-Van Beuningen, where you can view *Tower of Babel* by the Flemish painter Pieter Bruegel the Elder.

The small inner-city harbour of Delfshaven was spared during the WWII bombings and its historic waterfront is lined with gabled buildings housing trendy cafés and galleries. The Pilgrim fathers set sail for America from Delfshaven in July 1620 after meeting in the local Pilgrim Fathers Church.

Back across the river at Katendrecht is Holland America's former flagship, Rotterdam V, permanently moored as a hotel, its hull painted the original gray.

Rotterdam **shore excursions** include a countryside drive to the preserved windmills at **Kinderdijk**, which is a UNESCO World Heritage Site located 20 miles (32 km) southeast of Rotterdam. Other area attractions (all accessible by rail) are the picturesque town of **Delft** (famous for its pretty canals and locally crafted porcelain), the university town of **Leiden** (birthplace of Rembrandt) and the **Hague**, where places of interest include the House of Parliament and the Mauritshuis Museum with works by Rembrandt and other Dutch masters.

Rotterdam's cruise quay is overlooked by the historic Hotel New York and World Port Center.

DENMARK

Smallest of the Scandinavian countries, the Kingdom of Denmark once ruled its larger Nordic neighbours and was so feared by the English they paid the Danes a medieval land tax called Danegeld to fend off raids. Today Denmark is better known for modern design than military conquest. Characterized by clean lines and an elegant yet functional style, Danish-designed products turned Finn Juhl and Arne Jacobsen, among others, into household names.

With a population of 5.6 million, Denmark is densely populated. It is also, by land area, one of the smallest countries in Europe at 16,600 square miles. A drive from the northern border to the southern border can be completed in about four hours. Denmark consists of Jutland (the mainland) and several hundred islands of varying size that are interconnected by bridges and ferries. Zealand is the largest island and is where Copenhagen is situated, at the entrance to the Baltic Sea.

Denmark's low-lying countryside contains rolling hills clad in green fields of rye grass and other crops bordered by groves of beech trees. Jutland's southern border abuts Germany and those who live along this castle-dotted frontier like to display their Danish patriotism by painting their houses white and their doors red – colours of the Danish flag.

Denmark is a constitutional monarchy and its reigning monarch is Queen Margrethe II, who was crowned in 1972. The Faeroe Islands and Greenland are self-governing dependencies within the Danish realm. The Danish West Indies were a former colony, sold to America in 1917 and renamed the Virgin Islands of the United States.

Lutheranism is the country's official religion, although relatively few Danes attend church on a regular basis. Danish is the official language and most Danes speak fluent English. The Danish alphabet is similar to the English alphabet, but with three

A street scene in Copenhagen

extra vowels at the end. The Danes' spelling of their country is Danmark. Denmark's country code for international calls is +45.

Denmark's unit of currency is the krone (DKK), which divides into 100 ore (pronounced *or-a*). The approximate exchange rate is US$1 = 6.5 kroner (£1 = 10 kroner). Major credit cards are widely accepted except when buying bus tickets. A 15% service charge is automatically added to hotel and restaurant bills and to taxi fares. On purchases of more than DKK 300, non-EU citizens can obtain a tax refund by first obtaining a tax-free form at the store of purchase. Global Blue has customer services offices at Illums Bolighus's downtown location (Amagertorv 10 on the Strøget) and their airport location (Terminal 2 Arcade). For instructions on obtaining a tax refund, visit www.global-blue.com.

Denmark's History

Denmark's earliest settlers arrived in the Jutland in about 10,000 BC but it wasn't until the age of the Vikings that the world began to take notice of the Danes as they launched repeated raids on Western Europe. During this era of Danish expansion, Harold Bluetooth – king of Denmark and conqueror of Norway – turned his back on Norse paganism and embraced Christianity for himself and his subjects. To commemorate this momentous event, Harold ordered the raising of a runic stone in the royal town of Jelling on the Jutland mainland. Now a UNESCO World Heritage Site, this 10th-century stone bears an inscription describing Harold's achievements and marks the creation of Denmark as a nation state.

In 1397, Queen Margrethe I instigated the political union of Denmark, Sweden and Norway, and had her grandnephew Erik of Pomerania crowned king of all three realms at Kalmar Castle in Sweden – a union that lasted for over a century. With a brilliant royal court, Denmark thrived. However, upon siding with Napoleon in the French Revolutionary Wars, Denmark was attacked by England and its naval fleet destroyed by Horatio Nelson in the Battle of Copenhagen (1801).

More setbacks came when Denmark was defeated by Prussia in 1864 and lost Schleswig-Holstein in the Jutland. Yet, despite losing a third of its territory, Denmark prospered by re-educating its farmers at rural folk schools. A modern system of public education was introduced in the early 1800s, which encouraged a flourishing culture of literature and philosophy led by Hans Christian Andersen and Søren Kierkegaard. In 1849 a new constitution was signed by Frederick IV, bringing to an end the country's absolute monarchy and establishing Denmark as a constitutional monarchy. This historic event is commemorated each June 5 with a national holiday called Constitution Day,

Denmark remained neutral during WWI and recovered North Schleswig in 1920. German forces invaded Denmark in 1940 and King Christian X, the popu-

lar "Equestrian King," symbolized Danish defiance by riding
alone on horseback through the
streets of Copenhagen. Most of
Denmark's Jewish population
(including refugees from other
countries) escaped to Sweden
with help from the Danish resistance. Liberated by British
troops in May of 1945, Denmark
joined the North Atlantic Treaty
Organization (NATO) in 1949
and the European Economic
Community in 1972 but has
retained its own currency.
Denmark's per-capita income is
among the highest in the world,
and its economy has been rated
among the world's freest for conducting business.

(Above) Queen Margrethe I
(Below) Royal guard outside
Amalienborg Palace

Copenhagen

Copenhagen is both historic
and hip, with a pleasing mix of
old world charm and modernist architecture. Considered one
of the world's most livable cities, Copenhagen is – in the words
of Danish architect Jan Gehl – a
reconquered city. Where cars
once clogged main arteries and
central squares, people now stroll
along the pedestrian-only streets
and gather in squares to enjoy the
fountains, public art and open-air
cafés. This transformation began
back in 1962 when the Strøget –
the city's high street – was closed
to car traffic. Additional streets
and squares were, over time, emp-
tied of cars, and today the city has
an extended network of pedestrian-only promenades connected by
dozens of bicycle paths.

Copenhagen is Denmark's
capital and largest city, with a
population of 1.2 million. *Koben*

Havn means *merchants' harbour* and the city began as a fishing village. By the early 11th century Copenhagen was an important trading port at the entrance to the Baltic Sea where it exacted tolls from ships passing through the narrow Øresund strait. In 2000, completion of the Øresund bridge between Copenhagen and Malmø provided southern Sweden with its first direct land-link to continental Europe.

Getting Around

Copenhagen has four cruise terminals, all located in the north section of the city. Furthest from the city centre is the new **Ocean Quay** (about 4.5 miles or 7 km to the city centre; 10 miles or 15.5 km to the airport) which is the turn-around-port for large ships. **Freeport** (Levant Quay) is two kilometres closer to the city centre, and Langelinie Pier is located in the city centre, as is Nordre Toldbod Quay, for small cruise ships. **Langelinie Cruise Pier** is within walking

distance of the downtown sights; simply follow the harbourfront promenade that leads past several attractions, starting with the Little Mermaid sculpture. Nordre Toldbod Quay is just south of the Little Mermaid.

If your ship is docked at Freeport on a port call, your options for getting into the city centre include walking to the Nordhaven train station (it's a 15-minute walk), boarding the No. 26 city bus, taking a taxi (the fare is about 200 kroner) or, if available, the ship's shuttle.

If you are boarding your ship at Freeport or Ocean Quay and travelling directly from Copenhagen Airport to the cruise port, the taxi fare is 400 to 550 kroner, depending on the time of day. A convenient option is to book a ship's transfer.

If you are heading to downtown Copenhagen from the airport, you can take the train to Central Station (opposite Tivoli Gardens) or take the metro to Norreport Station, then walk or

Shore Excursions

COPENHAGEN

Ship-organized excursions include a variety of city tours – by coach, bicycle, kayak or canal boat. Guided walking tours are also offered. Special-interest tours include Danish design and architecture. The picturesque village of Dragør, south of Copenhagen, is often included in a Copenhagen sightseeing tour. Check your cruise line's website for details on specific excursions being offered.

If you prefer to buy a tour once you arrive in Copenhagen, red sightseeing buses depart regularly from Langelinie Pier. Hop on and off these buses as you please. The complete city tour takes approximately 80 minutes and tickets can be bought from the bus driver. For the independent-minded traveller, see **Getting Around's sightseeing options** for more suggestions.

take a taxi to your hotel. Outside rush hour, a 30-minute taxi ride from Copenhagen Airport to the city centre is about 230 kroner.

To reach Freeport or Ocean Quay on public transit from downtown entails taking the train from Norreport Station to Nordhavn Station, followed by a 15-minute walk to Freeport or a 45-minute walk to Ocean Quay. Another option is to catch the No. 26 bus from Osterport Station but there's no bus service on the weekend and boarding with luggage could be inconvenient. A taxi or ship's transfer are easier ways to get to Ocean Quay or Freeport from downtown.

If you're disembarking at Ocean Quay, a ship's transfer is recommended due to traffic congestion at the port and long waiting times for taxis.

A visitor information centre is located at the Langelinie Cruise Pier, and the city's main tourist information centre is located opposite Tivoli Gardens on Vesterbro Gade.

(Above) The Little Mermaid near Langelinie Cruise Pier. (Below) Street art and cafés on the Strøget.

A Copenhagen Card (sold at airports and tourist offices) offers free or discounted admission to dozens of museums and attractions, as well as free travel on public transportation (www.visit-copenhagen.com).

Copenhagen's city centre is compact and very walkable, but other **sightseeing options** include

(Top) A sightseeing canal boat.
(Above) Hotel D'Angleterre in King's New Square.

taking the hop-on/hop-off red buses that run regularly between major downtown sites, or taking a boat tour with Stromma Canal Tours – these one-hour guided tours (DKK 75 per adult) depart from Nyhaven and Gammel Strand. There is also a hop-on/hop-off waterbus service that can be boarded at Nyhaven (www.stromma.dk). Free walking tours are conducted twice daily, departing from City Hall. For more information on guided tours, the city's official website is VisitCopenhagen.

Bicycling is another option. City Bikes can be rented using a credit card for DKK 25 per hour. For more information, visit www.bycyklen.dk.

Admission is free to state museums such as the National Museum, Thorvaldsen Museum, Danish Resistance Museum and National Gallery. Ny Carlsberg Glyptotek has free admission on Sundays. **Most museums are closed Mondays and on Constitution Day (June 5).**

Where to Stay

Copenhagen's five-star hotels include the Hotel D'Angleterre, a storied grand hotel in the heart of downtown at King's New Square. The iconic Radisson Blu Royal Hotel (the former SAS Royal) was designed by Arne Jacobsen in the 1950s and is located near Tivoli Gardens and the central train station. On the other side of the Tivoli Gardens is the Marriott Copenhagen – a modern glass-and-brick building overlooking the inner harbour.

Four-star hotels include the Copenhagen Admiral Hotel, housed in a converted 18th-century warehouse building, and Radisson Blu Scandinavia overlooking a lake on the edge of Christianshavn.

Dining

A classic Danish lunch consists of open-face sandwiches on rye bread topped with pickled herring, salami and cheese. Danish beer, brewed from locally harvested barley, is among the world's best. The Danes are also known for their layer cakes, kringles and

Viennese-style pastries, and their love of coffee. When strolling the streets of Copenhagen, you'll find numerous sandwich stands, cafés and coffeehouses to pause at for lunch or light refreshment. The Reinh Van Hauen bakery on Ostergade (near King's New Square) sells mouth-watering pastries, including a cinnamon roll called *kanel-snegl*.

Outdoor cafés lining Nyhavn are popular for their lively harbourfront atmosphere. Quieter venues include the Winter Garden at Ny Carlsberg Glyptotek where the in-house café offers light lunch dishes and pastries from its bakery. Lunch fare is served in the courtyard café of the Royal Copenhagen flagship store (Amagertorv 6 on the Strøget).

La Glace patisserie opened its doors at Skoubogade 3 (just off the Strøget) in 1870 and people have been coming ever since to enjoy the freshly brewed coffee and delicious layer cakes, including a chocolate and coffee mousse creation to honour the Danish author Karen Blixen, who once owned a coffee plantation in Kenya and wrote *Out of Africa* under the name Isak Dinesen.

Copenhagen's most famous restaurant is Noma, rated one of the best in the world for its authentic Nordic cuisine prepared using traditional cooking methods.

(Top) Copenhagen's sidewalk cafés and (above) Danish pastries at the Ny Carlsberg. Glyptotek's cafe.

Located at 93 Strandgade, across the water from Nyhaven, this Michelin-starred restaurant takes reservations months in advance.

For a uniquely Danish dinner experience, the Sankt Gertrud's Kloster (Hauser Plads 32) is housed in a former monastery and serves classic Danish-European cuisine in an intimate atmosphere created by the flickering light of 1,200 candles.

Tivoli Gardens also has a variety of restaurants, including the trendy Café Ketchup (formerly Divan I) where you can enjoy drinks and dinner on the glass-enclosed terrace.

Shopping

Danish design and craftsmanship are well represented in the shops of Copenhagen, many of which are located on or near the Strøget – one of the world's longest pedestrian shopping streets. About a mile long, the Strøget consists of five interconnecting streets – Østergade, Amagertorv, Vimmelskaftet, Nygade and Frederiksberggade – and runs from Kongens Nytorv (King's New Square) to City Hall Square.

The Magasin department store at Kongens Nytorv 13 carries a wide range of outstanding Danish product lines, including bed and table linens, damask (a lustrous fabric in a satin weave), glassware, porcelain, jewellery and handicrafts.

Other recommended stores in the vicinity of Kongens Nytorv

Magasin department store

include a Bang & Olufsen outlet (Kongens Nytorv 26) and a House of Amber outlet and museum at Kongens Nytorv 2. House of Amber carries a wide selection of amber jewellery in silver and gold settings, and has outlets at Langelinie Cruise Pier and City Hall Square.

Dozens of shops line the Strøget, including the flagship store of Royal Copenhagen Porcelain (Amagertorv 6). This centuries-old company, purveyor to Danish royalty, is famous for its handpainted porcelain and classic Blue Fluted patterns.

Rosendahl, which distributes product lines by numerous Danish designers, has retail locations throughout downtown Copenhagen, including Illum department store at Østergade 52 (the Strøget) and Illums Bolighus at Amagertorv 10 (the Strøget). Rosendahl's award-winning products include Grand Prix cutlery and wooden toys by Kay Bojesen, and wristwatches by Flemming Bo Hansen. Rosendahl also carries timeless productions by Arne Jacobsen, whose flatware was selected for the movie *2001: A Space Odyssey* for its futuristic appearance, and whose lightweight chairs (the Swan, Egg, Ant and Number Seven) are international design classics.

More shops line the side streets leading off the Strøget, including Georg Jensen Damask at Ny Østergade 19, featuring damask tablecloths, quality handicrafts, and fine table linens. Gammel Strand's outdoor flea market is held on Fridays and Saturdays.

City Attractions

A waterfront promenade leads from Langelinie Cruise Pier to the **1 The Little Mermaid**. This famous statue was commissioned in 1913 by Carl Jacobsen (whose father founded Carlsberg breweries) and was sculpted by Edvard Erikson. She sits demurely on a rock near shore where she is photographed almost daily, often posing with fans. Small in stature, she is arguably Denmark's most famous celebrity. And like all celebrities, she is occasionally mistreated by her public. Her head was cut off in 1964 and although the homicide squad was called in (which in Denmark investigates desecrations of national monuments, as well as murders) the case remains unsolved. In 1984, two teenagers sawed off her right arm but returned it the next day, after they had sobered up. And on a September night in 2003, she was blasted from her stone base. Fortunately the statue on display is a copy of the original, which is held in an undisclosed location by the sculptor's heirs.

(Above) The Little Mermaid
(Below) Gefion Fountain and
St. Alban's Church

A short distance past The Little Mermaid is the massive **2 Gefion Fountain**. Completed in 1908, its sculpture depicts animal figures being driven by the legendary goddess Gefjun. Beside the fountain is the **Kastellet (The Citadel)**, which was built in the mid-1600s, and **3 The Museum of Danish Resistance**, which portrays the history of the Danish resistance during the German occupation of 1940-45. Close by is **DesignMuseum Danmark**, exhibiting Danish design classics.

(Above) Amalienborg Square
(Below) Frederick's Church

Restored waterfront warehouses line Larsens Plads, where a replica of Michelangelo's *David* stands in front of a red-brick building called Vestindisk Pakhus, which houses the Royal Danish Cast Collection.

The next place of interest along the waterfront promenade is **4** **Amalienborg Square** – a large octagonal plaza with an equestrian statue of Frederik V in the centre. Facing this expansive courtyard are four identical rococo mansions which comprise Amalienborg Palace – the winter residence of the Danish monarch. A museum occupies the ground floor of one of the mansions with exhibitions covering the reigns of four kings from 1863 to 1972.

Frederick's Church 5 (popularly known as Marble Church) can be seen when looking up the street leading west from Amalienborg Square. The church, designed in 1740, was completed in 1894, and its massive dome is the largest in Scandinavia.

Looking in the opposite direc-

Getting About
Although Langelinie Pier and Nørdre Toldbod Quay are short walks to town, the other cruise docks will require a cab ride or shuttle. Free Port Cruise Terminal is about 3 miles or five km to the city centre while Ocean Quay is 4.5 miles or about seven km.

Ocean Quay Cruise Terminal

Free Port Cruise Terminal

Trelleborggade
Sandkaj
Nordhavn
Bassin

COPENHAGEN

ØSTERBRO

Fælledparken

Pedestrian Street

0   500

Yards

N

Willemoesgade
Classensgade

Langelinie Cruise Dock

Garnisons
Kirkegard

KRISTIANIAGADE
Trondhjemsgade

Holmens
Kirkegard

Langelinie

CITY ATTRACTIONS
(1)   The Little Mermaid
(2)   Gefion Fountain
(3)   Museum of Danish Resistance
(4)   Amalienborg Square
(5)   Frederick's Church
(6)   Opera House
(7)   Nyhaven
(8)   Kongens Nytorv
(9)   Christiansborg Palace
(10) Thorvaldsen Museum
(11) Stock Exchange Bld
(12) Royal Library
(13) The National Museum
(14) Ny Carlsberg Glyptotek
(15) Tivoli Gardens
(16) City Hall
(17) Cathedral of Our Lady
(18) Round Tower
(19) Rosenborg Castle
(20) Danish National Gallery

Stockholmsgade

Ostre
Anlaeg

BERNADOTTES ALLE

Kastellet

1

Nordre Toldbod Cruise Terminal

Østerport Station

GRONNINGEN

ØSTER VOLDGADE

Haregade

Gernersgade

3

2

ESPLANADEN

SOLVGADE

Rigensgade

Adelgade

Adelgade

STORE KONGENSGADE

Kongens
Have

20

Design Museum

Amaliegade

LARSENS PLADS

Botanisk
Have

Rosenborg

19

5

Amalienborg

4

Kronprinsessegade

Borgergade

BREDGADE

Amaliegade

TOLDBODGADE

GOTHERSGADE

Abenra

Operaen

6

Orsteds
Parken

NORRE VOLDGADE

Nørregade

Krystalgade

Skinder-

KØBMAGERGADE

18

Kongens
Nytorv

8

NYHAVN

Nihauns Bro

Herluf

7

Skt. Peders Stræde

17

Studiestræde

Frederiksberggade

STRØGET (Østergade)

Kongens
gade

Brannbo...

CHRISTIANSHAVN

Niels JUELS GADE

Peder
Gade

Skrams

Holbergsgade

CHRISTIANIA

16

H.C. ANDERSENS BLVD

LÆDERSTRÆDE

TIETGENSGADE

Gammel Strand

Laksegade

BØRSGADE

Holbergsgade

HOP-ON HOP-OFF BOAT

Vester Voldgade

Vindebrogade

10

9

Christiansborg

11

KNIPPELSBRO

13

Frederiksholms Kanal

SLOTSHOLMEN

Christians Brygge

Tivoli Gardens

15

14

Copenhagen
Central Stn

LANGEBRO

12

Airport 30 min
by taxi

tion across the harbour, you will see the **Opera House 6**, which opened in 2005. The building's modernist design features the extensive use of glass, marble and maple wood, along with state-of-the-art acoustics and lighting. The Opera House can be reached by waterbus from several points along the waterfront.

Continuing south from Amalienborg Square you will soon reach **Nyhavn (New Harbour) 7** – a narrow arm extending from Copenhagen's main harbour. Nyhavn is lined with lovely old buildings and is one of the city's main gathering places. Locals and tourists alike linger here at the open-air cafes where they can enjoy the passing pageantry of people and canal boats, and soak up the

(Above, left) Opera House
(Left and below) Nyhavn

nautical atmosphere provided by the old wooden schooners moored alongside the stone quay. Hans Christian Andersen lived at 20 Nyhavn in his early years as a writer and later lived at 67 Nyhavn.

Kongens Nytorv (King's New Square) lies at the head of Nyhavn and is overlooked by the Royal Theatre (home to the Royal Danish Ballet) and the 17th-century Charlottenborg Palace, which houses The Royal Danish Academy of Art. Also overlooking this large central square is the luxury **Hotel Angleterre** and the **Magasin** – originally a hotel with H. C. Andersen one of its regular guests. The Magasin became a high-end department store in 1889 and it marks the entrance to a mile-long pedestrian shopping street called the **Strøget**.

About a third of the way along the Strøget, a side street leads south to **Slotsholmen** – a small island surrounded by a moat on three sides and the harbour on the fourth. The complex of buildings on this small island includes **Christiansborg Palace** – home of the Danish parliament, supreme court and foreign office. Built in the 18th century on the former site of two medieval castles (both of which were demolished) and two palaces (both of which burned down), the current palace was restored in 1916. Its richly adorned Royal Reception Rooms include the Throne Room which provides access to the balcony where Danish monarchs are proclaimed. The palace and its underground ruins are open to the public, with guided tours available.

Other buildings on Slotsholmen include the **Thorvaldsen Museum** (exhibiting a large group of works by the neo-classical sculptor Albert Bertel Thorvaldsen), the 17th-century **Stock Exchange Building** with its unique spire of twisting dragon tails, and the harbourfront **Royal Library** (Denmark's national library), which is housed in a 1906 building. Its new 'Black Diamond' annex overlooking the harbour was built in 1996, its design consisting of two massive black marble cubes joined by a multi-storey glass atrium.

The National Museum – Denmark's largest cultural-historical museum – is housed in a classical 18th-century mansion (a former royal residence), which

Stock Exchange Building

stands opposite the main entrance to Christiansborg, on the other side of Frederiksholms Kanal.

Ny Carlsberg Glyptotek 14 is an art museum, founded in 1897 by the brewing magnate Carl Jacobsen, which houses Northern Europe's largest collection of ancient art from Egypt, Greece and Italy, as well as 19th- and 20th-century sculptures, including a collection of works by Rodin. Glyptotek means 'collection of sculpture' but the museum also houses paintings by French Impressionists and Post-Impressionists, and by Danish artists. An elegant café is located in the bright and airy Winter Garden in the museum's domed courtyard.

Tivoli Gardens 15, named for a stylish resort town near Rome, first unveiled its eight-hectare fantasyland of twinkling lights, gardens, rides and restaurants in August 1843. The park's wooden rollercoaster debuted on the eve of World War I and still carries over one million riders each year on its

(Above, left) National Museum
(Left and below) Ny Carlsberg Glyptotek

Hans Christian Andersen

H. C. Andersen, the son of a shoe-maker and a washerwoman, was born in 1805 in Odense. Shy and homely, Andersen struggled with his lessons but his parents instilled in him a love of literature and theatre. After his father's death, Andersen moved to Copenhagen at the age of 14 to find work in the theatre. He failed as an actor but his poems won him patrons and by 1835 Andersen had achieved some success as a playwright and novelist. But his genius revealed itself only when he began writing fairy tales. Famous worldwide, these include *The Little Mermaid, The Little Match Girl, The Snow Queen* and *The Ugly Duckling.* Considered the father of the modern fairy tale, Andersen identified with society's misfits and outcasts. His own life was often sad and lonely, for he habitually fell in love with women who didn't return his affections, includ-ing the opera singer Jenny Lind. An avid traveller, Andersen never married and was described as a "bony bore" by the daughter of Charles Dickens after Andersen overstayed his wel-come at their home in London. Shortly before his death in 1875, Andersen

consulted with a composer about the music to be played at his funeral, stating that, "Most of the people who will walk after me will be children, so make the beat keep time with little steps." In death, Hans Christian Andersen has achieved immortality. His birthday, April 2nd, is celebrated as International Children's Book Day, and the statue of The Little Mermaid, erected in Copenhagen Harbour on his birthday in 1913, has become Copenhagen's most famous landmark and a national icon.

scenic railway-style ride over fake mountains and through tunnels at a leisurely speed of 30 mph. A new high-tech roller coaster has been added to the park, as has one of the world's highest carousels from which riders can enjoy sweeping views over the city. Tivoli was the brainchild of entrepreneur Georg Carstensen, whose venture was authorized by King Christian VIII upon hearing the convincing argu-ment that people amusing them-selves do not think about politics. When Walt Disney began planning Disneyland, he drew inspiration from the magical atmosphere cre-ated at Tivoli Gardens.

(Above) Statue of H. C. Andersen opposite Tivoli Gardens (below).

(Above) City Hall
(Below) Round Tower

Across from Tivoli Gardens in Rådhuspladsen (City Hall Square) stands **City Hall** 16, a red-brick building completed in 1905 , its design inspired by the medieval civic architecture of Siena, Italy. Its façade is graced with a golden statue of Absalon, a 12th-century Danish archbishop and statesman. On display in the foyer is Jens Olsen's World Clock (an advanced astronomical clock) which was set in motion in 1955 by King Frederick IX.

City Hall Square marks the eastern entrance to the Strøget shopping street, which leads in a general direction back toward the cruise piers. Several landmarks lie just north of the Strøget, starting with **Cathedral of Our Lady** 17, which is two blocks off the Strøget on Nørregade. This neo-classical cathedral was built in the early 1800s and contains sculptures by Albert Thorvaldsen. In May 2004, Crown Prince Frederick married his Australian bride Mary Donaldson here.

From the cathedral, several pedestrian streets wind to Købmagergade where the famous **Round Tower** 18 rises above the surrounding buildings. This stone tower, built in the late 1600s as an astronomical observatory, was used by the astronomer Tycho Brahe. The rooftop platform, providing sweeping views of the city, is reached not by stairs but by a spiral ramp that winds to the top and was designed for wheeling heavy instruments into the tower.

A few blocks from the Round Tower is the landscaped Royal Garden where tree-lined pathways lead to **Rosenborg Castle** 19, built outside the ramparts of Copenhagen in the early 1600s as a country residence for Christian IV. Rosenborg is now a museum displaying a wealth of royal treasures, including the crown used for coronations since 1670 and the crown jewels, which date to the early 1700s and are used by Denmark's current queen for important events.

Opposite the Botanical Gardens is the **Danish National Gallery** [20] Here you can view works by Italian Renaissance artists, masterpieces of the Danish Golden Age (1880-1900), and 20th-century paintings by such masters as Matisse and Edvard Munch. Admission is free and tours in English are provided.

Across the harbour from the city centre in Christianshavn is where the counter-culture enclave of **Christiania** has thrived since the early 1970s when a group of hippies moved into a derelict military barracks and established an alternative-lifestyle community.

The original **Carlsberg Brewery**, located in the city's eastern Vesterbro neighbourhood (2 km from Tivoli Gardens) has been converted in a visitor centre offering daily tours (visitcarlsberg.dk).

Other Ports & Attractions

If your cruise begins and/or terminates in Copenhagen, the pre- and post-cruise opportunities include renting a car for touring the Danish countryside or utilizing the country's efficient rail service. Accommodations include castle or manor house stays.

Places worth visiting include **Dragør**, a fishing port founded in the 12th century. Located south of Copenhagen, this charming village of winding lanes lined with traditional Danish houses has an historic harbourfront and several museums.

The **Open Air Museum**, located on a rural estate a 30-minute drive north of Copenhagen, has recreated Danish country life

(Above, right) Rosenborg Castle
(Right) Street scene in Dragør.

Fredensborg Palace

as it was at various times in the past with buildings that include a cottage, water mill and country manor. Admission is free; closed Mondays.

The port of **Roskilde** was Denmark's capital from the 10th century until it was replaced by Copenhagen in 1443. Its magnificent 12th-century cathedral is the final resting place of generations of Danish kings and queens whose elaborate tombs and monuments fill the chapels. The city's Viking Ship Hall houses five reconstructed Viking ships salvaged from the waters of Roskilde Fjord.

One of the prettiest castles in Europe is located in the town of **Hillerød** (about 20 miles from Copenhagen), which developed around the Renaissance-style **Frederiksborg Castle**. Built of brick and marble between 1602 and 1620, Frederiksborg's fairytale setting consists of three small islands on Castle Lake. For two centuries, until 1840, Denmark's kings were crowned here in the castle church. Frederiksborg was restored to its original rococo opulence following a fire in 1859, and the former royal residence now houses a museum of national history. Nearby, in the little town of

Fredensborg, is **Fredensborg Palace** – Queen Margrethe's spring and autumn residence.

The coastal port of **Helsingør** (called Elsinore in Shakespeare's *Hamlet*) is famous as the location of Kronborg Castle, first built in 1574 and reinforced in the late 1700s. It was one of Denmark's most important fortresses, overlooking the Øresund at its narrowest point, with Halsingborg, Sweden, lying opposite. Until the mid-19th century, any foreign ship passing through the Øresund beneath the ramparts of Kronborg Castle had to pay a toll to the Danish crown. Shakespeare chose this castle as the setting for his famous play, and its courtyard and battlements have, over the years, been the stage for numerous performances of *Hamlet*. The castle, declared a UNESCO World Heritage Site in 2000, is now a museum.

Six miles south of Helsingor is the **Louisiana Museum of Modern Art** – a seaside sculpture garden displaying works by Henry Moore and other modern artists. Continuing south past palatial homes overlooking sandy beaches, the coastal route leads to **Rungstedlund**, the family estate of Karen Blixen, which is now a museum dedicated to the famous author who wrote such works as

Out of Africa and *Babette's Feast* under the pen name Isak Dinesen.

Aarhus, the second largest city and principal port in Denmark, began as a fortified Viking town, its centre a pagan burial site. Aarhus is today a university city, its modern architecture in contrast to the historic quarter's medieval buildings. These include the 12th-century Aarhus Cathedral (with the longest nave in Denmark) and the 11th-century stone Church of Our Lady. Modern architecture in Aarhus includes City Hall, designed by Arne Jacobsen, and the ARoS art museum.

The cruise ships dock opposite the town centre, within easy walking distance of most major attractions, including the quiet narrow lanes of the Latin Quarter, which are filled with cafés and small specialty shops. Other attractions are the Old Town open-air museum depicting Danish town life in the 1700s and 1800s, and Marselisborg Palace, a summer retreat for the Danish royal family (a changing of the royal guard takes place outside the palace at noon when the queen is in residence).

Out-of-town excursions from Aarhus can be made to several places of interest on the Jutland peninsula. **Jelling**, a UNESCO World Heritage site, is where

Kronborg Castle, Helsingør

ancient runestones commemorate the reign of King Bluetooth.

Also nearby is the **Legoland** theme park, located in the town of Billund. The Lego factory was founded in the 1930s by a carpenter named Ole Kirk Christiansen who called it Lego (a combination of *leg godt* which is Danish for 'play well'). The first toys were made of wood, and the interlocking plastic bricks were developed in the early 1950s by the founder's son. Legoland opened in 1968, across from the factory, and it features small-scale versions of famous landmarks from around the world, including the Acropolis, Statue of Liberty, and a model of Copenhagen's city streets.

The port of **Fredericia** offers easy access by rental car to Egeskov Castle – a beautifully preserved moated castle from the 16th century, located on the island of Funen. (Sixt Car Rental will have a car waiting at the dock.) Another option is to take the train from Fredericia to the historic city of **Odense**. This city's 13th-century cathedral is considered one of the finest examples of Danish Gothic architecture. Hans Christian Andersen was born a few blocks from the cathedral in 1805. Admission to the nearby

Hans Christian Andersen museum includes entry to this house.

The seaside town of **Skagen** at the northernmost tip of the Jutland was once a remote fishing port. In the late 1800s it became an artists' enclave, as painters and writers escaping the city were drawn to Skagen's dramatic setting of wave-swept beaches and shifting sand dunes. Today it's a popular summertime beach resort of low yellow houses with red roofs, where attractions include Buried Church, a 19th-century lighthouse and historic Brøndums Hotel.

The Danish island of **Bornholm** lies off the south coast of Sweden in the Baltic Sea, and has changed hands several times over the centuries between Denmark and Sweden. During WWII, Bornholm was seized by Germany, then bombarded and eventually captured by Soviet forces in 1945, which left a year later. **Rønne** is the island's port of call, its ship harbour within easy walking distance of the town with its winding cobblestone streets and half-timbered houses. The main historic attractions are the ruins of a 13th-century fortress with a panoramic view overlooking the sea. Cycling and motor tours of the scenic countryside are popular, with more than a dozen medieval churches dotting the island, four which are round churches.

Greenland & Faeroe Islands

Both Greenland and the Faeroe Islands, self-governing dependencies within the Danish realm, are visited by cruise ships. The volcanic **Faeroe Islands** lie north of Scotland and consist of 18 main islands – the largest of which contains the capital **Torshavn** – and four small uninhabited islands. Fishing ports and sheep farms thrive on these rugged islands, which were first colonized by Norsemen in the 8th century, followed by Norwegian settlement in the 14th century, then passing under Danish rule in 1380.

Greenland, the world's largest island, is capped by an ice sheet that spreads outwardly in all directions, some of its glaciers flowing into the sea where massive icebergs break free. Those discharged into Davis Strait often reach the Atlantic shipping lanes. Greenland's coastal areas and offshore islands are free of ice and are where the Inuit (Eskimo) inhabitants were living when the Norse chieftain Eric the Red landed on their shores in 982. He named their island Greenland to make it sound more appealing to potential settlers, but only stone ruins remained of a Norse colony when the British explorers John Davis and Martin Frobisher rediscovered Greenland in the 16th century.

Lying largely within the Arctic Circle, Greenland was a magnet for Arctic explorers seeking the Northwest Passage. Recolonized by Norwegian missionaries in the

Nanortalik, Greenland

early 1700s, Danish trading posts were established soon afterwards, but the island remains sparsely populated to this day. With 80% of the island's land mass covered in ice most the year, there are no highways connecting its 18 towns. The United States established military bases in Greenland during World War II, and home rule was introduced in 1979. Greenlandic Inuit is the official language and most of the island's 60,000 residents are Inuit. Greenland's traditional subsistence economy has become modernized in recent years and commercial fishing is now an important industry.

Ports of call include **Qaqortoq**, founded in 1775, where sights include colonial buildings and an historic fountain-filled town square. Greenland's natural attractions are numerous – pristine fjords, massive glaciers, giant icebergs and coastal waters frequented by whales and other marine mammals.

A few cruise ships stop at Greenland during trans-Atlantic crossings, while Hurtigruten makes regular sailings to this remote region.

(Top) Prince Christian Sound.
(Below) A young Greenlander.
(Bottom) Port of Qaqortoq.

NORWAY

CRUISE ROUTES

ROUTES: -------------

0   60

Miles

N

Inset map

North Cape

VESTERÅLEN

Lopphavet

Altafjorden

Porsangen

Lakselfjorden

Vardø

Tromsø

Alta

Lofoten

Vestfjorde

Russia

Narvik

S w e d e n

F i n l a n d

Main map

ARCTIC CIRCLE

NORWEGIAN SEA

Seinkjer

Trondheimsfjorden

Trondheim

Kristiansund

Trollheimen 1672m

Molde

Romsdalsfjord

Andalsnes

Alesund

N o r w a y

S w e d e n

Volda

Stranda

Geiranger

Nordfjord

Olden

Jotunheimen

Sandane

Jostedal Glacier

Skjolden

Askvoll

Urnes

Ardal

Sognefjorden

Flåm

Lillehammer

Ringsaker

Elverum

Hardangerjokulen 1862m

Hamar

E45

Bergen

Hardangerfjord

Eidfjord

Hardangerjøkulen Glacier

Trolltunga

Hardangervidda

Oslo

Drammen

Haugesund

Boknafjord

Lysefjord

Skien

Fredrikstad

Stavanger

Sandnes

Tanum

Uddevalla

Kristiansand

NORWAY

Norway is a land of boundless beauty with its breathtaking fjords and snowcovered mountain peaks. First attracting ship-borne tourists in the late 19th century, this rugged scenery has also shaped Norway's national character – posing a challenge to survival but ultimately providing an abundance of natural riches.

Barely a quarter of Norway's total land area is productive with just five percent cultivated, but the country's forests are an excellent source of timber, its fertile waters support a large fishing fleet and its offshore seabeds contain oil deposits that have made modern Norway – which began as a network of farflung Norse settlements ruled by chieftans – into one of the world's wealthiest nations.

Norway at a Glance

Sparsely populated Norway is about three-quarters the size of California and has a population approaching five million. From 1825 to 1925, more than 800,000 Norwegians (about one-third of the population) immigrated to North America, many of them settling in the midwest of the United States where they farmed the fertile, flat land that was so scarce in their native Norway.

A mostly mountainous country dominated by a deeply indented coastline, Norway's northern territory extends well beyond the Arctic Circle where the Sami of Lapland have herded Arctic rein-

Geirangerfjord is one of many stunning fjords hidden along Norway's intricate coastline.

(Above) Sami live in Norway's north. (Below) Fresh berries are a summertime treat in Norway.

deer for centuries. The sun never fully sets in summer in Norway's northern regions, and in southern Norway there are 21 hours of daylight (from about 3:00 a.m. to 11:00 p.m.)

Norway is a parliamentary democracy and constitutional monarchy. Harald V has been the country's king since 1991. May 17 is Constitution Day and this flag-flying holiday is celebrated nationwide with parades, festivities and the wearing of traditional dress.

Norwegian and Sami are the country's two official languages, but English is widely spoken. The state religion is Lutheran.

The **unit of currency is the Norwegian krone** (kr or NOK), which divides into 100 øre. The approximate rate of exchange is $1 US = 7 krone; £1 British pound = 11 krone.

The cost of living is high in Norway, and this is reflected in prices charged for goods and services. Tipping is appreciated (5 to 10 per cent) but a service charge is automatically added to hotel and restaurant bills. Major credit cards are accepted at most stores and restaurants, and by taxi drivers.

Norway's country calling code is +47.

Dining

Seafood is a popular dish in Norway, where locally caught cod, herring, shrimp and salmon are featured on restaurant menus. Pork-and-veal meatballs are also popular, as are such delicacies as smoked elk and reindeer sausage.

Waffles (thin, heart-shaped and served with whipped cream and strawberry jam or berries) are popular, as are *sveler* – Norwegian pancakes served with a spread of sugar and butter.

Domestic cheeses include the famous Jarlsburg cheese – a semi-firm, yellow cheese that's distinctive for its slightly sweet and nutty flavour and for its small, round holes. Restaurant and bar prices in Norway are very high, with a glass of beer costing about $12.

Shopping

Shopping items to look for include hand-knitted sweaters in Nordic designs and wood-carved items decorated with patterns inspired by the Norwegian folk art of rose-maling (rose painting).

Another unique Norwegian craft is Hardanger embroidery, which traditionally utilized white thread on white cloth to create a geometric block pattern (diamonds, squares, etc.) for decorating *bunads* (long aprons). Today, coloured thread is also used in traditional and contemporary styles for embroidering cushions and table linens.

Other souvenirs include handmade pewter jewellery, trolls (dolls representing creatures from Norse mythology) and a wide range of Viking-themed mementos.

Stores displaying a tax-free shopping logo will issue a tax-free voucher for the amount of Value Added Tax you paid on purchases exceeding NOK 315. Visit www.globalblue.com for details on obtaining a refund.

(Above) Serving up fresh shrimp at a food stand. (Below) High-quality Norwegian knitwear.

Norway's History

King Harald, who claimed to descend from the Viking gods, was the first chieftan to unite Norway under one ruler in about 900. He then set his sights on lands lying to the west, conquering the Shetlands and Orkneys. Skilled seafarers, the Norsemen proceeded to raid parts of Western Europe, establishing the Norse duchy of Normandy and laying claim to Iceland and Greenland. But dynastic feuds threatened to tear the country apart until King Sverre was able to consolidate royal power. Throughout the 13th century Norway enjoyed peace and prosperity, and its capital, Trondheim, was an important Christian centre and place of pilgrimage.

All this changed in the 14th century with the political union of Denmark, Sweden and Norway (the Kalmar Union), which resulted in Norway being ruled by Danish governors for the next four centuries. This period of Norwegian history was later characterized by the playwright Henrik Ibsen as "twice two hundred years of darkness." The 19th century was the turning point for Norway, which was ceded by Denmark to Sweden in 1814. Despite Sweden recognizing Norway as an independent kingdom, their union was strained by a rising Norwegian nationalism, which culminated in Norway's peaceful separation from Sweden in 1905. The majority of Norwegians voted in favour of a constitutional monarchy versus a republic as their nation's form of government, and a Danish prince was chosen to be their new monarch. He was crowned Haakon VII, but the man who best personified Norway's newfound nationalism was Fridtjof Nansen.

An explorer, scientist, statesman and humanitarian, Nansen first caught the world's attention when, in 1888, he led an expedition on skis across the Greenland ice sheet. However, the achievement for which he has earned enduring fame – and an iconic status in Norway – was his amazing attempt a few years later to reach the North Pole. His ship, the *Fram* (which means *forward*), got stuck in the pack ice but – as Nansen had predicted – the prevailing ocean currents carried it slowly toward the North Pole. However, after a year spent drifting westward aboard the ice-locked *Fram*, Nansen and crewmember Hjalmar Johansen left the ship and attempted to reach the North Pole with skis, kayaks,

Norwegian polar explorer
Fridtjof Nansen.

Norway's Arctic waters

sledges and sled dogs. Enduring brutal conditions, they came within 226 miles (364 km) of the North Pole before turning south toward Franz Josef Land where they were rescued a year later upon a chance encounter with a British explorer named Frederick Jackson.

Nansen and Johansen returned to a hero's welcome in Norway, as did the crew of the *Fram* a few weeks later. Not only had Nansen proved his theory about a polar current, he had discovered that the Arctic was an ocean capped by an ever-shifting ice pack. Nansen became an international celebrity and the information he gathered on his brilliant exploit became the basis for all future Arctic work. He took on the role of statesman when working toward Norway's independence from Sweden in 1905, and he won a Nobel Peace Prize in 1922 for his international work with refugees.

German forces occupied Norway during World War II, but the majority of Norwegians fought back with armed resistance or civil disobedience, while the country's large merchant navy played a key role in Allied war operations, from the evacua-tion of Dunkirk to the Normandy landings. King Haakon, married to an English princess, headed a government in exile from London during the German occupation of Norway from 1940 to 1945.

Norway joined NATO after the war, and many of the state-controlled economic measures imposed during the war were continued as the country pursued a mixed economy of both extensive government ownership and free market activity. Norway joined the European Free Trade Association in 1959 but the Norwegian people have rejected joining the European Union.

The Norwegian government largely controls Norway's oil and gas reserves and has established a state-owned pension fund – the largest such fund in Europe, with assets in the hundreds of billions of dollars.

Norway has come under criticism from environmentalists and animals rights activists for its stance on whaling (a centuries-old tradition in northern Norway) and its fish farming industry, despite concerns about contaminants in pen-raised salmon.

Oslo

Oslo, with a population of about half a million, is the largest city in Norway. It is scenically situated at the head of island-dotted Oslofjord where pine-forested hills overlook the city. A transportation hub with cruise ships, car ferries and tour boats docking along the harbour-front, Oslo is also Norway's cultural centre with its many museums, art-adorned parks and historic buildings.

Oslo was founded by the Norse king Harald III in about 1000 AD and became Norway's national capital in 1299, but the city lost its importance when Norway was incorporated into the Kingdom of Denmark. Following the devastating fire of 1624 during which most buildings (built of wood with turf roofs) were destroyed, a spacious new town was begun using brick and stone under order of King Christian IV, who renamed it Christiania.

When Norway was ceded to Sweden in 1814, Christiania – although merely a small town

Cruising down Oslofjord

– was reinstated as the country's capital. A building boom followed, along with a massive influx of rural Norwegians seeking employment. The city's Royal Palace became home to Norway's new king when the country gained independence in 1905. The city's name was officially changed back to Oslo in 1925. Oslo hosted the Olympic Winter Games in 1952, and celebrated its 1000th anniversary in the year 2000.

Getting Around 🚶 🚲

There are four cruise piers in Oslo. Søndre Akershus pier is located beneath the ramparts of Akershus Fortress, and directly south is Vippentang pier. On the other side of the peninsula is Revierkai pier. All three are within walking distance of the city centre where the main attractions can be explored on foot.

The fourth pier is located on the other side of Oslo's harbour, near the new Tjuvholmen waterfront development.

A **hop-on/hop-off bus** stops near the cruise terminals and can be taken around the city centre and to the museums on the

Bygdøy Peninsula. **Passenger ferries** also provide transport from the harbourfront to Bygdøy.

There is a tourist information office on Akershusstranda beside the cruise terminal. The city's main tourist information office is opposite City Hall.

A **city card** (sold at tourist information offices) provides unlimited travel on **public transportation** (boats, buses, trams, trains) and free or reduced admission to most museums (www.visitoslo.com). National museums are closed Mondays and have free entry on Sundays; other days the adult admission is 50 NOK.

Taxi stands are situated throughout the city and taxis can be hailed on the street, but the ride will be expensive. The meter starts at about NOK 50 and the per kilometre fare varies from 14 to 30 NOK.

Shore Excursions – Oslo

Excursions include a selection of city driving tours with stops at such attractions as Vigeland Sculpture Park, Holmenkollen Ski Jump or several of the museums on the Bygdøy Peninsula. City walking and biking tours are also offered, as well as guided hikes in the hills above Oslo. Check your cruise line's website for details on shore excursions offered.

(Above) Oslo harbour. (Below) The harbourfront tram car can be taken to Vigeland Sculpture Park. (Bottom) One of the many bike stations in Oslo.

(Above) Hard Rock Cafe.
(Below) Shopping in Oslo.

Drivers accept credit cards and a tip is not expected.

Numerous **bike stations** are situated in the city centre and require an electronic smartcard to release a bike, which must be returned within three hours to any of the bike stations. (You can pick up another bike at the same or any other bike station.) Tourist smartcards can be rented for 24 hours at the Tourist Information Centre near City Hall for NOK 100 and must be returned to the same office.

Lunch Stops

A variety of restaurants can be found on and around Karl Johans Gate, including a Hard Rock Cafe located between the Grand Hotel and the Royal Palace. Establishments steeped in tradition include the Grand Hotel's street-level Grand Café, where Henrik Ibsen lunched every day (the proprietor would have a beer waiting at his table). Ibsen also had a regular table at Engebret Café on Bankplassen (Bank Square), as did Edvard Grieg and Edvard Munch. Another café popular with the city's artists is Theatercaféen, located across the street from the National Theater. Waterfront restaurants and bars are concentrated in the revitalized dockside area of Aker Brygge and the adjoining new harbourfront at Tjurholmen.

Shopping in Oslo

Oslo's main shopping area is the pedestrian precinct centred on Karl Johans Gate and its side-streets. Here you will find chain stores and Norwegian clothing stores such as Vero Moda.

Exclusive shops can be found along Akersgata.

An Oleana store, carrying a prize-winning collection of knitwear, silk scarves and silver jewellery, is located on Stortingsgata overlooking Spikersuppa (Michelle Obama purchased several Oleana sweaters while visiting Oslo in December 2009.)

A Holm store carrying Norwegian souvenirs and sweaters by Dale of Norway is located next to City Hall. The House of Oslo department store on Ruseløkkveien (in between the Royal Palace and Nobel Peace Center) opened in 2006 and features Scandinavian-designed housewares in its 20 shops (including an Illums Bolighus).

Most museums have excellent gift shops selling high-quality souvenirs. A handful of shops selling quality sweaters and souvenirs is located inside the Akershus cruise terminal

Akershus Fortress

Local Attractions

Akershus Fortress & Castle **1** was first constructed in about 1300 and it was from here that Denmark's Queen Margrethe ruled Norway. Damaged in the 1624 fire, Akershus Castle was remodelled as a Renaissance palace. The Norwegian fascist leader and Nazi collaborator Vidkun Quisling was imprisoned here at the end of World War II while awaiting execution as a traitor. Admission is charged to visit the castle's chapel and Royal Mausoleum. The castle grounds also contain the **Resistance Museum**, which documents Norway's resistance to the Nazi occupation of 1940-45. The fortress area is open free of charge, and in summer members of the King's Guard gather daily in the fortress square to begin their daily

parade to the Royal Palace via Kirkegata and Karl Johans Gate.

Kirkegata leads past Bankplassen (Bank Square), location of the **Museum of Contemporary Art** 2 and the **National Museum of Architecture** 3, both administered by the National Museum. Engebret Café, Oslo's oldest restaurant, is also located in this historic square.

To the east, along on the waterfront, is Oslo's **Opera House** 4, which opened in April 2008. Input from the public played a role in the architectural planning of its striking modernist design. Partially submerged, the building's gently inclined roof resembles two tidewater glaciers converging and flowing seaward into the fjord. People are allowed to walk onto the roof, which has become a big draw for skateboarders attracted to its smooth marble slopes.

A few kilometres northeast of the city centre is the **Munch Museum** 5, which houses a collection of paintings, drawings and prints the artist bequeathed to the city of Oslo upon his death in 1944 at the age of 80. Edvard

Oslo's modern Opera House

Munch was a pioneer of expressionism and his paintings, initially considered brutal and disturbing, reflect his profoundly unhappy childhood. Born in 1863, Munch was raised in Oslo by his father after his mother died when Munch was five. A sickly boy, Munch later wrote that he "inherited the seeds of madness" from his father, who was morbidly pious and obsessed with the macabre. One of Munch's sisters died in childhood (the subject of *The Sick Child*) and another became mentally ill. Stalked by death, Munch expressed his anguish in his art, his most famous work being *The Scream*, of which he created several versions – two paintings and two pastels. A painted version (and a pastel) is housed in the Munch Museum (the other is at the National Gallery). In August 2004, two masked gunmen entered the Munch Museum and stole Munch's *Scream* and *Madonna* in a daylight heist. The paintings were eventually recovered. The fourth version (a pastel)

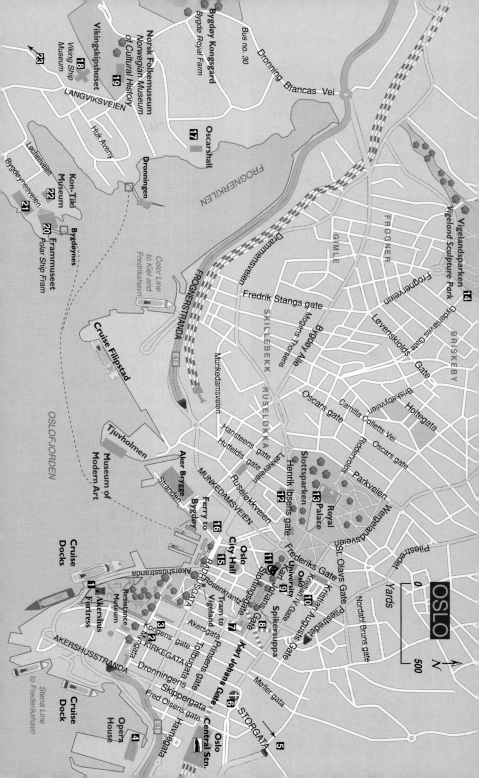

(Above) The Scream by Edvard Munch. (Below) Grand Hotel.

of *The Scream* is privately owned and was auctioned for a record-settting $120 million at Sotheby's in New York in 2012.

The **Oslo Cathedral** **6**, built of red brick and inaugurated in 1697 as Church of Our Saviour, is located at Stortovet Square and is where public events such as royal weddings and funerals are held. In 2001, Crown Prince Haakon married Mette-Marit Hoiby at the cathedral, which contains its original pulpit and altar, and has stained glass windows by Emanuel Vigeland. The eastern end of the square is enclosed by a curved building called the Bazar, into which is integrated the tower of the Fire Watch (Oslo's main fire station from 1860 to 1939).

Oslo's high street, Karl Johans Gate, leads from the Cathedral to the civic centre where notable buildings overlook several city blocks of fountains, lawns and flower beds, called **Spikersuppa**. At one end of Spikersuppa is the **Storting** **7** (Grand Assembly) building, which was completed in 1866 and houses the Norwegian parliament. Across the street is the stately **Grand Hotel** **8**, which opened in 1874 and which hosts the annual Nobel Peace Prize banquet, with the prize winner staying in the five-star hotel's Nobel Suite. U.S. President Barack Obama, recipient of the 2009 Nobel Peace Prize, and his wife Michelle viewed the traditional torch light procession from the balcony.

Near the western end of Karl Johans Gate is **Oslo University** **9** founded in 1811. Behind the university buildings, on Kristian Augusts Gate, is the **10** **National**

Gallery (part of the National Museum) which focuses on works by 19th- and 20th-century Norwegian artists, including a painted version of Munch's *The Scream*.

The **National Theater** , across from the university, is one of Norway's most revered cultural institutions and a showcase for the plays of Norway's famous playwright Henrik Ibsen. Before becoming a major film star in the 1960s, Liv Ullmann performed regularly at this theatre in productions such as *A Doll's House*.

The **Henrik Ibsen Museum** , located on Henrik Ibsens Gate, is the restored apartment where the playwright spent the last 11 years of his life with his wife Suzannah, living modestly and writing his final two plays. Considered the father of dramatic realism, Ibsen left his native Norway in 1864 to escape its stifling conformity and write the controversial plays for which he is famous – *A Doll's House, Hedda Gabler* and *An Enemy of the People*. When he returned 27 years later, the groundbreaking modernism he had introduced to western theatre had begun permeating all aspects of Norwegian life.

The **Royal Palace**  is situated on a sweeping rise at the end of Karl Johans Gate where a circular drive leads to the palace entrance. Designed by a Danish architect and completed in 1849 this neo-classical building was

(Top to bottom) Storting;
Spikersuppa; National Theater.

(Above and below) Royal Palace and its guards. (Bottom) Vigeland Sculpture Park

occupied only for short periods by visiting Swedish-Norwegian kings until Norway gained independence in 1905, at which time it became the permanent residence of the Norwegian monarch. Guided tours are available from mid-June to mid-August (some of which are in English) but tickets tend to sell out in advance. The park behind the palace, open to the public, is a peaceful setting of lawns and pathways leading down to an ornamental lake. In summer, the daily changing of the guard takes place in the palace forecourt at 1:30 p.m.

About a mile west of the Palace grounds is **Vigeland Sculpture Park 14**– one of Norway's best-known cultural attractions. Occupying 80 acres within Frogner Park, the Vigeland Sculpture Park was conceived and created by Gustav Vigeland, who spent 40 years of his life planning and designing groups of nude sculptures that illustrate the development of man. Of the park's many colossal sculptures, most impressive is the Monolith – a towering granite column of intertwined bodies. Vigeland was initially commissioned in 1907 to

create a fountain for the city, and this became the starting point for the sculpture park. In 1921, Vigeland agreed to donate all of his works to the city in exchange for a custom-built studio and residence in which to complete his sculpture park. Today this building, adjacent to the park, is a museum containing the sculptor's original works. Entry to Vigeland Sculpture Park is free and the grounds can reached by tram car from the harbourfront.

City Hall 15, located on the harbourfront, was inaugurated in 1950. This brown-brick building emulates the traditional northern-European town hall with its two towers and large clock with a 49-bell carillon that plays every hour. The hall's interior is decorated with works by Norwegian painters and sculptors, its massive main hall featuring colourful murals. The Nobel Peace Prize is awarded here each December, the ceremony attended by members of the Norwegian royal family.

Close to City Hall is the **Nobel Peace Center 16**, which opened in 2005 and commemorates the life and vision of Alfred Nobel as well as the lives of various Nobel

(Top) Nobel Peace Center
(Above) Oslo's City Hall

Laureates. Housed in a refurbished, 19th-century train station, the centre's film, video and photo exhibits are presented with state-of-the-art technology and interactive installations. The Peace Prize is the only Nobel prize awarded outside of Sweden, and the recipient of this illustrious award is selected by a five-member committee elected by the Norwegian parliament.

Another harbourfront attraction is **Aker Brygge** – a former shipyard that's been converted into a pedestrian area filled with shops and restaurants, as is the adjacent

Tjuvholmen harbourfront where the new **Museum of Modern Art** (designed by Renzo Piano) is a major attraction.

Passenger ferry boats dock at the head of Oslo's harbour, including one that makes regular 10-minute crossings from Pier 3 to the Bygdøy Peninsula where five museums are located, including the Fram Museum, Kon-Tiki Museum and Viking Ship Museum. The ferry stops at two docks, the first (Dronningen) is located a half-mile walk to the Viking Ship Museum and

Norwegian Folk Museum; the second stop (Bygdøynes) is right beside the Fram, Kon-Tiki and Maritime museums. All five museums are open daily throughout the summer.

Bygdøy is an exclusive residential area with parks, beaches, a royal farm and a summer palace called **17 Oscarshall**, which was built in the Neo-Gothic style in the mid-19th century by Oscar I to showcase Norwegian artistry and craftsmanship. Resembling a small castle , Oscarshall sits on a rise overlooking the water and is surrounded by manicured parkland. Originally a private royal residence, in 1881 Oscar II opened the palace to the public.

The **Viking Ship Museum 18** houses two of the best-preserved Viking ships ever found. Discovered in royal burial mounds, the ships date from the 9th century and were used to transport the remains of high-ranking chieftains on their final voyage to

(Left) A Bygdøy residence.

(Below) Viking Ship Museum.

"the other side." Jewellery, weapons and other artifacts found in their graves are also on display.

The open-air **Norwegian Folk Museum** 19 contains reproductions of traditional houses and a 13th-century stave church, constructed entirely of wood. Hosts dressed in folk costumes provide assistance and demonstrate various activities.

The **Fram Museum** 20, shaped like an inverted V, was specially constructed to preserve the wooden schooner *Fram* as a national monument. The brainchild of the Norwegian polar explorer Fridtjof Nansen, the ship was specially built to withstand the crushing pressure of pack ice as it drifted across the Arctic Ocean. The *Fram* was also used by Otto Sverdrup to explore the islands northwest of Greenland and, in 1910, Roald Amundsen sailed her to the Antarctic where he and four crewmembers made history by being the first to reach the South Pole. Amundsen's other famous ship, the *Gjøa*, used to be displayed at the nearby **Norwegian Maritime Museum** 21, but in

(Above) The passenger ferry to Bygdøy. (Below) Fram Museum.

2009 plans were set in motion to build extra exhibit space at the Fram Museum to better display and preserve this famous vessel – the first to sail through the Northwest Passage.

The **Kon-Tiki Museum** 22 is a tribute to the Norwegian explorer and anthropologist Thor Heyerdahl who, with the help of five crewmen, built a wooden raft in 1947 and sailed it across the South Pacific Ocean from Peru to an island in the Tuamotos. The wooden raft, called *Kon-Tiki*, is on display as is *Ra II* (another papyrus

The famous Kon-Tiki raft

raft built by Heyerdahl) and statues from Easter Island.

About about a mile from Bygdøynes pier, housed in the former residence of the Nazi collaborator Vidkun Quisling, is the **23 Holocaust Centre**. Quisling was executed for treason in 1945 and his home, Villa Grande, now houses a permanent exhibition on the fate of Norwegian Jews during World War II (closed Mondays).

One of Oslo's most popular out-of-town attractions is the **Holmenkollen Ski Museum and Jump Tower**. The museum traces 4,000 years of skiing history with exhibits that include ski equipment used by the famous polar explorers Nansen and Amundsen. The premises also feature a ski jump simulator, gift shop and café. The views are sweeping from atop the ski jump, originally built for the 1952 Winter Olympics but recently dismantled and a new one built for the 2011 Nordic World Championship. The Metro 1 bus travels to Holmenkollen.

Kristiansand

Located near the southernmost tip of Norway, this harbour city has long been a popular summer destination for vacationing Norwegians. The waterfront boardwalk leads past parks, a public beach and a 17th-century fortress with exceptional sea views. The waterfront bustles with a busy fish market and café on every corner, and the visitor information centre provides maps of self-guided walks through the charming old town, founded by King Christian IV in 1641.

A bridge connects Kristiansand with the island of Odderoya, a former naval base where remaining ramparts and 18th-century buildings can be explored. Other tours include a boat trip to the pretty village of Lillesand, and a visit to Setesdal Mineral Park, its amazing collection of minerals and crystals housed in caverns within a mountain.

The Fjords of Norway

Not until the late 1800s, when the Norwegian government undertook an extensive nautical survey of its long and intricate coastline, were the remote fjords and coastal communities of western and northern Norway connected by regular steamship service to the southern part of the country. The initial steamship service – transporting passengers, cargo and mail – expanded over time to connect more and more harbours. This nautical lifeline became known as Hurtigruten ("the express route") because it was much faster than travelling overland. In the 1980s, Hurtigruten (then called Norwegian Coastal Voyage) began launching larger and more luxurious ships to appeal to the growing tourist market. Today, Hurtigruten's fleet offers year-round cruises out of Bergen, while the major cruise lines offer summertime sailings to the fjords of Norway.

The Norwegian climate is ideal for summer cruising, with the days lengthening the farther north your ship travels, and the warm ocean currents providing coastal towns with relatively warm weather at these northern latitudes. Green valleys lying at the head of glassy fjords where villages cluster around country churches and farmhouses cling to mountainsides.

Stavanger

Called the Shortcut to the Norwegian Fjords, the Stavangar region occupies the southwestern corner of Norway and is where the Viking king Harald the Fairhair built his first royal residence after uniting Norway into one kingdom in 872 AD. Three swords set into the mountain rock above Hafrsfjord Bay serve as a memorial to King Harald I.

The shipbuilding and fish processing port of **Stavanger** is situated at the mouth of Stavanger Fjord, one of many arms of the extensive Boknafjorden. The cruise ships dock in the city centre, a short walk to Old Stavanger's narrow, cobbled lanes lined with white wooden buildings built two centuries ago and now housing craft shops, gal-

A Hurtigruten ship pulls into one of Norway's scenic fjords.

leries and museums. Local attractions include the Fish Market and the town's 12th-century Cathedral of St. Swithin, built of stone in the Anglo-Norman style, is a scaled-down replica of Winchester Cathedral in England.

Excursions offered in Stavangar include city walking and sightseeing tours, with visits to the Norwegian Canning Museum and the Norwegian Petroleum Museum (North Sea oil is refined here, earning Stavanger the title of Petroleum Capital of Norway). An eight-hour driving tour can be taken into the mountainous area of Gloppedalen to view Europe's largest boulder scree, while a shorter, four-hour trip can be made to Norway's only preserved medieval abbey (Utstein Abbey) which was a royal estate of Viking kings. Helicopter tours provide breathtaking aerial views of the Stavanger region.

Boat tours include one to Avaldsnes Karmøy, site of King

Harald's first royal residence, to visit the Long House of Bukkøy.

An hour's boat trip from Stavanger is Lysefjord, where Pulpit Rock, a heartstopping clifftop plateau, looms 2,000 feet above the deep blue water of the fjord. Even higher, at 3,000 feet, is Kjeraag cliff. It was from this precipitous perch that a 32-year-old daredevil named Thor Axel Kappfjell, who had successfully parachuted from some of the world's tallest buildings, attempted his last illegal leap in July 1999. He likely lost his bearings in the night fog and crashed into the cliff face while descending, for his body was found at the base, his parachute open.

Eidfjord (Hardanger)

Hardangerfjord, the second largest fjord in Norway, winds for 114 miles (183 km) inland before branching into several smaller fjords, including 15-mile-long (24 km) Eidfjord. The scenic val-

leys and cascading waterfalls of the Hardanger region make it a favoured tourist area, once known mostly for its Hardanger fiddle (similar to a violin and considered the national instrument of Norway) and its famous Hardanger embroidery (Hardangersøm). This craft flourished from 1650 to 1850 and became the classic ornamentation of the *bunad* – a traditional Norwegian costume consisting of a long apron worn over a white blouse and a full skirt .

Some cruise ships visit the village of **Ulvik**, a tender port hidden at the head of Hardangerfjord where passengers are tendered ashore to tour the scenic valleys and fruit orchards. The major port in this area is **Eidfjord**, from which excursions can be taken to view such scenic wonders as Hardangerjøkulen Glacier and Vøringsfossen – Norway's most famous waterfall with its free fall of 535 feet. Kjeasen, nestled on a mountain ledge above Simafjord, is touted as "the most inaccessible mountain farm in Norway" and offers a spectacular view of Eidfjord.

Eidfjord is also the gateway to Hardangervidda, which is the largest high-mountain plateau in Europe and Norway's largest national park. Hardangervidda Nature Centre, located five miles (8 km) from the cruise port, is a modern facility housing interactive exhibits about the natural and cultural heritage of the area, with a cafe and gift shop on the

Traditional Norwegian dress with Hardanger embroidery.

premises. Other manmade attractions include Sysendamman (one of Norway's biggest stone-filled dams) and Sima Power Plant, built right into a mountain.

The Troll Train takes visitors on a one-hour sightseeing tour along the shores of the fjord, with a stop at a Viking burial ground and medieval stone church. An outdoor activity centre provides bike/canoe rental as well as paddling instruction for beginners.

Bergen

Surrounded by the timeless grandeur of mountains and fjords, Bergen is known as the Gateway to the Fjords of Norway. The second-largest city in Norway, with a population of a quarter million, Bergen has managed to retain a village feel along its harbour. It was once the largest city of medieval Norway and a member of the Hanseatic League, its wealthy merchants imposing their unpopular rule from the mid-1300s to mid-1500s. Many of Bergen's

Bergen's Hanseatic waterfront

churches and monasteries were destroyed during social upheavals of the Reformation, but it retained its role as Norway's leading city until the rise of Oslo in the 19th century.

The ships dock either at Skoltegrunnskaien Pier (which is a short walk to the historic harbour) or at a pier further away (in which case, a ship's shuttle is provided). Bergen is very walkable, while brightly painted open trains on wheels and hop-on hop-off buses offer tours of the city.

The old Hanseatic Quarter of wooden warehouses and narrow, winding streets (called Bryggen) has been declared a World Heritage Site. The old Hanseatic wharf consists of a colourful row of quayside warehouses, rebuilt in their medieval gabled style after a fire in 1702. Today they house shops, art studios and restaurants. Of historic note are the Hanseatic Museum, the 12th-century St. Mary's Church and the 13th-century Bergenhus fortress containing Haakon's Hall (built when Bergen was the political centre of Norway

and rebuilt following damage sustained during WWII). In the 1560s, the governor of Bergenhus built himself Rosenkrantz Tower, which served as a residence and fortified tower.

The bustling Bergen Fish Market is at the far end of the harbour, about a five-minute walk from Bryggen, and nearby is the Ulriken cable car ride up Mount Ulriken, highest of the seven mountains surrounding Bergen. The Bergen Aquarium is at the harbour entrance, and the modern Bryggens Museum is a third of a mile (.5 km) from Skoltegrunnskaien Pier. Bergen's art galleries are clustered around a small, centrally located lake and admission is free with the purchase of a Bergen Card.

Bergen has long been a cultural centre, attracting the best of Norway's musical talent. Edvard Grieg was born in Bergen in 1843 and his former residence, located in the suburbs of Bergen, is a museum.

The Fløibanen Funicular (also free with a Bergen Card) is located in the centre of town. It's a six-minute ride to the 1,000-foot summit of Mount Floyen, where visitors can enjoy splendid views of the city and hiking paths.

Shore excursions in Bergen include a visit to Edvard Grieg's home, called Troldhaugen, which was built in 1885 and is now a museum. The lakeside property also contains the studio in which Grieg composed much of his music and a modern concert hall where chamber music is performed. Another notable attraction on a driving tour is the Fantoft Stave Church, first built in 1150 and rebuilt following a 1992 fire.

Flam and Skjolden (Sognefjord)

The village of **Flam** lies at the head of Aurlandsfjorden, and the village of **Skjolden** lies at the head of Lustrafjorden, two of the innermost arms of Sognefjord – Norway's longest and deepest fjord at 110 miles and depths exceeding 4,000 feet. Sognefjord branches into the Jotunheimen Mountains (Norway's tallest) where Jostedalsbreen Glacier is the largest on the European mainland. In some places the mountainsides plunge a sheer 900 feet into the water on both sides of the fjord. **Naerøyforden** branches off Aurlandsfjorden and is listed on

A mountaintop view of Flam.

UNESCO's World Heritage List for its exceptional beauty and wilderness.

The most famous attraction at Flam is the spectacular, 12-mile train ride that takes visitors on a journey through some of the wildest and most magnificent scenery Norway has to offer as it winds from the narrow Flamsdalen Valley up to a high, snow-covered mountain plateau. The steep climb along this standard-gauge railway – past cascading waterfalls, through spiralling tunnels and across narrow gorges – is made in locomotives powered by hydroelectricity.

Other shore excursions in Flam include kayaking or boat rides to explore the fjord landscape and perhaps spot some seals or dolphins. Hiking maps are available in the cruise terminal building, outlining walks that range from 30 minutes to three hours. Driving tours visit nearby villages and provide dramatic views overlooking the fjords where idyllic farms cling to the steep mountainsides. Along the mountain road between Aurland and Laerdal is a viewing platform called Stegastein, which overlooks Aurlandsforden from a height of 2,000 feet.

Shore excursions in Skjolden include coach tours to Jotunheimen National Park along the spectacular Sognefjell Mountain Road, and to Urnes Stave Church, Norway's oldest stave church and a UNESCO World Heritage Site. Skjolden is the world's first port to use the Norwegian-invented SeaWalk (a temporary floating pier structure that connects from ship to shore and replaces tendering).

Olden (Nordfjord)

The picturesque town of Olden lies at the inner end of Nordfjord, nestled in a beautiful valley at the base of glacier-clad mountains. The village centre is a ten-minute walk from the cruise pier where Old Church, built in 1759, stands on the site of a 14th-century stave church. On the other side of Olden is the Singer Home, where the American painter William Singer lived with his wife Anna from the early 1900s until his death in 1945. After inheriting a fortune from his family's steel company in Pittsburgh, Singer and his wife travelled to Paris and the Netherlands in search of artistic inspiration, which the post-impressionist painter finally found in the solitude and serenity of the Norwegian fjords. The region's snowcapped mountains and sunlit meadows became his muse, and the Singers became generous benefactors to the local community.

Local tour operators in Olden focus on the outdoors with rafting tours of Nordfjord and hiking to Mt. Huaren. Ship-organized excursions include boat trips on scenic Lake Olden and Lake Loen, as well as several tours to various arms of massive Jostedals Glacier, which covers approximately 300 square miles (777 square km). One glacier excursion features trail hiking to the face of Briksdal Glacier while another is a coach tour that ascends the Stryn Mountains to Lake Stryn to visit Justedal National Park Centre, a botanical garden and a geological park.

Another coach tour, this one to Boyabreen Glacier, entails travelling through a four-mile-long (6 km) tunnel built in 1986 under Jostedals Glacier to reach the town of Fjaerland and the nearby Norwegian Glacier Centre.

Alesund

A major fishing port situated on three islands at the mouth of Storfjorden, Alesund is considered one of Norway's prettiest towns with its art nouveau architecture of turrets and towers which lend the town a fairytale atmosphere. The town was rebuilt in this style following a devastating fire that struck one winter's night in 1904. The cruise ships dock in the centre of town, where a hop-on hop-off offers local tours.

Out-of-town attractions include an open-air museum, 2.5 miles (4 km) east of town, which displays buildings from the Middle Ages. A nearby stone church dates from the early 13th century.

Alesund is a pretty port filled with art nouveau architecture.

One excursion features a boat ride to the island of Langevag where the Devold factory once produced woolen sweaters, hats and mittens used by the polar explorers Nansen and Amundsen. The original factory, which opened in 1853, is now a museum but the factory outlet still sells traditional Norwegian sweaters and woolen blankets. Another excursion features a visit to the Saga Islands, birthplace of the Viking chieftan Rollo (who founded Normandy in 911) along with a stop at Atlantic Sea Park (the largest aquarium in Norway).

Included in most bus tours is Mt. Aksla Viewpoint – providing breathtaking views of Alesund and the surrounding islands, fjords and mountains. Mt. Aksla hiking excursions are also available.

One of the region's most famous attractions is Trollstigroad (Path of the Trolls), which has been voted Norway's most scenic drive. Also called **Trollstigen (Troll's Ladder)**, this road – cut into the mountainside and flanked by stone walls, ascends 2,815 feet above sea level and has 11 hairpin bends. A drive to Trollstigroad

from the Alesund cruise dock includes a stop at Gudbrand's Gorge – 80 feet straight down to the foaming river. Another stop is Trollstigen View Point before descending along the Path of the Trolls, past needle-sharp mountain peaks, to Andalsnes on the shores of Romsdalsfjorden. Highlights of the drive include crossing the 585-foot-high Stigfoss Waterfall and passing the Troll Wall – the highest vertical mountain wall in Europe at over 3,000 feet.

Geiranger

Of all the beautiful fjords in Norway, the fairest of them all is Geiranger. Lying at the very head of Storfjorden, the sublime Geirangerfjord is a UNESCO World Heritage Site and has been rated as the best cared for by National Geographic. The fjord's pristine beauty is punctuated by abandoned farms perched on clifftop plateaus, one of which is reached by climbing a rope ladder.

Cruise ships anchor at the head of Geirangerfjord and passengers walk ashore along a temporary floating pier structure connecting the ship to the tender dock in the

(Above) Troll's Ladder.
(Below) Viewpoint overlooking Geirangerfjord.

resort village of Geiranger. From here motorcoaches take visitors on tours into the mountains where the roads wind past lakes and waterfalls. Several viewpoints provide spectacular views of the fjord, including one at 4,500 feet (1372 m) from which the ship looks like a toy in the fjord below.

Shore excursions often include a visit to the Fjord Centre art facility which opened in 2002 and illustrates the extreme living and working conditions fjord farmers faced over the centuries. One excursion features a visit to a mountain farm where goats are raised for making cheese. Hiking to a waterfall or kayaking in Geirangerfjord are also offered.

Molde/Andalsnes

The charming fjord town of Molde is noted for its panoramic view of 222 mountain peaks. It's also known for its proximity to the scenic **Atlantic Road**, completed in 1989 and voted as Norwegian Construction of the Century. Touted as the world's most beautiful road trip, the Atlantic Road's many bridges connect the islands and skerries

(rocky islets) lying at the mouth of the area's fjords.

Molde is situated on Romsdalsfjord, as is the smaller port of **Andalsnes**, located near the word-famous Trollstigroad – Path of the Trolls. The cruise ships dock in the town centres of both ports, from which shore excursions can be made to the area's scenic highlights. In addition to the Atlantic Road and Path of the Trolls, other places of interest are the Mount Varden viewpoint for panoramic views and the fishing village of Bud. The Ergan Fortification – a WWII fort overlooking the Bjornsund Islands – is now a museum with an underground network of bunkers, headquarters and soldier's quarters.

One coach tour includes a boat trip – in a replica Viking ship – from Geitoya Island to the fishing community of Haholmen, which is the island home of adventurer Ragnar Thorseth, who builds and sails Viking ships around the world. Other excursions include hiking Mount Varden, or visiting an open-air museum with folk dancing demonstrations.

Trondheim

The first capital of Norway, Trondheim was founded by Olaf I in 997 on a peninsula in Trondheimsfjord. Its original name was Nidaros and it became an important Christian centre and place of pilgrimage with construction of a cathedral over the tomb of St. Olaf (King Olaf II). Considered the finest

Romsdalsfjord leads to the scenic town of Molde.

Gothic cathedral in Scandinavia, its design was overseen by the Archbishop of Nidaros who, after visiting Canterbury Cathedral in England, ordered his architects to incorporate several of its design features. (The cathedral was rebuilt in 1869, after several fires, using Norwegian blue soapstone and white marble.)

The Reformation diminished the importance of Nidaros as a religious centre, and the city was renamed Trondheim in 1537. Eventually eclipsed by the trading port of Bergen, Trondheim regained some of its former prominence when the first king of a modern, independent Norway was crowned in Trondheim Cathedral in 1906. All coronations since have taken place in Trondheim Cathedral, and the crown jewels are kept here. Another building of note in Trondheim is the royal residence of Stiftsgaard, built in the late 1700s and used by Norway's king and queen when they visit Trondheim.

Local museums include the Archbishop's Palace, built in the 12th century, which houses original sculptures from Nidaros Cathedral and national regalia in the palace's medieval vault. The National Museum of Decorative Arts features Norwegian craftsmanship through the centuries, and Trondheim Art Museum contains Norway's third-largest art collection with an emphasis on Norwegian art. The open-air Folk Museum features wooden buildings (including a 12th-century stave church) situated around the ruins of a medieval castle.

Trondheim's famous cathedral

Kristiansten Fort, built after the great city fire of 1681, repelled a Swedish conquest in 1718 but was overtaken by German forces during WWII and used for executing members of the Norwegian Resistance. The fort provides a sweeping view over Trondheim.

Northern Norway

Norway's northern region, which straddles the Arctic Circle, is the land of the midnight sun and the reindeer-herding Sami.

Tromsø, situated on the island of Tromsøy at latitude 69°, lies above the Arctic Circle and is the largest city in northern Norway with a population of 65,000. The Sami were the area's earliest inhabitants, followed by the Vikings. By the end of the 19th century, Tromsø

Erosion from ice and water formed the hole in Torghatten on Torget Island, although legend says the hole was created by the arrow of a troll. North of Torghatten is the Arctic Circle Monument (below), which marks that famous line of latitude. (Bottom) Tromsø.

was an important trading centre and base for Arctic expeditions, with explorers such as Nansen and Amundsen often recruiting crew here. Today the port of Tromsø is a base for shipping, herring fishing and seal hunting. In summer the sun doesn't set between May 21 and July 21. In winter, when darkness descends, the northern lights are a common sight in the skies over Tromsø.

A university town, Tromsø is home to both historic and modern attractions, including its wooden cathedral (built in 1861), the Polar Museum (housed in an 1830s wharf building) and the Tromsø Museum (established in 1872 and now part of the University in Tromsø). Mack Brewery is where you can have a pint at the northernmost brewery in the world. Polaria is a modern adventure centre featuring panoramic films and an aquarium with Arctic sea mammals. Tromsø's best-known landmark is the modernist Arctic Cathedral, symbolizing the strength of pack ice. Constructed in 1965, this iconic building stands on the mainland looking across the water to the city centre, which is connected by bridges.

Other attractions are the cable car ride up Mount Storsteinen for breathtaking views of the Troms Valley and surrounding mountains, and a visit to the Tromsø Wilderness Centre where visitors can experience Sami culture. The fishing village of Sommarøy is 38 miles (60 km) west of Tromsø. A one-hour drive from Tromsø is the world's northernmost 18-hole golf course – open 24 hours a day in summer.

Alta lies at the head of Alta Fjord, its forested setting a contrast to the region's generally desolate landscapes. Cruise passengers are tendered ashore at Alta, where local rock carvings dating to c. 4200 BC are listed on UNESCO's World Heritage List. The Alta River has carved Norway's largest canyon and made headlines in the fall of 1979 when the local Sami and environmentalists protested the construction of a dam and hydroelectric power plant that would create an artificial lake and inundate a Sami village. Construction of the power plant went ahead, but was scaled down to cause less flooding of Sami land and less disruption to reindeer migration and wild salmon stocks.

North Cape, Europe's northernmost point, is marked by a dramatic cliff that rises 1,000 feet (305 m) above the ocean. The sun doesn't set here in summer (from the second week in May until the last week in July) and doesn't rise in the middle of winter, when the only respite from darkness are the northern lights that shimmer across the sky. **Honningsvag** is the port at North Cape and it bustles with cruise ships at the height of summer while free-roaming reindeer graze on the tundra at the outskirts of town.

Beyond North Cape is **Spitsbergen** – the largest island of the Svalbard archipelago, which lies halfway between mainland Norway and the North Pole. Excursions from the port of Longyearbyen, the world's northernmost town, include hiking to a mountain plateau and a boat trip to view nesting seabirds.

Cruising around Spitsbergen

SWEDEN

Sweden seems to have it all – beautiful scenery, attractive cities and one of the highest living standards in the world. Universal education and health care are core values and conservation is taken seriously, with the Swedes recycling just about everything and their children raised to be environmentally conscious. Public access to nature is enshrined in the country's constitution, and this 'right to roam' allows hikers to cross private property and even camp there temporarily, providing they ask permission and don't pitch a tent within sight of someone's house.

Sweden's longstanding neutrality has placed the country in a unique position as an international mediator and a favoured destination for asylum seekers and refugees – a role Sweden played during World War II when it received children evacuated from Finland and thousands of Jews escaping from Nazi-occupied Denmark and Norway.

Sweden at a Glance

The southern one-third of the country is where the majority of Sweden's 10 million people live. The land here is low-lying and productive for farming, while the northern two-thirds of the country is mountainous and sparsely populated.

Pastoral islands dot the waters off Stockholm.

Stockholm (pop. 1.4 million) is the capital and largest city. Sweden became a member of the European Union in 1995 but has not joined the single European currency. **Sweden's currency is the Swedish krona** (SEK) and 1 krona = 100 ore. The approximate rate of exchange is $1 USD = 8 kronor (£1 = 12 kronor). The euro is not widely accepted.

The official language is Swedish, and English is widely spoken, and the major religion is Lutheranism. The country calling code is +46. Public holidays include National Day (June 6) and Midsummer's Day (the Saturday that falls between June 20 and 26)

Sweden's History

A people called Svear inhabited northern Sweden in early historic times, eventually conquering and

merging with their neighbours in southern Sweden. The Swedish kings warred for centuries with the Danes and Norwegians while pushing seaward from their eastern frontier, conquering Finland in the 12th century.

The rise of a feudal class weakened royal authority, as did the influence of German merchants of the Hanseatic League, and in 1397 Sweden became part of the Kalmar Union, instigated by Denmark's Queen Margrethe. But the Swedes chafed at this arrangement and regents chosen by the Swedish parliament held the real power in Sweden.

When Denmark's Christian II ordered a massacre of Swedish nobles at Stockholm in 1520, resistance in Sweden hardened. One of the senators killed at the massacre was the father of Gustavus Vasa, who later defeated the Danes and in 1523 was crowned the new king

Sweden's military heritage is reenacted daily in summer at Stockholm's Royal Palace.

of Sweden, marking the beginning of the Swedish modern state.

Within a century, having seized territory from Russia and Poland, Sweden was the dominant Protestant power of continental Europe under the leadership of the great warrior king Gustavus Adolphus, who died on the battlefield. His daughter Christina made Stockholm the official capital in 1634, reigning over a court filled with music and poetry, attracting scholars such as Descartes.

By the end of the 17th century Sweden had become a European power, controlling Finland, Latvia, Estonia and other parts of the Baltic seaboard. Sweden's great period of empire came to an end in the Northern War of 1700-1721 when the rising Russian Empire dealt Sweden a crushing defeat. Fraught internally with civil strife and political intrigue, Sweden suffered several *coup d'etats* as rival factions of the nobility sought power. Gustavus IV was forced to abdicate in 1809 and his aged, childless uncle was placed on the throne while Sweden's parliament (the Riksdag) searched for a suitable successor. Seeking an alliance with Napoleon, the search ended with the French general Jean Baptiste Jules Bernadotte.

Elected crown prince of Sweden and adopting the name Charles John, Bernadotte was a popular choice with the Swedish public due to the kindness he had shown Swedish prisoners during one of his campaigns. He was also a brilliant military commander who ultimately allied Sweden not with Napoleon but with Russia and England, helping to defeat his former commander at the battle of Leipzig in 1813 and marching the Swedish army into Denmark. This was the last war in which Sweden has participated. Peace prevailed during Bernadotte's reign as Charles XIV (1814-44) and subsequent kings from the House of Bernadotte oversaw a foreign policy of armed neutrality.

The nation's current monarch, King Carl XVI Gustaf, serves a ceremonial role, with legislative power vested in the elected Riksdag. The king's eldest daughter, Crown Princess Victoria, is next in line to the Swedish throne. In 2010, Victoria married her former fitness instructor, Daniel Westing, who grew up in the lake town of Ockelbo, located 100 miles north of Stockholm and far removed from high society. Victoria had to overcome her father's objections to the match, but in the end true love prevailed and a committee of royal courtiers spent several years tutoring and grooming the friendly country boy into a popular prince.

A ship threads its way through the Stockholm Archipelago.

Stockholm

The approach by ship to Stockholm is one of the most scenic anywhere as your vessel weaves its way past the treed islands of the Stockholm Archipelago. Tens of thousands of islands, islets and skerries comprise this archipelago, and it takes a cruise ship about three hours to navigate through the Northern Stockholm Archipelago. (Some ships instead pull into the port of Nynashamn, located 36 miles south of Stockholm.)

The archipelago's outer islands are barren rock, but those closer to Stockholm are verdant with trees and gardens. About 150 of these islands are inhabited, their 19th-century mansions and summer cottages overlooking grassy slopes that run down to the water's edge. A popular recreation area, the islands are connected by waterbus service to Stockholm. In winter the channels freeze over and people ice skate between the islands. They wear extra-long skate blades, use ski poles and carry safety gear in the event they fall through the ice and have to pull themselves out.

Stockholm occupies a cluster of islands where Lake Malaren flows into the Baltic Sea. Founded in the mid-13th century on the site of a fishing village, modern Stockholm is considered one of the world's finest cities with its broad streets, waterfront parks and well-planned housing projects. The city's historic core – Gamla Stan (Old Town) – is a medieval warren of narrow, winding streets, and the adjacent island of Sodermalm provided the setting for Stieg Larsson's Millennium Triology.

Getting Around

Most ships embarking and disembarking passengers in Stockholm will dock at the Frihamnen cruise terminal, located about two miles (3 km) northeast of Gamla Stan (about 10 minutes by taxi; 20 minutes by public bus). Ships making a port call in Stockholm will dock at one of several cruise piers in the city's harbour, or possibly pull into Nynashamn, located 37 miles (60 km) south of Stockholm. Passengers tendered ashore at Nynashamn can reach Stockholm by train, shore excursion or motorcoach shuttle; trains run twice hourly to Stockholm.

The main cruise pier in Stockholm's harbour is Stadsgarden, on the island of Sodermalm, which is connected by bridges to Gamla Stan. (Small ships often dock right at Gamla Stan.) It takes about 30 minutes to walk the 1.5 miles (2.4 km) from Stadsgarden into the city centre (follow the blue line). A less strenuous way to get there is to take the Hop-On Hop-Off Boat that docks near the Stadsgarden cruise quays opposite Fotografiska (Photography Museum). An all-day ticket (160 kronor) can be pre-purchased online (stromma.se) or you can purchase a single-use ticket (40 kronor) when boarding the boat and ride it to the Nybroplan dock where a ticket booth sells all-day tickets. An all-day ticket allows you to disembark and re-embark at various stops around the harbour, and this can be combined

Hop-On Hop-Off Boats are an ideal way to explore the city.

Shore Excursions

STOCKHOLM

The wide selection of ship-organized excursions includes driving tours, canal trips, kayaking or hiking expeditions, and cycling around Djurgarden's parkland. Tours of Gamla Stan include stops at the Royal Palace and City Hall. The Vasa Museum or Absolut Ice Bar can also be visited on an organized tour. Full-day tours often feature a scenic drive to the shores of Lake Malaren to visit fortified Gripsholm Castle, built by Gustav Vasa (Gustav I) in 1526, or the idyllic town of Sigtuna with its wooden houses and narrow alleys.

Check your cruise line's website for detail on the shore excursions being offered.

The Nybroplan waterfront

with the red Hop-On Hop-Off Bus, which follows a route past most of Stockholm's sights. Bus passengers can get on and off at any of the 21 stops, including the cruise piers at Stadsgarden and Frihamnen. A combination all-day bus-and-boat ticket is 380 kronor; an all-day ticket for the Red Sightseeing buses is 260 kronor.

Most cruise lines offer an all-day shuttle service into Gamla Stan from Stadsgarden or Frihamnen that drops off in front of the National Museum or the Royal Opera. You can also take the public bus (6 kronor) from the cruise piers into Gamla Stan. Taxis are available, but expensive (credit cards accepted).

Stockholm's airport is connected to the city centre by high-speed trains (the Arlanda Express), which depart every 15 minutes on the 20-minute journey between the airport and the central train station

in Norrmalm (the city's business and shopping area). The same trip by taxi takes about 45 minutes. An airport shuttle services the major downtown hotels. The Stockholm Card (525 kronor for one day) provides free access to museums, attractions, public transportation and sightseeing boats.

Where to Stay

Hotels near the Arlanda Express train station include the four-star Nordic Light Hotel and Nordic Sea Hotel, which is home to the world's first Absolut Icebar. A few blocks south of central station, near the waterfront, is the Sheraton Stockholm Hotel. The stately five-star Grand Hotel is a city landmark overlooking the harbour that opened its doors in 1874.

The Hilton Stockholm Slussen is located on the Sodermalm

(Above) A cafe near the Cathedral. (Below) Naglo restaurant at Gustav Adolfs Torg. (Bottom) King's Garden

waterfront, opposite Gamla Stan, and just a few minutes' walk from many of the significant sites mentioned in the Millennium Trilogy. (Guides at the nearby Stockholm City Museum lead Millennium tours of the area.)

Dining

Smorgasbord is a Swedish dining tradition and the most elegant place in town to enjoy this classic Scandinavian feast is at the Grand Hotel's Veranda restaurant, which serves six courses of delicacies, including herring dishes and smoked salmon.

Den Gyldene on Osterlanggatan in Gamla Stan is Stockholm's oldest restaurant, serving classical Swedish dishes in a candle-lit setting. More restaurants and cafés are located along **Storkyrkobrinken** (which leads from the House of Nobility to the Cathedral) and Trangsund (which winds from the Cathedral to the Great Square).

Kungstradgarden (King's Garden) in Norrmalm is where locals and tourists come to enjoy restaurants at either end of the tree-lined park with its sunken

fountain, outdoor chess matches and live performances on the tent-covered stage.

Shopping

Sweden is famous for its fine glassware, stainless steel kitchenware and Nordic folk art, including brightly painted wooden handicrafts.

The city's main shopping area is centred around **Sergels Torg**, near the northwest corner of King's Garden, which is where the department store NK (Nordiska Kompaniet) is located.

Crystalware by Orrefors and Kosta Boda is available at their outlet on Birger Jarlsgatan (a few blocks from Nybroplan) and at Nordika Kristall (Kungsgatan 9), which houses an art-glass gallery. Another Nordika Kristall outlet is located in Gamla Stan on Osterlanggatan.

The famous interior design store Svenskt Tenn is located on Strandvagen, a waterfront boulevard leading off Nybroplan.

(Right) Storkyrkobrinken in Gamla Stan. (Below) Stockholm's harbour.

Souvenir shops are concentrated on Vasterlanggatan and Osterlanggatan in Gamla Stan.

Value Added Tax (VAT) is added to most purchases but can be re-claimed on large amounts with a Tax Free Receipt issued by participating retailers.

(Above) Military bands perform at the Royal Palace during the daily changing of the guard.

City Attractions

Gamla Stan, the historic heart of Stockholm, occupies three interconnected islands and contains numerous historic buildings as well as shops, restaurants and outdoor cafes. The adjacent mainland is where the city's shopping and theatre district is located. The main tourist information centre is located on the north side of King's Garden (Kungstradgarden) in Norrmalm.

The **Royal Palace** **1** is a highlight for most visitors, especially if you time your arrival in its outer courtyard to coincide with the mid-day Parade of Guards held daily in June, July and August (12:15 Monday-Saturday; 1:15 Sunday and official holidays). This massive palace was built in the Italian baroque style and completed in 1754, replacing the original medieval castle which was destroyed by fire in 1697 (apart from the north wing). It contains 680 rooms, which include offices for members of the royal family and their staff. Parts of the palace are open to the public, and guidebooks are sold at the entrance desks. Guided tours are also available. Highlights include the State Apartment (where gala banquets are held during state visits), the Bernadotte Apartments, and the Royal Chapel. Museums within the palace walls include the Tre Kronor Museum (with exhibits on the original medieval castle), Gustav III's Museum of Antiquities (displaying classical sculptures), the Treasury (containing the state regalia) and the Royal Armoury, housed in the palace vaults.

Stockholm's cathedral **2**, called Storkyrkan (Great Church) began as a village church in the late 13th century. Rebuilt follow-

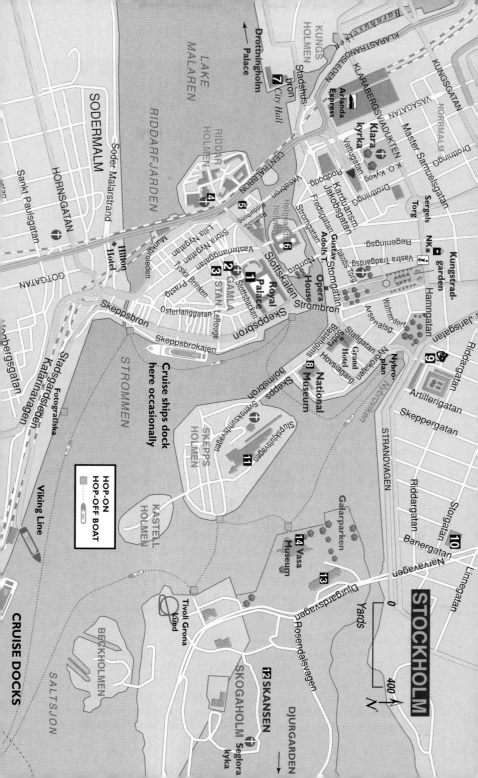

(Above and right) The interior of Stockholm's cathedral.

ing a fire, the church underwent major conversions throughout the 15th century and emerged as a late-Gothic structure. Lavish adornment was added in the 17th century and highlights include a 12-foot-high bronze candelabra and a 15th-century altar monument depicting St. George slaying a dragon. In 1942 the church received cathedral status. Royal weddings, coronations and baptisms take place in the cathedral, with Crown Princess Victoria marrying Daniel Westing here on June 19, 2010.

Immediately south of the cathedral is **Stortorget (Great Square)** **3**, the oldest square in Stockholm. It is relatively small compared to the main squares of other medieval cities and is surrounded on three sides by tall narrow houses originally owned by wealthy merchants and shopkeepers. The only civic building – the Stock Exchange Building – stands on the square's north side. This 18th-century, French rococo building currently houses the Swedish Academy, Nobel Library and **Nobel Museum**, which was inaugurated in 2001 and celebrates the work and ideas of Nobel laureates over the past century. The museum is open daily in summer, from 10 am to 5 pm, and guided tours in English are at 11:15 am and 3 pm.

Riddarholmen (Knights' Island) contains numerous 17th-century palaces (now civic buildings) such as those surrounding the central public square of **Birger Jarls Torg**, in the centre of which stands a statue depicting Birger Jarl, founder of Stockholm. Nearby is **Riddarholm Church** **4**, easily spotted with its distinc-

Alfred Nobel

An inventor and industrialist with a love of poetry and English literature, Alfred Nobel was born in Stockholm on October 21, 1833. When Nobel was five years old, his father moved the family to St. Petersburg where he had established a successful business designing naval mines for the Tsar to protect St. Petersburg from a British sea attack. Educated by private tutors, Nobel was fluent in five languages by age 17. He travelled widely as a young adult, training with the world's foremost chemists and engineers. Upon returning to Sweden, he developed nitroglycerine as an explosive, performing experiments on a barge in Lake Malaren.

In 1867 he patented his most famous invention – dynamite – and also invented a detonator (blasting cap), which together were used widely in all forms of construction work – from blasting rock to drilling tunnels to building canals. Nobel eventually founded dozens of factories and laboratories in over 20 countries, and he ultimately held 355 patents for his various chemical inventions. His intensive work and travel schedule left little time for a personal life and he never married. He also developed what were then considered radical views, for he became inclined toward pacifism and held misgivings about his inventions and their potential use. Thus, when he died without issue in 1896, his will instructed the executors (two young engineers) to use most of his immense fortune for the awarding of annual prizes in the fields of physics, chemistry, medicine, literature and peace (economics was added in the 1960s).

Although Nobel's will was contested by relatives, the Nobel Foundation was eventually formed and the first Nobel Prizes were awarded in 1901. With the exception of the Peace Prize (which is awarded in Oslo to a recipient selected by the Norwegian parliament) the Nobel Prizes are chosen by Swedish academies. The selection process is long and rigorous.

Accomplished individuals in each area of expertise are invited to submit nominations, which are kept secret and scrutinized by a committee which forwards a preliminary list to experts in that discipline. They reduce the list of nominees from 200 to 15 and submit this, with recommendations, to the appropriate academy whose members vote to select the winner.

The Nobel Prizes are presented annually by the King of Sweden on December 10, the anniversary of Nobel's death. This ceremony takes place at Stockholm Concert Hall in Hotorget Square, followed by a lavish banquet in the Blue Room of Stockholm City Hall.

(Above) Alfred Nobel (Below) U.S. President Obama in Oslo receiving the 2009 Peace Prize.

(Above) A statue of Stockholm's founder stands in the centre of Birger Jarls Torg. (Below) Riddarholm Church.

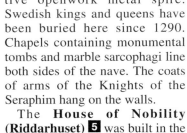

tive openwork metal spire. Swedish kings and queens have been buried here since 1290. Chapels containing monumental tombs and marble sarcophagi line both sides of the nave. The coats of arms of the Knights of the Seraphim hang on the walls.

The **House of Nobility (Riddarhuset)** 5 was built in the mid-1600s (two wings were added in 1870) to hold meetings of Swedish nobility during the Swedish parliament's Diet (Assembly) of Four Estates (nobles, clergy, burghers and peasants). Hanging on the walls are the coats of arms of aristocratic families that have, over the centuries, belonged to the House of Nobility. Also on display is a 17th-century chair carved in ivory and ebony.

The **Riksdag (Sweden's parliament)** 6 is housed in a late 19th-century building on the island of Helgeandsholmen, which is connected by bridges to the main part of Gamla Stan opposite the Royal Palace. The Riksdagshuset's curved facade faces west, and an information centre outside the main entrance is where you can sign up for a guided tour.

City Hall (Stadshuset) , built between 1911 and 1923, is situated on King's Island over-looking Lake Malaren. Designed by Swedish architect Ragnar Osterberg, the red-brick building is a modern interpretation of the Scandinavian Renaissance style. Take an elevator or walk the 365 steps to the bell tower, which offers panoramic views over Stockholm. City Hall is famous worldwide for the annual Nobel Banquet held in its Blue Hall. Guided tours only are available of this ceremonial hall and of the Golden Hall (splendid with gold mosaics). Daily tours in English are held on the hour (except 1 pm) from 10 am to 3 pm, June through August. Most cruise lines offer organized shore tours of City Hall.

The **National Museum** , Sweden's largest art museum, is housed in a 19th-century building which faces, across the water, the Royal Palace. The museum's vast collection of fine and decorative art includes drawings, paintings and sculptures. Dutch and Flemish artists, such as Rembrandt and Rubens, are represented, as are numerous 18th-century French artists. The museum also houses an art library and restaurant. Open daily in summer; admission is 100 SEK.

(Top to bottom) House of Nobility; Riksdag; City Hall.

(Above) The National Museum viewed from Helgeandsholmen.
(Below) Royal Dramatic Theatre.

The **Royal Dramatic Theatre** **9**, founded in 1788, is famous for its acting school, which produced a long list of famous actors and directors including Ingmar Bergman, Greta Garbo, Ingrid Bergman, Bibi Andersson and Max von Sydow.

East of the Royal Dramatic Theatre, in the upscale residential district of Ostermalm, is the **History Museum** **10** (Historiska Museet), which features historic Viking exhibits.

The **Moderna Museet (Museum of Modern Art)** **11** is located on the harbour island of Skeppsholmen and houses a comprehensive collection of modern art, including works by Dali, Picasso, Matisse and Andy Warhol. (Admission is 120 SEK; closed Mondays.)

Djurgarden, once a royal hunting grounds, is a park-like island of green spaces and outdoor attractions, including a harbourside amusement park called Tivoli Grona Lund. Beside it is the new **ABBA Museum**, dedicated to the legendary Swedish disco group of the 1970s with extensive displays of memorabilia and stage costumes, and interactive exhibits such as a vocal recording booth.

Nearby is the sprawling open-air museum at **Skansen** **12**, which replicates pre-industrial Sweden with traditional farm houses, a manor house and a 19th-century town. Skansen and the nearby **Nordic Museum** **13** were founded by the 19th-century Swedish scholar Artur Hazelius whose goal was to preserve Swedish folk culture before it was completely eroded by modern industrialization. The Nordic Museum is housed in a late-19th-century building designed in the Danish Renaissance style.

A popular attraction on Djurgarden is the **Vasa Museum** **14**, home to the only surviving example of a 17th-century warship. Sweden was an ascending sea power when King Gustavus Adolphus ordered the construction of the 64-gun *Vasa* at the dockyard in Stockholm, where she was launched amid much fanfare in August 1628. The Swedish king was away at the time, waging war in Poland, and didn't witness the disaster viewed by the hundreds of spectators lining the shoreline. Hailed as the mightiest warship ever built, the *Vasa* had barely left the ways when she began to heel over, take on water through her open gunports, and sink 110 feet to the bottom of the harbour where she lay in her muddy grave for over 300 years.

The raising of the *Vasa* took place on April 24, 1961, and the entire country watched the televised event. To prevent the wooden hull from breaking up, it had been slowly raised into shallow water before the final lift to the surface. To prevent decay the moment the ship was exposed to air, all woodwork was promptly treated with a preservative. The ship is now on display in the specially built, climate-controlled Vasa Museum, as are many of the preserved artifacts found on board the ship. The museum is open daily; admission is 130 SEK. The gift shop sells books, prints and replicas of jewellery and other items recovered from the *Vasa*.

If you're spending more than a day in Stockholm, consider a visit to **Drottningholm Palace**, which is a UNESCO World Heritage Site. This palace has been the Swedish royal family's official residence since 1981, when King Carl Gustav and Queen Silvia decided its parklike setting was more suitable for raising a young family. Beautifully situated on Lovon Island, overlooking Lake Malaren, the 18th-century palace and formal gardens were inspired by the Palace of Versailles, but on a smaller scale. Much of the palace, including its perfectly preserved theatre, is open to public tours. Queen Desiree, the French-born consort to King Charles XIV (founder of the House of Bernadotte), spent her summers at Drottningholm – a welcome respite after the long, dark, snow-laden months of a Swedish winter. In summer, a one-hour tour-boat ride can be taken from the City Hall jetty to Drottningholm Palace.

Vasa Museum and Nordic Museum to its left.

Visby

A small city on **Gotland Island**, Visby is a popular summer resort with its preserved medieval architecture and rose-filled gardens. Cruise ships anchor in the harbour and tender their passengers ashore where the walled town is easy to explore on foot. A ship's biking tour is a good way to see more of the island.

Visby began as a Viking settlement, trading port and pagan religious centre. When German merchants of the Hanseatic League settled here in the 11th century, they established Visby as a commercial centre, building stone fortifications and numerous churches. Today, the medieval walled town

Almedalen Park, near the seafront in central Visby.

Drottningholm Palace

is a UNESCO World Heritage Site. The Ring Wall encircles the town's winding cobblestone streets and Gothic church ruins. On warm summer days, visitors linger at the sidewalk cafés or browse the boutiques selling crafts, clothing and jewellery such as pendants replicating Norse talismans made with ancient moulds. Historical highlights include the restored Cathedral of St. Mary's with gargoyles carved into fantastic beasts, demons and angels, and the Historical Museum's two dozen exhibit halls, including the medieval collection housed in a 13th-century warehouse.

From the late 13th-century until the mid-17th century, Gotland changed hands several times between the Danes, Swedes and Hanseatic League, until finally becoming a possession of the Swedish crown.

Gotland, which is a limestone plateau with a steep coastline and few hills, has fertile soil for farming and sheep raising. Its major industries are fishing, cement making and tourism. A ferry connects the north end of Gotland to its smaller, sister island of Faron. Also known as **Faro**, this remote rural island of fine beaches was the decades-long home of the renowned and reclusive movie director Ingmar Bergman.

Helsingborg

The port of Helsingborg is popular for its access by ferry across the narrow Øresund strait to **Helsingor** – home of the Danish castle famous as the setting of Shakespeare's *Hamlet*. Other attractions in Helsingborg are its medieval tower built by the Danes over six centuries ago when the Danish crown controlled both sides of the Øresund. Massive fortresses stood on either side of the strait to exact a levy from all trading vessels passing through its narrowest part. With a population approaching 100,000, Helsingborg is a pleasant city of stone-built churches, half-timbered houses and a pedestrian shopping street (Sweden's first). It is also the international corporate headquarters of Ikea.

Helsingborg shore excursions include guided walking tours, ferry trips to Helsingor to visit Kronborg Castle, and driving tours to Sofiero Castle – the favourite summer residence of King Gustav VI Adolf with its beautiful gardens and expansive lawns, which are sometimes used for large outdoor concerts, including performances by Bob Dylan and Bryan Adams.

Steps lead to Helsingborg's
Danish-built fortress.

Gothenburg (Goteborg)

Sweden's second-largest city and major shipping port. Gothenburg is situated at the mouth of the Gota alv River. Cruise ships dock at one of several quays: Arendal and Skandia are in the outer harbour, about 20 minutes from the city centre on a ship's shuttle bus; America Quay accommodates small cruise ships and is just over a mile (2 km) from the city centre, which can be reached by tram or ship's shuttle; Freeport (Frihamnen) is less than a mile (about 1 km) from the city centre, reached by walking over a bridge.

Founded in 1621, Gothenburg thrived as a trading port, with wealthy merchants building imposing stone houses alongside the city's canals. Modern industrial wealth (Volvo was founded here in 1927) is reflected in the city's numerous parks, gardens, and museums. The charming pedestrian street of Haga Nygata is lined with preserved wooden houses, boutiques and cafés. Gothenburg is known for its seafood restaurants and the local fish market, housed in a church-like hall built in 1874, draws visitors to its fresh shrimp stands.

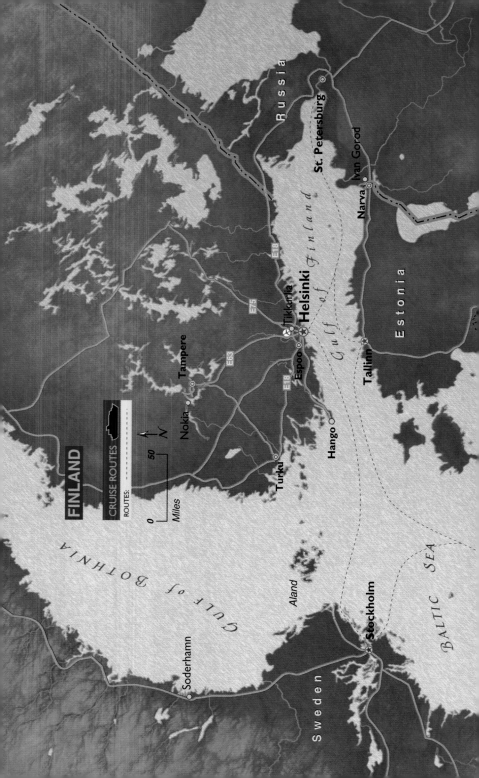

FINLAND

Finland has long been caught in the middle – between the warring empires of Sweden and Russia, then between the West and the Soviet Union. This political predicament has shaped much of Finland's national character, as has the predominance of winter ice and snow. Ice skating originated in Finland when the early settlers strapped blades to their boots for crossing the frozen lakes that dot the countryside. Cross-country skiing is popular on the country's vast central plateau of lakes and pine forests, where Finnish regiments fought the invading Soviets on skis during World War II. The heartiest of Finns practise the extreme sport of ice swimming – leaping into a hole (an *avantouinti*) that has

Helsinki's Senate Square

been cut in the ice. The sauna has long been a popular family pastime in Finland, where the stones of a steaming hot sauna were traditionally heated with wood fires.

A History of Finland

Finland's northernmost area lies above the Arctic Circle where the Sami people inhabit the treeless tundra, their distant ancestors having arrived in Finland during prehistoric times. When nomadic Finnish-speaking hunters and fishers began migrating into the region, they pushed the Sami and their reindeer herds northward. Christian missionaries were the next to arrive, followed by Swedish troops in the 13th century. In 1581, Finland became a grand duchy of Sweden, enjoying extensive independence under Swedish rule while widely adopt-

ing the language and culture of the Swedes. Sweden's recurring wars with Russia caused much suffering in Finland, however, including the famine of 1696 in which a third of the Finnish people perished.

When Russia gained control of Finland during the Napoleonic Wars, the Finns began to chafe under foreign rule. Nationalism became a powerful movement, inspired initially by the epic poems of Johan Runeberg, and later by the stirring orchestral works of Jean Sibelius, who composed *Finlandia* in 1900 at a time when the democratic autonomy Finland had once enjoyed under Czar Alexander II was being curtailed by the imperial decrees of Czar Nicholas II. When the Bolsheviks deposed Nicholas during the Russian Revolution, Finland proclaimed

Uspenski Orthodox Cathedral is the largest Eastern Orthodox church in Western Europe.

its independence. In the ensuing civil war, the Finnish-nationalist White Guard – led by General Mannerheim – defeated the Soviet-backed Red Guard. Finland was not totally free of Russian dominance, however, for the Soviet Union attacked again in 1939. Finnish troops were superior at winter warfare and, aided by volunteers and supplies from Sweden and Norway, were able to initially repulse the Russians. However, Finland was ultimately no match for the USSR and was forced to sign a peace treaty in early 1940.

When Germany attacked the Soviet Union in June of 1941, Finland allied itself with Germany in an attempt to regain territory seized by the Soviets. By the end of the war, Finland was again the loser. Its northern region had been devastated by fighting between German and Soviet troops, and its shattered economy was burdened with $300 million in reparations owed to the USSR. Still, Finland managed to repay this heavy debt

by 1952 and, despite Soviet influence on domestic politics, the Finnish-Communist Party gradually lost influence in the 1970s. However, Finland's reluctance to provoke the communist superpower living next door resulted in what was dubbed the Finlandisation of the country in which the media, schools and libraries censored any material critical of the USSR.

The collapse of the Soviet Union in 1989 allowed Finland to become increasingly European, and the country has thrived as a highly industrialized, free-market economy. Finland, which joined the European Union in 1995, is admired for its high quality of public education and social welfare, which includes giving all expectant mothers a "baby box" filled with clothes, diapers and bathing products, and fitted with a small mattress so the box can be used as baby's first bed. This tradition began in the 1930s when Finland was a poor country and was designed to give all children a good start in life.

Finland at a Glance

The population of Finland is 5.2 million, and the majority (94%) speak Finnish – a language similar to Estonian and Hungarian. The Finnish language is unrelated to the North Germanic languages spoken in the rest of Scandinavia and relies heavily on the use of suffixes and compounds. Spoken by the peasantry under Swedish rule, the Finnish language received official status in 1863. Swedish, once the language of Finland's nobility, is spoken by 6% of the populace and is Finland's second official language. Street signs are posted in Finnish and Swedish. About 60% of Finns understand English.

Following centuries of rule by Swedish kings and Russian czars, the modern nation of Finland

Finland's National Library is a repository of the nation's literary heritage, including books published in the Russian Empire.

– after fighting its way to independence in 1917 – chose not to adopt a monarch as head of state but instead became a parliamentary republic headed by a president.

(Above) A busker on Helsinki's harbourfront. (Below) A waitress in a Helsinki restaurant.

The majority of Finns (80%) belong to the Lutheran church, with 1% belonging to the Eastern Orthodox Church.

The unit of currency in Finland is the euro. The country calling code is +358.

Helsinki

Helsinki, situated on a peninsula, is a natural sea port and the capital of Finland. Founded in 1550 by Gustavus I of Sweden, the port (which is blocked by ice in winter) is sheltered by a group of islands upon which the Swedes constructed a sea fortress to defend its eastern frontier from Russian naval attacks.

Helsinki was destroyed by fire in 1808 and rebuilt on a grand scale after Czar Alexander I moved the Finnish capital there in 1812 from Turku. Helsinki hosted the 1952 Summer Olympic Games and in 1975 the Helsinki Conference on Security and Cooperation in Europe, which achieved the signing of the Helsinki Accords.

Helsinki, with a population of 1.2 million, is the cultural heart of Finland. The city contains dozens of museums and art galleries, and enjoys a thriving café culture. It is also the nation's commercial centre, with industries ranging from textile mills and clothing factories to machine shops and shipyards that build cruise ships, naval vessels and ice breakers. The famous Kvaerner Masa shipyard (which has launched numerous cruise ships) is located a short distance from the cruise piers at Hernesaari.

Getting Around

There are numerous piers in Helsinki servicing cruise ships as well as local ferries to Stockholm and Tallinn. The **Munkkisaari quays at Hernesaari** are located about 2 miles (3 km) west of the city centre. It's a pleasant 30-minute walk into town from Hernesaari along the park-lined waterfront or through the upscale neighbourhood of Eira and the shop-filled Design District. Some cruise ships docking at Hernesaari will provide a shuttle that drops off near the Swedish Theatre.

If there's no shuttle, one option is to catch the public bus (#14) along Hernesaarenranta and get off at one of the stops along Fredrikinkatu (the fare is 3 euros). The red Hop-On Hop-Off bus sometimes stops at the cruise pier or can be boarded at Eira as it follows a circular route from Senate Square to the city's major attractions (25 euros). The taxi fare from Munkkisaari pier to Market Square is about 12 euros.

A tourist information booth is located at the Munkkisaari cruise pier. The Helsinki City Card, which is sold online (36 euros) and at locations throughout the city, provides free admission to top attractions and public transport.

The other cruise piers are located in the **South Harbour** in front of the Olympia Terminal (a 10-minute walk into the city centre) and at Pakkahuone Quay (a five-minute walk to Market Square).

The city core can be explored on foot or hop aboard Tram 2 (formerly Tram 3T) at its stop near the Olympia Terminal to travel the

Shore Excursions

Helsinki

Ship-organized excursions focus on the major sights of Helsinki and include coach tours, walking tours and harbour cruises. You can visit Suomenlinna Island Fortress by ferry on an organized tour, or tour the Finnish Archipelago by speedboat. You can also explore Helsinki's unique variety of architecture on a tour that includes an out-of-town visit to lakeside Hvittrask – the studio home of Eliel Saarinen before moving to the United States where his son Eero Saarinen, a leader of the International style, became one of the 20th century's foremost architects. Another popular excursion is the coach trip to Porvoo, an idyllic waterfront town (Finland's second oldest) located an hour's drive from Helsinki where boutiques, galleries and cafes line its medieval cobblestone streets.

"sightseeing route" past the major attractions to the Olympic Stadium and back. You can get on or off the tram at any stop, or complete the entire loop in about an hour. Tram tickets are valid for one hour and can be purchased from the driver; the cost is 3 euros.

Tram cars are an economical way to visit city attractions.

The Helsinki Tourist & Convention Bureau is located near the east end of the Esplanade, at Pohjoisesplanadi 19.

Shopping

Finnish design is highly regarded and has been successfully applied to clothing, jewellery, tableware and furniture. The famous glassware manufacturer Iittala, founded in 1881, carries an extensive line of classic and contemporary works, including its signature Aalto vase. Iittala's flagship store is on the north side of Esplanade at Pohjoisesplanadi 25. Other items designed by Alvar Aalto can be found at Artek, also on the Esplanade (Etelaesplanadi 18).

Finnish textiles are recognizable for their bold and colourful prints, exemplified by the innovative creations of Ritta Immonen who co-founded Marimekko in Helsinki in 1951. The sleeveless, cotton dresses designed by Marimekko were elevated to international status when Jackie Kennedy wore several during the 1960 U.S. presidential campaign. Marimekko shops are located at the west end of the Esplanade (Pohjoisesplanadi 2) and in the Kamp Gallery (beside the Hotel Kamp on the north side of the Esplanade).

Finnish designer products are featured at Design Forum Finland, located a few blocks south of the Esplanade in Helsinki's Design District – home to antique shops, interior decorating studios, and clothing and jewellery boutiques.

Helsinki's main shopping streets are Mannerheimint, Aleksanterinkatu and both sides of the Esplanade. Stockmann is Helsinki's largest department store (occupying the entire block at the corner of Aleksanterinkatu and Mannerheimint) and carries an enormous selection of items. One block west of Stockmann is the historic Hotel Torni, its top-storey bar providing sweeping views of the city.

The recently revitalized Tori Quarters (the neoclassical city blocks between Market Sq. and Senate Sq.) contain design and craft shops, including the latest

Finnish handicrafts are sold at Market Square.

fashions at Kiseleff House on the south side of Senate Square.

One of the best places to browse for Finnish handicrafts is at Market Square where local artisans set up outdoor tables to display their wares. Alongside Market Square stands Old Market Hall where specialty food shops sell Finnish coffee, cheeses, sweets and tinned delicacies.

For information on claiming VAT returns on purchases worth a minimum total of 40 euros, see www.globalrefund.com.

Dining

Finns traditionally dined on simple food that was available during the long winters, such as game meat, root vegetables and smoked or pickled fish. Today Finnish cuisine features fresh seafood and sauces flavoured with garden herbs. Numerous cafés line the Esplanade, including the glass-roofed Café Kappeli, which has been a favourite Helsinki gathering place since it opened in 1867, and which remains the place to pause for a light lunch. The bar serves European beers on tap and wines by the glass. The luxurious Hotel Kamp, which opened in 1887 on the north side of the Esplanade at Pohjoisesplanadi 29, serves a lavish afternoon tea, while the cozy Café Esplanade at Pohjoisesplanadi 37 serves delicious cinnamon rolls, and soup and sandwiches at lunch time. The seaside Café Ursula at Embassy Park is a pleasant spot to pause for refreshment on the large terrace if you're walking to or from Hernesaari cruise port.

(Above) Sofiankatu leads past sidewalk cafes to Senate Square. (Below) Cafe Kappeli.

17 **16** **OPERA HOUSE**

18 **Sibilius Monument**

Olympic Stadium

Hesperiankatu

Museok

Toolonlahti

RUNEBERGINK

Toolonkatu

15 **Finlandia Hall**

12 **National Museum**

19 **'Rock' Museum**

14 **Parliament**

ARKADIANKATU

10 **Museum of Contemporary Art**

13 **Helsinki Central Stn.**

Elaintarhanlahti

Hakaniemenranta

Kaisaniemenranta

Kluuvi Gloet

UNIONINKATU

Liisankatu

FABIANINKATU

Helsinki Cathedral ✝

Kirkkokatu

Hallituskatu

POHJOISRANTA

Yiopistonkatu

Aleksanterinkatu

19

UNIONINKATU

Stockmann

Hotel Kamp

POHJOISESPLANADI

ETELAESPLANADI

1

Shuttle Drop off

7

6

Sofiankatu

4

Mkt. Sq.

2

3

Cafe Kappeli

5

Kanavakatu

8

Katajanokan

Katajanokka

Ferry & Waterbus to Suomenlinna

SIMONK

MANNERHEIMINT

Anneg Armank

FREDRIKINKATU

Kalevankatu

LONNROTSG

BULEVARDEN

BULEVARDI

UUDENMAANKATU

RUOHOLAHDENK

Punavuori Rodbergen

ROOBERTINKATU

Ratakatu

Design District

Hogbergsg

Kaserngatan

UNIONINKATU

Fabiansg

9

Korkeavuorenk

Kasarmikatu

SODRA KAJEN

Argelandent

Olympia Terminal

Punavuorenkatu

Skeppareg

Jagaregatan

Bergmansgatan

Mannerheim Museum

11

Itainen Puistotie Ostra Allen

ULRIKASBORG

FABRIKSGATAN

Pietarinkatu

Puistokatu

KAIVOPUISTO BRUNNSPARKEN (Embassy Park)

TEHTAANKATU

Peramiehenk

Telakkatu

Armfeltint

Huvilakatu

Kapteeninkatu

MERIKATU

Ehrensvardintie

Docksg

HAVSGATAN

Eirastranden

Merisatamanranta

Hylkeenpyytajank

Laivak Skeppsg

Munkkisaari

Hernesaarenranta

Cruise Docks

HELSINKI

0 ——— 1/4

Miles

↑ **N**

City Attractions

The cruise ships' shuttle drops off passengers near the Swedish Theatre at the western end of the **Esplanade 1**, a broad boulevard that runs down to the harbour-front and serves as the social hub of Helsinki. Outdoor cafes and design shops line both sides, and running down the middle is a narrow park lined with linden trees where locals and tourists gather to watch the buskers or relax on park benches.

The **Havis Amanda Fountain**, located near the eastern end of the Esplanade, features a centrepiece bronze sculpture of a young woman symbolizing Helsinki's rebirth. Each spring on the eve of May Day she is washed by university students while thousands of onlookers gather to watch this fun-filled ritual.

Market Square 2 lies at the harbourfront end of the Esplanade and is where local artisans set up tables displaying their wares. Sightseeing boats and passenger ferries to **Suomenlinna Sea Fortress 3** (a 15-minute trip) depart from piers beside Market Square. Suomenlinna is a UNESCO World Heritage Site and is situated on six islands connected by bridges. Visitors can join guided tours or independently explore the 18th-century fortifications (including many tunnels). The historic maritime fortress also features numerous museums, shops and cafes.

City Hall 4, originally built as a hotel in 1833, overlooks Market Square (the mayor's office is located above the large balcony).

(Above) The Esplanade. (Below) Havis Amanda. (Bottom) City Hall.

Two blocks east is the **Presidential Palace** (entrance allowed only as part of a guided tour). Once used by the Russian czar, it is now a venue for presidential functions.

Sofiankatu leads north past the **City Museum** 6 to **Senate Square** 7 where Helsinki's landmark cathedral looms above the neoclassical buildings surrounding the monumental centre of Helsinki. The Prussian-born architect Carl Ludvig Engel, who had trained in Berlin before working abroad in various cities including St. Petersburg, was chosen by Czar Alexander I to design a civic square in keeping with Helsinki's new role as capital of the Grand Duchy of Finland. The **Palace of the Council of State** was completed on the eastern side of Senate Square in 1822 and the **main University building**, on the opposite side of the square, was completed 10 years later. Beside it is the **National Library**.

The **Church of St. Nicholas** (now **Helsinki Cathedral**) was modelled after Saint Issac's Cathedral in St. Petersburg's Senate Square and was com-

The main University building

pleted in 1852, twelve years after Engel's death. Standing at the top of a broad but very steep flight of steps, the neo-classical Cathedral was built in the Greek-cross plan with a central dome and four smaller domes. A statue of **Czar Alexander II** stands at the bottom of the steps, the figures at the base of the pedestal representing the law, culture and peasantry. Senate Square is used for various public events, including outdoor concerts and snowboard happenings. It has also posed as a Russian square in such movies as Warren Beatty's *Reds* (1981) and John Huston's *The Kremlin Letter* (1970).

Standing on a hilltop near the harbour is **Uspenski Orthodox Cathedral** 8, designed by a Russian architect in the 1860s in the Russian Byzantine revival style. It is the largest Eastern Orthodox church in Western Europe and symbolic of Finland's Russian connections with its golden cupolas and red-brick facade.

Helsinki is home to dozens of excellent museums, including the **Design Museum** 9 (in the heart of the city's Design District), the **Museum of Contemporary Art Kiasma** 10 (housed in a contemporary building designed by American architect Steven Holl) and the **Mannerheim Museum** 11, which was the home of the military hero Baron Carl Gustav Emil Mannerheim, who led Finnish forces to independence in 1918 and later served as president of Finland.

The **National Museum of Finland** 12, which opened in 1916, is housed in a building designed in the national romanticist style by Eliel Saarinen. Its entrance hall is adorned with frescoes depicting the *Kalevala* – an epic poem compiled from Finnish folklore by the 19th-century writer Elias Lounrot.

Eliel Saarinen also designed the **Helsinki Central Railway Station** **13**, which opened in 1919. It represents the country's architectural transition from National Romanticism to a Functionalist style. Its features include a clock tower, with much of the building clad in Finnish granite.

Parliament House 14 home to Finland's 200-seat parliament, is an example of Nordic Classicism. Designed by J.S. Siren and completed in 1931, the building's red granite facade features a row of Corinthian columns.

Finlandia Hall 15 overlooking Toolonlahti Bay, was designed by the legendary Finnish architect Alvar Aalto. Completed in 1975, this magnificent concert and meeting hall is an example of Modernism at its finest; 30-minute guided tours are available. Also standing on the shores of Toolonlahti Bay is the **Finnish National Opera 16**, its building completed in the 1990s.

The **Olympic Stadium 17** – built for the 1952 Olympic Games – is located near the north end of Toolonlahti Bay. The stadium's Functionalist design includes a tower that is 72 metres high and provides spectacular views over the city. Nearby is the flower-filled Winter Garden.

The **Sibelius Monument 18** is situated in Sibelius Park,

which was named in 1945 to honour the 80th birthday of the composer Jean Sibelius. The monument itself, made of stainless steel tubes, is the work of Eila Hiltunen and was unveiled in 1967.

One of Helsinki's most unusual attractions is **Temppeliaukio 'Rock' Church 19**, quarried out of the natural bedrock. Designed by Timo and Tuomo Suomalainen and constructed in 1969, the Rock Church is used both for religious services and as a venue for concerts with its excellent acoustics.

Uspenski Orthodox Cathedral

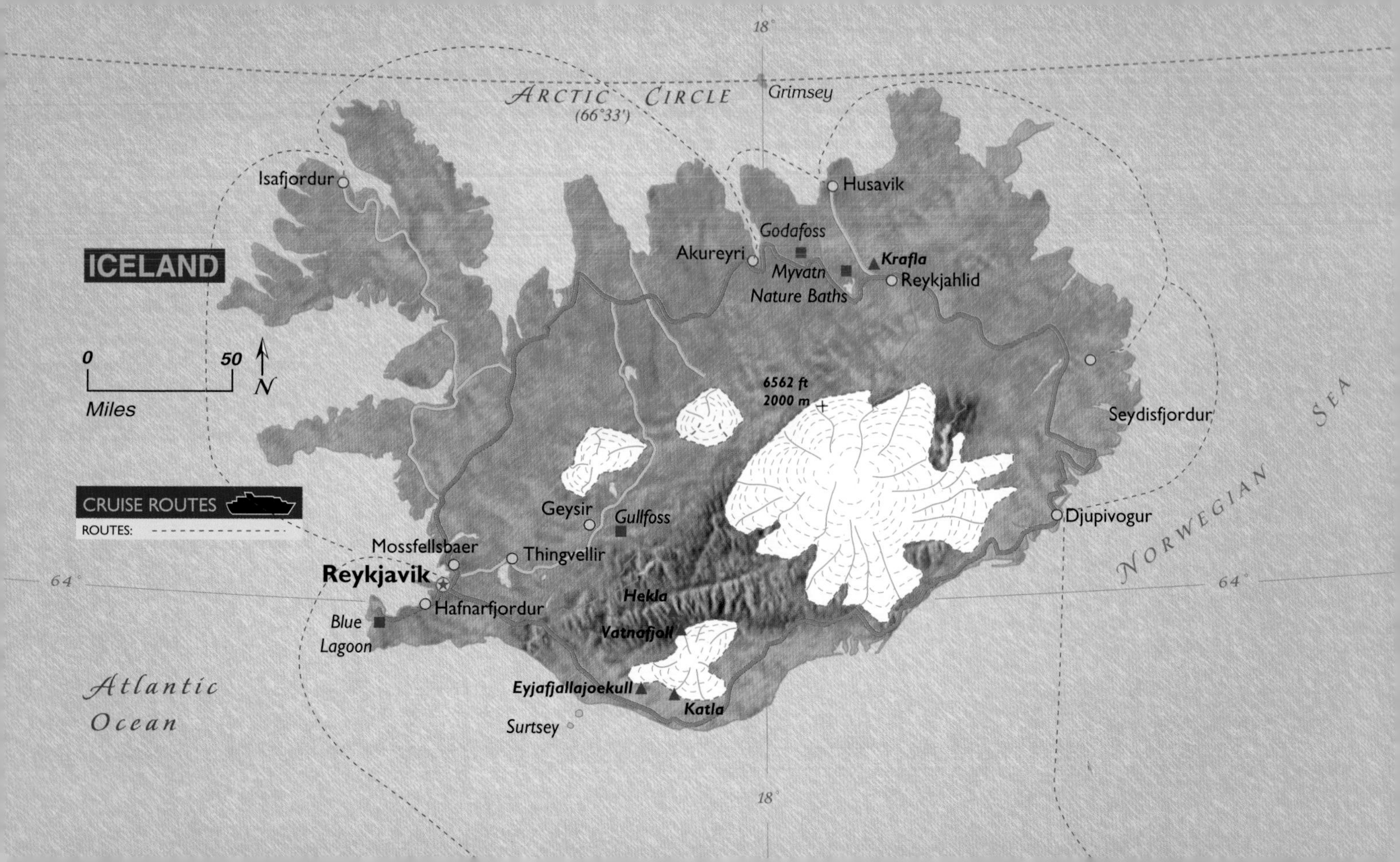

ICELAND

NORWEGIAN SEA

ARCTIC CIRCLE
(66°33')

Grimsey

Isafjordur

Husavik

Krafla ▲
Reykjahlid

Godafoss ■
Myvatn ■
Nature Baths

Akureyri

Seydisfjordur

Djupivogur

6562 ft
2000 m +

Gullfoss ■
Geysir
Thingvellir

Hekla ▲
Vatnafjol
Eyjafjallajoekull ▲
Katla ▲

Surtsey

Mossfellsbaer
Reykjavik ☆
Hafnarfjordur

Blue
Lagoon ■

N

0   50
Miles

CRUISE ROUTES
ROUTES: -----

Atlantic
Ocean

18°

18°

64°

64°

ICELAND

The island nation of Iceland is an isolated place of stark beauty. Deep fjords indent its rugged coastline, volcanic peaks rise above silent expanses of ice and snow, and glacial meltwater feeds thundering waterfalls which spill into river gorges. The opening scenes of Ridley Scott's *Prometheus* were filmed in Iceland and featured Dettifoss – the most powerful waterfall in Europe. Iceland also contains vast fields of lava rock and rolling plains of soft, dusty sand which served as a lunar-like landscape for NASA astronauts training for their first moon landing.

Lying in the mid-Atlantic just south of the Arctic Circle, Iceland is geographically a young basalt plateau (a raised part of the Earth's crust), which straddles

Gullfoss is one of many spectacular waterfalls in Iceland.

the Mid-Atlantic Ridge (a volcanic submarine mountain range). Because Iceland sits atop a mantle plume (hot spot), the country has about 200 volcanoes, many of which are active, and an abundance of hotsprings, which provide a cheap and non-polluting source of heating for homes and outdoor swimming pools.

Iceland is Europe's second largest island (after Great Britain) and over half of the country's total population of 300,000 live in the capital of Reykjavik, which is an Old Norse name meaning Smoky Bay, so named for the misty geothermal steam rising from the water.

Iceland's History

First visited by Irish monks, Iceland was settled by Vikings in the mid-9th century. The Norse chieftain Eric the Red arrived a century later, having left Norway

with his exiled father. They sailed to Iceland, where his son Leif Ericsson was born. Others seeking sanctuary in Iceland have included the American chess champion Bobby Fischer, who defeated the Soviet Union's Boris Spassky in a celebrated chess match held in Reykjavik in 1972. Icelanders, who are passionate about chess, returned the favour in 2005 by granting citizenship to their adopted national hero.

Fischer died in Reykjavik in 2008, the same year Iceland's rapidly expanding economy nearly collapsed amid the global financial crisis. The country's currency went into a freefall and the Icelandic government, facing

The Leif Ericsson statue in front of Hallgrimskirkja in Reykjavik.

national bankruptcy, turned to oil-rich Russia for an emergency loan. This is not the first time Iceland has faced looming disaster. In the 17th and 18th centuries, Danish trade monopolies and repeated pirate raids ruined the country's economy, while epidemics and volcanic eruptions killed many.

After centuries of poverty and hardship, the 19th century brought a rebirth of national culture and a longing for independence. Icelandic literature flourished just as Old Norse literature had until the 13th century, when Iceland came under Norwegian, then Danish, rule. In 1918 Iceland became a sovereign state in union with Denmark, but this agreement was peacefully terminated in 1944 when Icelanders voted to become an independent republic.

Iceland's parliament had first convened at Thingvellir in the year 930, making it the world's oldest. The country's language is so well preserved that modern Icelandic is virtually the same as Old Norse, which is why Icelandic schoolchildren can read sagas written in medieval times.

Iceland's isolated location has also resulted in animal breeds unique to these shores. Icelandic sheep, brought by Vikings, grow fleece in two layers – a long, outer layer (tog) and a short, fine underhair (pel). The early Icelanders spun the tog into strong cord for weaving, while the finest wool (similar to mohair) was used for lacy shawls and embroidery. The Icelandic horse, also brought by the Vikings, is a small, hardy animal with a heavy winter coat and was bred for farm work in harsh conditions. A friendly, easy-to-handle breed with no diseases, the Icelandic horse is protected by a law that prohibits the importing of horses into Iceland.

With limited agricultural land, Iceland's major industry has always been fishing. The abundance of fish also attracts whales, which feed in local waters from May through September. Seabirds such as puffins and kittiwakes nest in sea cliffs, their rocky ramparts washed by waves that have eroded nearby sea stacks into shapes with names such as The Giant and The Hag – inspired by Old Norse legends.

Modern artists include the avante-garde singer-songwriter Bjork, and the post-rock band Sigur Ros, who have performed on the television show *Game of Thrones*, scenes from which were shot in Iceland near Lake Myvatn. The band's recording studio is located in the coastal town of Mosfellsbaer, about ten miles north of Reykjavik, where they converted a drained, abandoned swimming pool (*sundlaug* in Icelandic) into a studio. The textile company Alafoss was founded here in 1896, taking its name from the local waterfall which provided energy for spinning wool.

Iceland at a Glance

Iceland's climate is similar to the Alaska Peninsula. Summers are warm and the sun barely sets in June and July. English is the second language and spoken by nearly all Icelanders. Iceland's **currency** is the krona. Approximate exchange: $1US = 130 ISK; £1GBP = 200 ISK.

Renting a car is one way to see the attractions near Reykavik. Traffic jams are rare and the roads are well maintained. Speeds are posted in kilometres and driving is on the right. Rentals start at about $85 a day and the best rates are obtained by booking online.

The fishing port of Husavik is also a whalewatching base.

Shore Excursions

ICELAND

Shore excursions in Iceland focus on the country's unique natural attractions, with driving tours to hotsprings, geysers, waterfalls and glaciers. On-the-water excursions include whalewatching, kayaking and river rafting. Land-based activities feature golf, horseback riding and 4X4 safaris. A popular tour from Reykavik is the eight-hour tour of the Golden Circle which takes in spectacular Gullfoss (Gold Falls), Kerio volcanic crater, Thingvellir National Park (a UNESCO World Heritage Site that encompasses the first Viking settlement in Iceland and the original site of the country's parliament) and Geysir (a geothermal area from which the English word 'geyser' is derived).

Shopping items to look for include woven and knitted textiles. Iceland is famous for its Lopi wool cardigan – made with a bulky weight yarn and featuring a distinctive circular yoke and patterned borders. The Alafoss factory outlet in Mosfellsbaer carries beautiful Lopi sweaters in a range of colours and patterns, as well as sheepskin hats, gloves and other items.

Ports of Call

Reykjavik is Iceland's capital, industrial hub and largest port. The city centre is compact and home to the nation's parliament (Althing), university, national theatre and national museum. A new concert hall and conference centre stand along the harbourfront. Notable monuments include a statue of Leif Ericsson given by the US Congress to the people of Iceland in 1930 to commemorate the 1,000th anniversary of the founding of the Althing. This statue stands in front of Hallgrimskirkja church, which rises above the Reykjavik skyline like a pinnacle of ice.

The dramatic countryside surrounding Reykjavik is a short drive away. Area attractions include the famous **Blue Lagoon** geothermal spa, situated in a field of lava rock on Reykjanes, which is a peninsula with active volcanism beneath its surface. A large, shallow swimming pool was built beside a geothermal power station to tap into its hot and mineralized water – a mixture of silky white silica mud and blue-green algae.

The pool's steaming hot, sulphuric water is not only relaxing and invigorating, its therapeutic qualities are recognized by Iceland's ministry of health in the treatment of various skin conditions, such as psoriasis, eczema and acne. Facilities at the spa include bathing suit rental, dressing rooms, showers, a cafe and gift shop.

Akureyri (pop. 16,000) is the main town of northern Iceland and lies at the head of Eyjafjord, the longest fjord in Iceland. The cruise dock is within walking distance of town, which is known for its Botanical Gardens, galleries and souvenir shops. Excursions at Akureyri include a visit to spectacular Godafoss Waterfall, the nature baths at Lake Myvatn (known for its abundance of bird life) or a flight to Grimsey Island (pop. 100), which lies on the Arctic Circle and is edged with sea cliffs. Whalewatching excursions originate in the nearby fishing port of **Husavik** in Skjalfandi Bay.

The small port of **Isafjordur** (pop. 3,000) occupies a spit of land in Skutulsfjordur, one of several fjords found in mountain-ringed Isafjordur. Home to historic merchant houses and fishermen huts, the town is a 30-minute boat ride to the seabird colonies of Vigur Island.

Seydisfjordur (pop. 750) lies nestled at the base of two mountains below a valley carved by a river that cascades over 25 waterfalls into a lagoon at the head of the fjord. The cruise dock is in the centre of town and features traditional wooden buildings. Ferries connect this eastern Iceland port with continental Europe.

The coastal village of **Djupivogur**, set amid scenic mountains and fjords, offers shore excursions to Glacier Lagoon. Formed by the retreating Jokulsarlon Glacier, this famous lagoon began forming in the 1930s. As the glacier tongue retreats, it calves ice into the lagoon, and these floating ice sculptures can be viewed on 40-minute boat tours. The lagoon was featured in the James Bond movie *Die Another Day*.

(Opposite) The geothermal waters of Blue Lagoon near Reykjavik. (Right) Djupivogur provides access to Jokulsarlon Glacier Lagoon.

Eastern and Central Europe

The collapse of the Soviet Union changed the political map of Europe. East Germany, Poland and the Baltic states of Lithuania, Latvia and Estonia all broke away from the Eastern Bloc, and Russia itself began opening up to the West. St. Petersburg is now the premier port of a Baltic cruise, with ships docking here overnight to allow passengers ample time to explore this magnificent city. Tallinn (Estonia) and Warnemünde/Rostock (for Berlin) are popular ports of call on a Baltic cruise, with Riga (Latvia), Klaipeda (Lithuania) and Gdansk (Poland) also receiving ships, though in fewer numbers. The German ports of Kiel and Hamburg (on the North Sea) also receive cruise ships.

CRUISE ROUTES
ROUTES:
RUSSIA
0
30
Miles
N
Russia
Lake
Ladoga
Finland
E18
E18
Helsinki
Ushkovo
Sestroretsk
Sertolovo
KAD
St. Petersburg
M-16
M-18
Lomonosov
Petrodvorets
(Peterhof)
Kolpino
Kirovsk
Pushkin
Pavlovsk
M-11
M-10
Gatchina
Gulf of Finland
Tallin
E20
Estonia
Narva
Kingisepp
Russia

RUSSIA

Russia is a nation forged by conquest but haunted by the fear of collapse. So massive in size it spans 11 time zones and borders 14 other countries, Russia has spent much of its turbulent history defending its frontiers from invasion. The country's western provinces lie in Europe but its vast eastern hinterland stretches across northern Asia to the Bering Sea where the winters – long, dark and bitterly cold – seem to symbolize the suffering the Russian people have endured over the centuries. None have escaped the despair brought by sieges and starvation, purges and poverty. Even the czars lived in fear, their enemies lurking in palace corridors or on the streets of St. Petersburg where worker unrest was brutally put down.

Today St. Petersburg is the premier port on a Baltic cruise. Most ships dock here overnight so their passengers can see as much as possible of this canal-woven city filled with palaces and churches built when St. Petersburg was the czarist capital of Imperial Russia.

Russia at a Glance

Russia is the largest country in the world in terms of land area, covering 6.6 million square miles (17 million sq km), but large tracts in the north and east, where the climate is harsh, are sparsely populated. Although Russia enjoys astounding natural wealth, with

A royal garden at Peterhof.

massive reserves of mineral and energy resources as well as the world's largest forest reserve, the standard of living of the average Russian remains low due to corruption and the economy's reliance on raw exports because of its lack of modernization.

Russia's population is 142 million, with about 12 million living in Moscow, the capital. St. Petersburg's population is close to 5 million. The average life expectancy for men is 64 years and for women it is 76 years. The major language is Russian and the major religion is Orthodox Christianity although relatively few Russians actively worship – a legacy of seven decades of Soviet rule.

(Above) 'Peter the Great' greets tourists in St. Petersburg.
(Below) A wedding party poses in front of the Winter Palace.

The Russian Federation is a semi-presidential republic governed by a president and prime minister. Because the president is allowed to serve only two consecutive terms under the Russian constitution, Vladimir Putin stepped aside as president in May 2008 and returned to his former office of prime minister while his hand-picked successor, Dmitry Medvedev, was sworn in as president. Managed elections returned Putin to the presidency in 2012.

Russia remains steeped in superstition, with many believing that the birthmark on Mikhail Gorbachev's forehead was a sign that he was destined to be a leader of Russia. Russian customs include winter bathing in a steaming hot *banya* (sauna) followed by a plunge into icy cold water; the temperature contrast is believed to make the body stronger.

Many Russians also believe that the rural way of life reflects the true Russian soul, which is why the tradition of owning a *dacha* – a rustic retreat in the country – remains the dream of most city dwellers. The building of *dachas* began in the 18th century when the privileged classes were rewarded with land for their loyalty and service to the czar. During the Soviet era millions of ordinary Russians were granted small plots of rural land where they could build a modest structure and grow vegetables. Today's *dachas* feature suburban-style houses and landscaped gardens which appeal to professionals seeking a weekend escape from the city.

Chess is a popular pastime in Russia, played year-round in city parks. Russian grand masters include Anatoly Karpov and Garry Kasparov, the latter becoming the world's youngest chess champion when he defeated Karpov in 1985, a title he held for two decades before retiring in 2005 to concentrate on Russian politics. Kasparov was jailed for five days in November 2007 for leading an anti-Putin demonstration in Moscow.

Russian holidays are determined by the Orthodox calendar. Christmas, which was officially forbidden during the Soviet era, is celebrated on January 7, with Christmas mass held on the eve of January 6. New Year's Eve is the biggest holiday in Russia, celebrated with feasting and other festivities to ensure a prosperous year ahead. Duck or goose, stuffed carp and jellied meats are often served, along with small pies or pastries (*pelmeni*) filled with cabbage, apple or meat.

For more history of Russia, turn to the History section in Part I.

Shopping

The country's monetary unit is the rouble (1 rouble = 100 kopecks). Shops and restaurants are not allowed to accept foreign currency but US dollars are widely accepted by street vendors (bring bills of various denominations and don't expect change). Outdoor souvenir markets are located beside the Church on Spilled Blood and in St. Isaac's Square. Shops are located at the Hermitage, offering high-quality souvenirs and artwork, where payment can be made in roubles or by credit card. Items to look for in St. Petersburg include lacquer boxes, porcelain tableware, hand-painted bowls, matryoshka nesting dolls and Fabergé fine jewellery.

Finely crafted Russian souvenirs.

St. Petersburg

At its height as the capital of czarist Russia, the city of St. Petersburg glittered with imperial splendour. Lavish dinner parties and opulent balls were hosted by the Russian nobility, their horse-drawn carriages whisking counts and countesses along the canal-lined city streets to call at the private palaces of aristocratic friends or to attend a performance of opera or ballet at the Mariinsky Theatre.

Immortalized in the novels of Tolstoy and Dostoyevsky, St. Petersburg was all that Peter the Great had envisaged in 1703 when he chose the city's building site at the mouth of the Neva River on land conquered from Sweden. Seeking a Baltic seaport, Peter spared no expense – both in money and human lives – constructing his new capital that would be a 'window looking on Europe.' The river delta's flood-prone marshes made construction difficult, but canals were dug,

bridges were built and noble families, under order of the czar, commissioned private palaces along the city's waterways. Thousands of workers and craftsmen were brought to St. Petersburg to work on Peter's grand project, and thousands of them died.

Peter, who had travelled throughout Europe, was an admirer of western culture and had hired Italian and French architects to design a city of spacious, classical beauty. He also built the fortress of Peter and Paul on one of the river delta's many islands to protect St. Petersburg from Swedish naval attacks. In 1712, Peter moved the Russian capital from Moscow to St. Petersburg, which reached its height as an international centre of literature, music, theatre and ballet in the late 19th century. The rich and reckless lifestyles of the Russian nobility, so masterfully described in the novels of Count Leo Tolstoy, were in stark contrast to the fate of the vast underclass of workers who toiled in the city's factories.

In 1914, when war broke out with Germany, the city was renamed Petrograd (the Slavic version of St. Petersburg), but the name change could not mask the simmering discontent of the city's soldiers, sailors and factory workers who spearheaded the Russian Revolution of 1917 that toppled Czar Nicholas and his German-born czarina. Replaced the next year by Moscow as the Russian capital, Petrograd was renamed

A St. Petersburg canal.

(Above) Sightseeing boats pro-
vide tours of the city's canals.
(Right) Constantine Palace.

Leningrad in 1924. The city came under terrible siege by German armies during World War II and hundreds of thousands died from famine and disease. A 1991 referendum restored the city's name to St. Petersburg, a choice favoured by younger Russians.

Vladimir Putin grew up in St. Petersburg where he lived in a two-room unit of a communal apartment block with his mother (a factory worker) and father (a conscript in the Soviet Navy). As President of Russia, Putin hosted his country's first Group of Eight summit at the opulent Constantine Palace overlooking the Gulf of Finland on the outskirts of St. Petersburg. Begun by Peter the Great, it had been long abandoned when Putin decided to reconstruct the crumbling palace to commemorate St. Petersburg's 300th anniversary in 2003. The city founded by Peter the Great is reclaiming its past glory and is once again a window to the West.

Getting Around

If you are visiting St. Petersburg for the first time, you're well advised to book shore tours. It is possible to explore St. Petersburg independently, but you must obtain a visa before leaving home and most taxi drivers don't speak English. You will make better use of your time if you take escorted tours ashore, either through the cruise line or directly with a local operator. **No visa is required for cruise passengers participating in tours organized by the cruise lines or by government-licenced operators (see Shore Excursions on next page.)**

Cruise ships visiting St. Petersburg no longer dock at the cargo quays but at one of two new

(Top) St. Petersburg's industrial port area. (Above) A tour guide in St. Petersburg. (Below) St. Basil's Cathedral in Moscow.

Shore Excursions

St. Petersburg

The extensive selection of shore excursions offered by the cruise lines consists of half-day, full-day and evening excursions. With advance planning, you can coordinate several excursions to take full advantage of your two days in port. Visit your cruise line's website to research and book your shore excursions online. Most tours are a combination of driving and walking. Boat rides on the city's palace-lined waterways are also offered, as is a ride on the city's subway system (the metro) which is tunneled deep under the city's waterways, its stations beautifully decorated with chandeliers, paintings, mosaics and statues. You can visit Moscow on a full-day trip that involves a one-hour flight each way. Your Moscow guide will take you to Red Square, St. Basil's Cathedral and the Kremlin.

The alternative to booking shore excursions with the cruise line is to book in advance an extensive one- or two-day tour with a local operator, such as **Denrus** (denrus. re/), **Red October** (redoctober.us/) or **SPB Tours** (spb-tours.com/). These government-approved operators are licensed to provide tours to cruise passengers. Once you have made a booking, they will send you an electronic tour ticket. Be sure to make a printed copy of your booking confirmation, which you must take with you when you go ashore to meet your tour group. Highly recommended is the two-day group tour with Denrus, which covers all of St. Petersburg's major attractions as well as some less-visited sites and includes lunch, rest stops and shopping opportunities, all overseen by a well-educated guide who explains the history and local customs.

ports dedicated to cruise ships. The main port is located on the west side of Vasilyevskiy Island, about 10 miles (6 km) from the city centre. A smaller port is located at the English Embankment, about half a mile from the city's central squares.

When heading ashore, be aware of pickpockets in crowded areas, such as outdoor souvenir markets or the entrances to metro stations. Take small US bills for tipping and using bathrooms.

Must See

Most of St. Petersburg's famous attractions are clustered in the city centre. Places you won't want to miss are Winter Palace/ Hermitage Museum in Palace Square, the Bronze Horseman monument in Senate Square, St. Isaac's Cathedral, Square of Arts (locale of the State Russian Museum) and Church of the Saviour on Spilled Blood. Be sure to visit at least one of the royal estates located outside St. Petersburg, especially Peterhof, which is famous for its fountains, gardens and ornate palaces.

St. Petersburg's Winter Palace

Local Attractions

St. Petersburg's premier attraction is the magnificent **Winter Palace** **1** , which is the main building of an architectural ensemble that houses the world-renowned State Hermitage Museum. When the Italian architect Rastrelli designed the Winter Palace for Empress Elizabeth in the mid-18th century, he created a long, three-storey rectangular building with a central courtyard accessed from Palace Square. The majestic grandeur of this Russian baroque palace derives from its four facades, each slightly different but all embellished by a two-tier colonnade and an abundance of moulded decoration. During the reign of Catherine the Great, the palace complex was expanded to house her growing collection of Western art. She oversaw construction of the Small Hermitage, the Great Hermitage and the Hermitage Theatre. These buildings were interconnected by passageways with the Winter Palace.

The palace's interior, which contains over a thousand rooms, was reconstructed in the neoclassical style following a fire in 1837.

Interior views of the Hermitage.

The Imperial Museum of the New Hermitage opened to the public in 1852. Since then, the museum's original collection has expanded to include more than three million works of art and artifacts, including sculptures, drawings and more than 8,000 paintings of the Flemish, French, Dutch, Spanish and Italian schools, with works by Rembrandt, Rubens, Picasso and Matisse. The massive museum is divided into sections, including one featuring a tribute to Peter the Great, and another devoted to the life and literary works of Pushkin. The palace itself is a work of art, built on a monumental scale to symbolize the wealth and power of imperial Russia with its vaulted ceilings, grand staircases, granite columns and rooms richly adorned with gilt and marble. (Visit hermitage-museum.org for a virtual tour of the palace and exhibit rooms.)

The Winter Palace overlooks **Palace Square 2** where the General Staff Building curves along the length of its southern boundary, creating an expansive public square. Constructed in the 1820s, this building is an excellent example of Russian Classicism, its two semi-circular wings connected by a triumphal arch crowned with a sculpture called Chariot of Glory. Originally housing government offices, gala rooms and the private apartments of the Russian chancellor, the building's east wing became part of the Hermitage in 1993 to house new exhibitions of the museum.

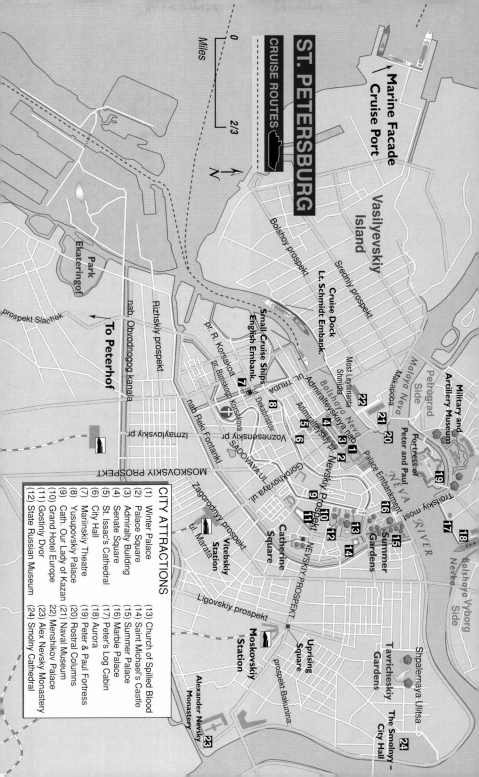

ST. PETERSBURG

CRUISE ROUTES

Marine Facade
Cruise Port

Vasilyevskiy Island

Cruise Dock
Lt. Schmidt Embank.

Small Cruise Ships
English Embank.

To Peterhof

Park
Ekateringof

prospekt Stachek

Riznskiy prospekt

nab. Obvodnogog kanala

Izmaylovskiy pr.

MOSKOVSKIY PROSPEKT

SADOVAYA UL.

Gorohovaya ul.

Voznesenskiy pr.

nab. Reki Fontanki

pl. Baispsoog Korsakova

pr. R. Korsakoa

ul. Dekabristov

ul. TRUDA

Admiralteyskaya nab.

Bolshaya Neva

Most Leytenanta Shmidta

Sredniy prospekt

Bolshoy prospekt

Malaya Neva

Makаroba

Petrograd Side

Military and Artillery Museum

Fortress of Peter and Paul

NEVA RIVER

Palace Embankment

Troitskiy most

Bolshaya Nevka

Bolshaya Vyborg Side

Summer Gardens

Catherine Square

Vitebskiy Station

Zagorodnyy prospekt

ul. Marata

Ligovskiy prospekt

Uprising Square

prospekt Bakunina

NEVSKIY PROSPEKT

Moskovskiy Station

Alexander Nevskiy Monastery

Tavricheskiy Gardens

The Smolny - City Hall

Shpalernaya Ulitsa

Miles

0   2/3

N

CITY ATTRACTIONS

(1) Winter Palace
(2) Palace Square
(3) Admiralty Building
(4) Senate Square
(5) St. Isaac's Cathedral
(6) City Hall
(7) Marrinskiy Theatre
(8) Yusupovskiy Palace
(9) Cath. Our Lady of Kazan
(10) Grand Hotel Europe
(11) Gostiniy Dvor
(12) State Russian Museum

(13) Church of Spilled Blood
(14) Saint Michael's Castle
(15) Summer Palace
(16) Marble Palace
(17) Peter's Log Cabin
(18) Aurora
(19) Peter & Paul Fortress
(20) Rostral Columns
(21) Naval Museum
(22) Summer Palace
(23) Alex Nevsky Monastery
(24) Smolny Cathedral

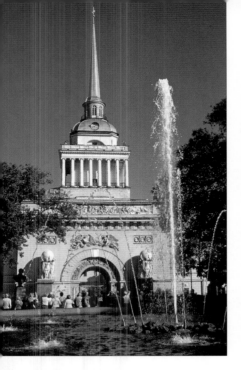

(Above) Admiralty Building.
(Below) The Bronze Horseman.

Standing in the middle of Palace Square is the Alexander Column, raised by Nicholas I to commemorate his brother Alexander I as victor over Napoleon in the Patriotic War of 1812. It took five years to raise this column, which rises 157 feet, making it the highest triumphal column in the world.

Next door to the Hermitage is the golden-spired **Admiralty Building** 3 , which originally housed the Admiralty Board and is now a naval college. Designed in the Empire style, it was built between 1806 and 1823. The writer Vladimir Nabokov, born in St. Petersburg in 1899, wrote a short story about this magnificent building entitled 'The Admiralty Spire.'

Beside the Admiralty Building is **Senate Square** 4 (originally called Peter's Square) and this is the site of an iconic equestrian statue of Peter the Great called The Bronze Horseman, the name given it in a famous poem by Pushkin. This statue, which has become a symbol of St. Petersburg (much like the Statue of Liberty is symbolic of New York City), was commissioned by German-born Catherine the Great to gain legitimacy in the eyes of the Russian people after seizing the throne in a palace coup. She chose a French sculptor named Falconet who shows the heroic figure of Peter mounted on his horse, which is rearing at the edge of a cliff while trampling a serpent beneath its hind hooves. The 20-foot-tall statue is mounted on an even higher pedestal of granite shaped from a massive stone slab that was found embedded in a marsh outside St. Petersburg. It took 400 men nine months to drag this massive slab of stone across four miles of countryside to the water's edge where a specially constructed barge was used to transport it to Peter's Square. During the siege of Leningrad (1941-44), the statue was protected from bombing and artillery fire with sandbags and a wooden shelter.

Peter's Square was renamed Decembrists Square in 1925 to commemorate the Decembrist Revolt that took place here 100 years earlier. In 2008 its name was changed to Senate Square, in keeping with the neoclassical Senate and Synod buildings, designed by Carlo Rossi and now housing the Constitutional Court of Russia, which occupy the west side of the square. The Admiralty Embankment runs along the waterfront side of the square, affording wonderful views of the Neva and palaces across the river.

Next to Senate Square is the golden-domed **St. Isaac's Cathedral 5**, an imposing structure of granite and marble designed in the Classical style by a young French architect named Ricard de Montferrand. It became his life's work, with construction begun in 1817 and the great gilded dome completed in 1842. Some 562 stairs lead up to the lantern atop this dome. The cathedral follows the Greek cross plan, its four

The exterior and interior of St. Isaac's Cathedral.

Peter the Great

Peter I was a large, powerful man of restless energy, keen intellect and a passion for the sea, acquainting himself firsthand with everything nautical – from ship building to navigation. The youngest child of Czar Alexis by his second wife, Peter was four when his father died in 1676 and he spent much of his youth exiled from the royal court in Moscow due to a struggle for succession between rival family factions. While growing up on the outskirts of Moscow, the future czar demonstrated his budding military prowess in war games with children of nobility and those who came from the roughest social background. He also befriended foreign officers serving in the Russian army and they introduced the young prince to the rudiments of warfare.

As czar, Peter travelled incognito throughout Europe where he learned about western industrial techniques, working for a time as a ship's carpenter in Holland. Upon his return to Russia to put down a rebellion led by his half-sister, Peter set about overcoming Russia's backwardness with wide-ranging reforms. One of his first acts was to personally cut off the long beards of his nobles and order them to replace their Muscovite attire, including their conical hats, with western-style clothing. He modernized the army, founded the navy and established technical schools. His decision to move the Russian capital from Moscow to the new city of St. Petersburg was symbolic of his dramatic reforms, which were met with widespread resistance. But Peter was a ruthless and determined leader whose disregard for human life extended to his oldest son Alexis – an outspoken critic of his father's reforms who paid with his life when arrested for treason and tortured to death. Peter the Great died in 1725.

façades graced with red granite columns standing 50 feet (16 m) tall. The light-filled interior is richly adorned with mosaics, paintings and gold-clad sculptures.

On the south side of St. Isaac's Square, facing the cathedral, is **St. Petersburg's City Hall** ▦ . It occupies a neoclassical imperial palace (Mariinsky Palace) which was built from 1839 to 1844 for the daughter of Emperor Nicholas, Grand Duchess Maria Nikolayevna. An equestrian statue of Nicholas I stands in the centre of the square, and the luxury Hotel Astoria (which opened in 1912) is on the square's east side, adjacent to the new Hotel Angleterre, built in the 1990s to replace the original (the Russian poet Sergei Yesenin hung himself in one of its rooms in 1925). Part of the square is actually an extremely wide bridge (the Blue Bridge) spanning a canal.

A few blocks west of city hall is the **Mariinskiy Theatre** ▦ , famous as the home of the Kirov

St. Petersburg's City Hall

Ballet. The modern Mariinsky II theatre opened next door to the original Mariinsky in 2013. Also in the vicinity is **Yusupovskiy Palace** 8 , where the infamous Rasputin was murdered by a group of right-wing patriots, including a cousin of the czar, in December 1916. Rasputin's scandalous hold over Empress Alexandra (who believed he possessed supernatural powers with which he kept healing her hemophiliac son) had undermined Emperor Nicholas II's increasingly tenuous hold on power when Prince Yusopov invited the much-resented "healer" to his palace. Rasputin was served poisoned cakes and wine, but when he showed no ill effects, his panicked assassins shot him repeatedly and threw his body into the Neva River.

(Above) Wax mannequins portray Rasputin's murder inside Yusupovskiy Palace. (Below) Kazan Cathedral. (Bottom) The monument to Pushkin outside the State Russian Museum.

Nevsky Prospekt, named after St. Petersburg's patron saint Alexander Nevsky, is the city's main avenue, which runs from the Admiralty through the central shopping and entertainment districts. Numerous churches also line this busy street, including the Empire-style **Cathedral of Our Lady of Kazan** 9 , built in 1811. Field Marshal Kutuzov, a national hero who led the Russian army to victory over Napoleon in 1812, is interred here. Across the street at the corner of Nevsky Prospekt and Mikhailovskaja Street stands the five-star **Grand Hotel Europe** 10, whose guests have included Tchaikovsky and Elton John.

A wide selection of stores is found on Nevsky Prospekt, most notably the elegant arcades of **Gostiniy Dvor** 11, the city's largest department store. Across the

street lies the Passage – a shopping gallery covered with an arched glass-and-steel roof – which leads off Nevsky Prospekt toward Square of Arts and the **State Russian Museum** 🔢. Home to the world's largest collection of Russian fine art, the museum is housed in Mikhailovsky Palace. Designed by Carlo Rossi and constructed between 1819 and 1825 for a son of Emperor Paul I, the palace is a masterpiece of Russian neoclassical architecture. Nicholas II acquired the palace for the state and transformed it into a museum, which opened to the public in March 1898. A monument to Pushkin, Russia's national poet, stands in the middle of square, which is also the locale of the Stray Dog Cafe – an early 20th-century gathering place for writers and poets (including Boris Pasternak) who met here in the cellar of the Dashkov mansion.

Standing alongside the Griboedov Canal behind the Russian Museum is the much-photographed **Church of the Savior on Spilled Blood** 🔢. Officially called the Cathedral of the Resurrection of Christ, its 19th-century design is a revival of Russian medieval architecture. Richly ornamented and featuring an array of colourful onion domes that rival those of celebrated St. Basil's Cathedral in Moscow, the church has an equally impressive interior of detailed mosaics covering all of the walls and ceilings. This spectacular church was dedicated solely to the memory of Czar Alexander II, who was assassinated at this site on March 13, 1881. He was riding in his carriage along the canal embankment when an anarchist threw a grenade which exploded and prompted the czar, who was shaken but unhurt, to get out of his carriage and remonstrate with his presumed attacker. This is when another conspirator exploded a second hand bomb and mortally wounded the czar. Bleeding heavily, he was taken to the Winter Palace where he died a few hours later. A shrine was erected on the exact spot of the attack, which was later enclosed within the walls of the church built by Alexander III as a memorial to his father. Work began in 1883 but was not completed until 1907, during the reign of Russia's last czar, Nicholas II. Ransacked and looted follow-

The Church on Spilled Blood

ing the Russian Revolution, the church became a temporary morgue during the Siege of Leningrad, then a warehouse for vegetables after the Second World War. Never a public place of worship, the restored church reopened as a museum in 1997 and is now one of St. Petersburg's major tourist attractions.

Another royal assassination took place in **Saint Michael's Castle**  (also called Mikhailovsky Castle or Engineers Castle) which is today a branch of the State Russian Museum, housing official portraits of Russian emperors and empresses. Completed in 1801 as a royal residence for Paul I, who feared an assassination plot, the castle was surrounded on all sides by canals and moats, its bridges guarded by sentries. Within weeks of moving into his new home, however, the unpopular czar was murdered in his bedroom by some noblemen who resented his autocratic policies. The palace subsequently became an engineering college attended by such illustrious Russians as Dostoyevsky.

The Summer Garden is part of the State Russian Museum and contains the **Summer Palace of Peter the Great** – a modest stone structure he had built in 1710 in which to spend his summers. Situated on a point of land where the Fontanka flows into the Neva, water would wash against the sides of the house and arriving boats would tie up alongside to mooring rings mounted on the facade. The palace's wooden floor beams were reminiscent of ship construction, and oak – a wood traditionally reserved for Russian shipbuilding

Peter the Great's Summer Palace

– was used for the palace doors, stairs and wall panels.

Lying to the west of the Summer Garden is the Field of Mars (a military parade ground) and the adjacent **Marble Palace**. Built in the late 1700s for Count Grigory Orlov (a favourite of Catherine the Great), the Marble Palace is an outstanding example of early neoclassicism in Russia, its facades and interior decorated with marble of various colours. The palace housed the Lenin Museum from 1937 to 1991, at which time it became a branch of the State Russian Museum housing permanent art collections.

Peter the Great's original residence – a **log cabin** – is situated directly across the Neva from the Summer Gardens. Built in three days by Swedish carpenters, this pine log cabin is where Peter first lived while planning his new city. The cabin's interior doors came from captured Swedish ships and the walls were covered with sailcloth. Peter would cross the Neva

in a light boat he built himself. The cabin is now a museum, perfectly preserved and protected from the elements by a red-brick pavilion.

The historic battleship *Aurora* **18** is docked a few hundred yards upstream from the Peter the Great's cabin and has been turned into a museum. At 2:00 a.m. on October 25, 1917, this ship gave the signal (by firing a blank shot) to storm the Winter Palace and seize power from the provisional government.

On Zayachy Island, a short distance downstream from Peter the Great's log cabin, is the **Peter and Paul Fortress** **19**. Built to defend St. Petersburg from Swedish attacks, it is the city's oldest structure and within its walls is the city's first stone church – the **Cathedral of St. Peter and St. Paul**. Designed by Trezzini in the early baroque style, the church's gilded spire is 404 feet high and crowned with a golden angel holding a cross. The cathedral's royal crypt contains the tombs of Peter the Great and most of his successors, including Nicholas II, who was reinterred here in 1998. The remains of this last czar, his wife and three daughters were found buried in a forest near Yekaterinburg in 1991, and the remains of his son and other daughter were found nearby in 2007. (Nicholas and his family

(Top to bottom) The battleship Aurora; Peter and Paul Fortress; interior of Cathedral of St. Peter and St. Paul. (Opposite page, top) Remains of Russia's last czar and his family.

were canonized by the Russian Orthodox Church in 2000, and formally rehabilitated by Russia's Supreme Court in 2008 with a ruling that their killings were pre-meditated murder.) The fortress also contained a high-security political jail where past prisoners included Dostoyevsky, Trotsky and Lenin's brother Alexander. Parts of the former jail are now open to the public.

Across the river from the fortress, standing on the Spit of Vasilyevsky Island, are the eye-catching **Rostral Columns** — constructed as oil-fired navigation beacons in the 1800s and studded with ship's prows. They flank the Stock Exchange, a white colonnaded building completed in 1810 which now houses the **Naval Museum** . Nearby are the side-by-side, red-and-white buildings of St. Petersburg State University, constructed in the early 1700s to house government ministries and given to the university in 1835. Famous scholars and important figures of Russian culture and politics have studied at this prominent university, including Lenin who passed his law finals in 1891.

Other buildings of note along University Embankment include the stately **Menshikov Palace** – built for Peter the Great's chief lieutenant Alexander Menshikov, who effectively ruled Russia for several years following the czar's death until his enemies forced him into exile. The restored palace is now a branch of the Hermitage, housing a collection of Russian cultural artifacts from the early 1700s.

(Above) Priests at the Cathedral of St. Peter and St. Paul.
(Below) The Rostral Columns.

Catherine the Great

Peter the Great's daughter Empress Elizabeth ruled Russia from 1741 to 1761, during which time she built the Winter Palace (now the Hermitage art museum) in the heart of St. Petersburg. She also chose a 15-year-old German princess as the wife for her nephew and heir, Peter III. Called Princess Sophie, she changed her name to Catherine, converted to the Eastern Orthodox faith and absorbed Russian culture – all the while enduring an unhappy marriage. Shortly after the death of Empress Elizabeth in 1761, Catherine and her fellow conspirators seized power from her dissolute husband and murdered him. Despite having no legal claim to the throne, Catherine enjoyed widespread support among the Russian nobility and took several of them as lovers, a few of whom became powerful political advisors.

Well read and a patron of the arts, Catherine began her reign intent on reform. However, a peasant uprising in 1773 led by a Cossack named Pugachev prompted her to become increasingly conservative, curtailing the rights of serfs while increasing the international power and prestige of Russia through diplomacy and military conquest. She also added wings to the Winter Palace, filled them with fine art collections and invited to her court such intellectual luminaries as Voltaire. Catherine intensely disliked her son and successor Paul I, who was resented by the nobility for his autocratic policies. He felt unsafe living in the Winter Palace after his mother's death and built himself a nearby moated castle, but within weeks of moving into his new residence in 1801 the demented czar was murdered in his bedroom by a group of Russian officers.

Outlying Attractions

Nevsky Prospekt, the city's main avenue, eventually leads out of the downtown core to the **Alexander Nevsky Monastery** 23, founded in 1710. Its extensive grounds contain two baroque churches, one neoclassical cathedral and two cemeteries. The graves of Dostoyevsky, Tchaikovsky, Rimsky-Korsakov, Mussorgsky and Glinka are at the Tikhvin Cemetery.

Smolny Cathedral 24 was intended as the centrepiece of a monastery being built to house Peter the Great's daughter Elizabeth, who had chosen to become a nun until a bloodless palace coup (led by her and the imperial guards) placed her on the throne in 1741. The cathedral was designed by Rastrelli, who also designed the Winter Palace, and this blue-and-white edifice is crowned with golden domes. The nearby Smolny Institute was constructed in the early 19th century as a school for girls of the nobility. It became Lenin's Bolshevik headquarters during the October Revolution in 1917. Sergei Kirov, one of Stalin's most trusted aides, was assassinated here in 1934, probably at Stalin's order. City administration has operated here since 1991, and Putin served at this office as deputy mayor before becoming prime minister (and then president) of Russia.

Royal Summer Palaces

The wealth and opulence of the Romanov dynasty spread outward from St. Petersburg to the numerous summer palaces and pavilions they built for themselves throughout the 18th and 19th centuries. These royal residences were occupied and destroyed by German troops during the Siege of Leningrad, but most have since been rebuilt and are today major tourist attractions.

The royal estate of **Peterhof** (20 miles west of the city) is often called the Russian Versailles for its ornate palaces, landscaped gardens and dazzling array of fountains and statues. The Grand Palace stands on a bluff, its terrace overlooking the magnificent Grand Cascade – a resplendent ensemble of 64 fountains, with water cascading in broad sheets past glittering gilt statues. The main fountain's centrepiece statue of Samson wrestling the jaws of a lion symbolizes Russia's defeat of Sweden in the Great Northern

(Above) A czarina's summer pavilion at Olga's Pond. (Below) The Grand Palace at Peterhof.

War. A natural spring in the Upper Garden behind the Grand Palace supplies the gravity-fed water system that operates the fountains.

The Lower Park contains an extensive array of individual fountains as well as Peter the Great's original seaside palace, called Monplaisir, which resembles a Dutch colonial mansion. He also built Marly Palace, inspired by Louise XIV's royal hunting lodge. Subsequent czars added to Peterhof's palatial grounds, with Empress Elizabeth hiring Rastrelli (the architect of the Winter Palace) to remodel the Grand Palace, and Nicholas I building Cottage Palace (a gothic mansion) in adjacent Alexandria Park.

Nicholas I also commissioned summer pavilions for his wife Alexandra and youngest daughter Olga, which are located on the edge of Olga's Pond opposite Peterhof's Upper Garden. The adjacent town of Peterhof was renamed Petrodvorets in 1944 but reverted to Peterhof (German for 'Peter's home') in the early 1990s.

The town of **Pushkin**, named in Soviet times to honour Russia's national poet, was originally called Tsarskoye Selo (Czar's Village) when founded by Peter the Great in 1708. The original **Catherine Palace**, built for Peter's wife, was later demolished and replaced with a palace of unsurpassed grandeur by their daughter Empress Elizabeth, who commissioned Rastrelli to create a palatial residence in keeping with her extravagant tastes. The palace's blue-and-white rococo façade is ornamented with gilded statues and its interior is famous for the Amber Room –

an entire chamber lined with panels of amber, gold leaf and mirrors. Destroyed by German forces during World War II, this room was recreated by craftsmen who worked on this painstaking project from 1982 until its completion in 2003. Nearby is Alexander Palace, home of the last Romanov czar, Nicholas II. Pushkin's vast royal park is filled with grottoes, canals and lakes.

(Opposite and below) Peterhof's Grand Cascade. (Bottom) The ballroom in the Grand Palace.

A few miles from Pushkin is **Pavlovsk**, named in honour of Paul I, who was given this royal estate by his mother Catherine the Great. The neo-classical palace is less ostentatious than Pushkin or Peterhof but is admired for its elegant design and English-style landscape garden.

Yet another imperial palace is at **Gatchina**, where Catherine the Great bought the local village and surrounding lands to build a palace and park for her favourite supporter, Count Grigory Orlov (one of the conspirators who placed Catherine on the throne by murdering her husband Peter III). Orlov had fallen out of favour by the time the palace was completed in 1781, and Catherine's son Paul was given the palace. Despite the estate's association with one of his father's assassins, Paul liked the palace's fortress-like appearance which he enhanced with cannons, sentry boxes and a moat.

Catherine Palace in Pushkin.

Russian Artists

St. Petersburg in the 19th century was a brilliant cultural centre, producing towering figures of the arts. Alexander Pushkin – the 'Russian Shakespeare' – was a young nobleman when exiled to the Crimea in 1820 but pardoned by the czar six years later. Pushkin's major works include his masterpiece *Eugene Onegin* and his famous poem *The Bronze Horseman*, inspired by the bronze equestrian statue standing in Senate Square. Pushkin was killed in a duel at the age of 38.

The times in which Pushkin lived among St. Petersburg society are captured in Leo Tolstoy's novels *Anna Karenina* and *War and Peace*, the latter vividly describing Napoleon's disastrous military invasion of Russia in 1812. Tolstoy, born in 1828, was a member of the Russian nobility and wrote firsthand about sumptuous balls and all-male dinner parties where copious amounts of liquor were consumed. Tolstoy wrote about what he knew, having enjoyed a profligate life in St. Petersburg before serving in the Russian army, followed by marriage and children. In his later years he adopted a doctrine of Christian love and non-violence, rejecting organized religion and personal possessions.

Tolstoy was a family friend of Boris Pasternak, who became a hero of Russian intellectuals during the Stalinist era. Pasternak's masterpiece is the novel *Dr. Zhivago*, for which he won the 1958 Nobel Prize in Literature. Pasternak was greatly influenced by Tolstoy, who is widely regarded as one of the world's greatest novelists, along with his contemporary Fyodor Dostoyevsky.

The son of an army surgeon, Dostoyevsky didn't enjoy the privileged lifestyle of Count Tolstoy. His father was a violent alcoholic who was brutally murdered by his own serfs when Dostoyevsky was 18. Shortly after graduating from military engineering school in St. Petersburg, Dostoyevsky was arrested for belonging to an illegal group of radical utopians and was sentenced to death, only to learn at the end of a pre-execution ceremony that he had been granted a reprieve. Sent to a Siberian penal colony for four years of hard labour, he endured great physical and mental pain, including repeated attacks of epilepsy, before returning to St. Petersburg. Dostoyevsky's powerful prose and psychological insights are showcased in such masterpieces as *Crime and Punishment* and *The Brothers Karamazov*.

The Russian temperament is also reflected in its legacy of classical music, which thrived in the latter half of the 19th century with a string of famous composers studying at the St. Petersburg Conservatory. These included Tchaikovsky, Moussorgsky (a former officer of the Imperial Guard) and Rimsky-Korsakov, who gave up a naval career to compose orchestral works. Rimsky-Korsakov's pupils included Prokofiev and Stravinsky, while Tchaikovsky strongly influenced his friend Rachmaninoff.

The St. Petersburg Ballet, known to the world as the Kirov, was founded in the 1700s as the Imperial Russian Ballet. In 1889 the company moved into the Mariinsky Theatre where it premiered Tchaikovsky's *Sleeping Beauty* and *Swan Lake*. During the Soviet era, the company's name was changed to honour the Bolshevik revolutionary Sergey Kirov and the name is still used when touring abroad. Famous dancers at the Kirov have included Rudolph Nureyev and Mikhail Baryshnikov. George Balanchine (born as Georgi Balanchivadz) studied dance and music in St. Petersburg, and eventually moved to the United States where he became the ballet world's foremost contemporary choreographer.

(Below) Count Leo Tolstoy

(Bottom) The Mariinsky Theatre

THE BALTIC STATES

The Baltic states of **Estonia**, **Latvia** and **Lithuania** captured the world's attention in August 1989. In a demonstration of solidarity against Soviet occupation, two million people joined hands and created a human chain that was nearly 400 miles long. Called the Baltic Way, this peaceful but powerful protest ran from Tallinn in Estonia to Vilnius in Lithuania. It was part of the Singing Revolution that had begun at the Tallinn Song Festival in June 1988 (during the early days of *glasnost*) when masses of people attending the festival began spontaneously singing patriotic songs that had been forbidden by the Soviets since annexing the three Baltic states in 1940.

Tallinn's restored Old Town

All three nations gained independence in August 1991, and they wasted no time promoting economic and political ties with Western Europe, joining NATO and the European Union in 2004. Cruise ships call at all three countries, with Tallinn receiving the most visitors.

Tallinn, Estonia

Tallinn, capital of Estonia, was founded by Danish king Waldemar II, who built a fortress here in 1219 (the Estonian words *Taani linn* mean 'Danish castle'). Tallinn was eventually sold to a German order of knights called the Livonian Brothers of the Sword, who ruled from their fortified hilltop while the powerful Hanseatic merchants conducted commerce in the walled Lower Town. A stroll through the winding streets of Tallinn is

like stepping back to the Middle Ages, with its variety of architecture reflecting the town's occupation over the centuries by Danes, Germans, Swedes and Russians. Tallinn was heavily damaged during World War II, but its restored Old Town was declared a UNESCO World Heritage Site in 1997.

Estonia at a Glance

The Republic of Estonia borders Russia and is about the size of Switzerland. Estonia's population is 1.4 million and the main language is Estonian – similar to Finnish – although one in three Estonians is Russian. Major religions are Evangelical Lutheran and Russian Orthodox, although much of the population is unaffiliated with a specific church. Government is a parliamentary republic, and the Estonian capital is Tallinn (pop. 400,000). The country's **currency** is the euro. The international dialing code is +372.

Shore Excursions

Estonia

Although Tallinn is a port that can be easily explored on your own, the cruise line's shore excursions offer historic background on the Old Town, with guided walking tours that are often combined with a folkloric show or chocolate-making demonstration. Countryside tours include mountain biking, kayaking and sportfishing. Local operators also offer guided tours, including well-regarded Denrus.

(Above left) A street leading to Alexander Nevsky Cathedral.

(Left) Estonian knitwear.

Getting Around

The cruise port is about a mile (1.6 km) from the gates of the Old Town, and it takes approximately 20 minutes to walk the distance. Most cruise lines provide a shuttle service for a small fee, with a drop-off outside the main entrance of the Old Town. A red Hop-On Hop-Off bus makes regular stops at the cruiseship terminal while following its route in and around the Old Town; the fare is 19 euros for a one-day pass. Taxis are also available but fares are unregulated, so be sure to check the operator's price list to determine his starting fare (2 to 5 euros) and metered fare per kilometre (.5 to 1 euro).

(Above) Almond seller in Town Hall Square (bottom). (Below) Shops line the Old Town streets.

Shopping

Tallinn is just across the Gulf of Finland from Helsinki, and the Scandinavian influence is evident in Estonian design, be it furniture, fashion or home textiles. Items to look for in Tallinn include Estonian knitwear, amber jewellery and glass art. The streets of the Old Town contain numerous art galleries, fashion shops and jewellery stores.

Dining

Outdoor cafés are plentiful in the Old Town, especially at Town Hall Square, where the Olde Hansa recreates a medieval atmosphere for diners with its traveller's luncheon of smoked herring, anchovies, liver paté, rye breads and thick soups. Cafes and restaurants are also tucked into the streets leading off the main square, such as Café Maiasmokk (Sweet Tooth Café) at Pikk 16, which is housed in a 200-year-old candy factory and serves wonderful cakes and coffee. Small packets of roasted sugared almonds – sold from food carts in Town Hall Square – are good for snacking as you walk the cobblestone streets.

Ascending to the Upper Town.

Tallinn Attractions

The Old Town is a delight to explore on foot, with cobblestone lanes leading to half-hidden courtyards and church squares. The following is a suggested walking route through the Lower and Upper Towns.

Viru Gate 1, marked by two 14th-century towers, is the main entryway leading into the Old Town along Viru Street. A busy shopping street, Viru leads to cafe-lined **Town Hall Square 2** (Raekoja Plats), site of Tallinn's medieval marketplace. This central square is still a hub of activity with outdoor concerts, festivals and crafts fairs held here. Residents dressed in medieval costume invite tourists to sample the medieval fare served in such restaurants as the Olde Hansa (housed in the old Packing Hall) or Peppersack

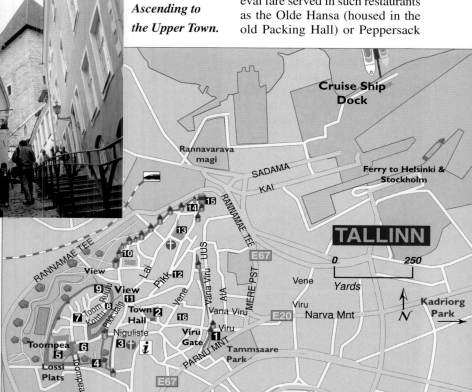

(housed in the residence of a Hanseatic merchant). The 14th-century Town Hall is open in summer to visitors, its cellar containing a model of 16th-century Tallinn, and a climb to the top of its tower (115 steep steps) provides sweeping views. The 15th-century Town Hall Pharmacy is one of the oldest in Europe that is still functioning at its original spot in the square.

Crossroads lead in all directions from Town Hall Square. If you follow Kullassepa to Niguliste, you will come upon the **(i) Visitor Information Centre** where you can pick up a detailed **walking map**. Niguliste Street runs along one side of **St. Nicholas's Church** ❸ (Niguliste Church), which was built by German merchants from the island of Gotland in the early 13th century. Restored following WW II bombing raids, the church is today a concert hall and museum dedicated to church art.

(Above) Town Hall. (Below) A street in Old Town.

Continuing along Niguliste Street to Luhike Jalg Street, which ascends to the Upper Town, you will pass the Danish King's Garden on your left before proceeding through a gate tower to **Toompea (Cathedral Hill)**, site of the Danish-built castle. Before heading to Toompea's main square (Lossi Plats), a detour to your left will lead to a 15th-century tower called **Kiek-in-de-Kok** (Peep in the Kitchen) ❹ so named for the vantage it provided into kitchen windows in the Lower Town. Today this cannon tower houses a museum featuring narrow stairways and access to the secret tunnels built beneath the Old Town.

(Above) Estonian Parliament building. (Left) Dome Church.

The original 13th-century Danish castle on Toompea has undergone much reconstruction over the centuries, including the addition of an 18th-century building that today houses the **Estonian Parliament 5**. Standing opposite is **Alexander Nevsky Cathedral 6**, designed by a St. Petersburg architect and completed in 1900 when Tallinn was part of Imperial Russia.

Nearby is **Toomkirk 7** (Cathedral of Saint Mary the Virgin), which is also called **Dome Church**. Its original stone structure dates to the mid-1200s, with additions and modifications added since. Kohtu Street leads from Toomkirk to **Kohtu Viewing Platform 8** from which you can enjoy a view overlooking the Lower Town. Another **viewing platform 9** is entered through an arch off Rahukohtu.

To return to the Lower Town, follow the long sloping street Pikk Jalg to the tower archway that leads onto several streets branching off in various directions. From here, you can continue to the far end of the Lower Town, or you can return to Town Hall square. Attractions to be seen on an extended walking tour include a section of the medieval wall that connects **Nunna, Sauna and Kuldjala Towers 10** where visitors can climb up to the ramparts to enjoy splendid views.

Major attractions on Pikk Street include the **Estonian History Museum 11**, housed in the preserved Great Guild Hall, which was built by the town's wealthy merchants from 1407 to 1417 and displays the Great Guild's coat of arms on its façade. Further along Pikk Street at #26 is the **House of the Brotherhood of Black Heads** 12, a military fraternity of bachelor merchants; their emblem is positioned above the doorway of this 16th-century building, which features an ornate façade reflecting the Dutch Renaissance style.

Near the end of Pikk Street stands **St. Olav's Church** 13 , a rebuilt Gothic church that was once the tallest in medieval Europe. Its soaring spire has been struck by lightening at least eight times and the church has burned three times. During the Soviet era, the spire was used by the KGB for sending radio transmissions. At the far end of Pikk Street are the **Three Sisters** 14 – the former residences of three Hanseatic merchants, which now house a luxury hotel.

Marking the very end of Pikk Street is the Great Coastal Gate and Fat Margaret's Tower, the latter housing Tallinn's **Maritime Museum** 15 . If you are planning to walk back to the ship, this exit from the Old Town is closest to the cruise piers. If you are planning to walk back through the Lower Town to the Viru Gates and catch the shuttle back to the ship, be sure to stroll through **St. Catherine's Passage** 16 – an enclave of craftsmen's workshops and artisans' studios lining a narrow medieval passageway that connects Vene and Muurivahe streets.

Doorway of House of the Brotherhood of Black Heads.

Outlying Attractions

The **Museum of Occupation and Fight For Freedom**, which opened in 2003, is located just outside the Old Town at Toompea 8. Housed in a modern building, the museum is dedicated to Tallinn's years of Soviet occupation.

The stately **Kadriorg** area, about a mile east of the Old Town, is where Peter the Great built a baroque summer palace and gardens for himself and his wife Catherine. Today the czarist palace houses the **Kadriorg Art Museum** and standing opposite, on the far side of the gardens, is the **Presidential Palace**. The palace's park-like setting encompasses several historic outbuildings, including Peter the Great Cottage, as well as the ornamental **Swan Lake**. Numerous foreign embassies are located in the

Kadriorg area, as is the **Kumu Art Museum**, which opened in 2006 and exhibits both classical and contemporary Estonian art. Also in the Kadriorg area is the **Song Festival Grounds**, with its modern amphitheatre and where the Singing Revolution began in 1988.

Riga, Latvia

Situated on a natural harbour lying upriver from the mouth of the Daugava River, Riga has been an important trading centre since the time of the Vikings and subject to foreign rule since the 13th century. When Latvia gained independence from the Soviet Union in 1991, Riga was initially plagued with poverty and crime, but has since revitalized itself and is a growing tourist destination. The old town has

retained its medieval character and the Art Nouveau district contains an unparalleled collection of Jugendstil buildings for which Riga's historic centre has been declared a UNESCO World Heritage Site.

Getting Around

The cruise ships dock at the ferry terminal, which is a half-mile (.8-km), 15-minute walk along the waterfront to Old Riga (the city's historic centre). Most cruise lines provide a shuttle for a small fee. Metered taxis are available (be sure your driver displays an operating licence). Tram cars connect the ferry terminal with the city centre.

Latvia at a Glance

The Republic of Latvia, wedged between Estonia and Lithuania, has a population of 2 million. The majority is ethnic Latvian, but a quarter of the population is Russian due to decades of Soviet domination. Latvian is the official language and schoolchildren learn English as a second language. Lutheran and Orthodox are the two major religions, and the system of government is a parliamentary democracy. Riga is the capital and largest city of Latvia with a population of 700,000. The city's most famous son is Isaiah Berlin, born in Riga in 1909 when Latvia was part of the Russian Empire. Latvia joined the European Union in 2004 and its unit of **currency** is the euro.

Riga's cathedral (left) and Freedom Monument (opposite).

Shopping & Dining

Amber jewellery and Soviet memorabilia are popular souvenirs in Riga. Cafes serving beef stroganoff and Latvian beer are numerous in the Old Town, especially at Cathedral Square. The city's Russian tea-rooms are perfect for an afternoon snack.

Attractions

Riga's old section (Hansa town) is encircled by a park-lined moat where the fortified city's walls were once protected by a series of medieval towers. **Powder Tower 1**, the only one remaining from the original walls, houses the Latvian Museum of War. The ancient **Castle of the Livonian Knights 2** has been rebuilt over the ages and is today occupied by the Museum of Latvian History, Museum of Foreign Art and the Latvian president's

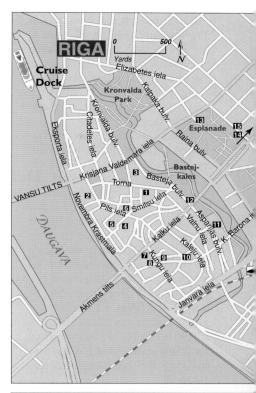

Shore Excursions

Riga

Riga shore excursions include a drive to the ruins of Bauska Castle and to Rundale Palace, a beautiful baroque palace designed by Rastrelli (the Italian architect who designed the Winter Palace in St. Petersburg). Riga's tragic Jewish history is revisited in a tour of several memorials, including the site of the 1941 burning of the Big Choral Synagogue, the Old Jewish Cemetery which contains the graves of Riga's Jewish residents killed by the Nazis, and the mass grave at the site of the Rumbula massacre. Check your cruise line's website for details on Riga shore excursions.

official residence. The **Latvian Parliament Building** , built in the 19th century on Jekaba Street, was barricaded by the Latvian Popular Front to prevent the Soviet Army from reaching it during the country's independence movement in the early 1990s.

Cathedral Square (Doma laukums) is the centre of the medieval town. Here stands the 13th-century **Dome cathedral**, which was built by Bishop Albert (Riga's founder) in 1221 and rebuilt in the 16th century. Beside it, housed in a converted monastery, is the **Museum of Riga's History and Navigation** which began with the private collection of a Riga doctor. The **Three Brothers** is a trio of stone houses on Maza Pils, the oldest being No. 17 (dating from the 15th century) and No. 19, now housing the city's architecture museum.

The box-shaped **Latvian Occupation Museum** chronicles the country's Soviet era of occupation, and the **House of the Blackheads** is a 14th-century inn featuring an ornate Dutch Renaissance facade that was reconstructed in honour of Riga's 800th birthday in 2000. Nearby is **St. Peter's Church**, first built in 1209, its soaring spire completed in 1746. Soviet engineers restored the church in the 1970s and installed an elevator in its tower for views over the city. On the next street is **St. John's Church**, a 13th-century chapel.

Richard Wagner was once music director of the local opera, and the city's neo-classical **National Opera House**, built in 1863 and rebuilt following a fire in 1882, is a monument to Riga's rich musical heritage. It stands on the edge of Vermane Park, which lies along Pilsetas Kanals – a canal that winds through the city, dividing the Old Town from the New Town. It's a short canalside walk from the Opera House to the **Freedom Monument**, unveiled in 1935 and rising high above the spacious plaza. The monument is a symbol of freedom and independence for Latvians, who would rally at its base during the Soviet era.

The **National Art Museum** showcases Latvian fine art and is located on the far side of the Esplanade, a parkland of formal gardens and period mansions. Lying northwest of the Esplanade

Art Nouveau architecture on Elizabetes iela.

is the **Art Nouveau District** where late 19th- and early 20th-century apartment buildings were designed in the Jugendstil (German for 'youth style'). The elaborate façades of these buildings include several by the Mikhail Eisentein, who was born in St. Petersburg of Swedish and Jewish-German ancestry. Buildings of note by Eisentein include Elizabetes iela 10b; Alberta iela 4, 6, 13 (the Belgium Embassy is on the 5th floor of No. 13); and Strelnieku 4 (housing the Stockholm School of Economics).

Outlying Riga attractions include the **Open Air Ethnographic Museum 14** , which is located about five miles (9 km) from the city centre, and the **Riga Motor Museum 15**, housed in a modern building which opened in 1989, its exhibits including Stalin's armoured limousine.

Lithuania

Once encompassing most of present-day Belarus and Ukraine, then forming a commonwealth with Poland in 1569, the large European state of Lithuania was eventually partitioned by surrounding countries to become the small republic of today. The country's Baltic port of **Klaipeda** has been ruled at various times in its history by the Teutonic Knights, Prussians, Germans and Soviets. Modern Klaipeda is an emerging port of call for visiting cruise passengers who stroll the cobblestone streets of the medieval Old Town to view such highlights as Theatre Square and the Amber Market. Excursions are offered to Zemaitija National Park, where a former Soviet nuclear missile launch site is nestled amid the forests and lakes of this scenic nature reserve. Also visited on an excursion from Klaipeda is the historic town of Kretinga, which is home to a Benedictine monastery.

Lithuania's population of 3.5 million is predominantly Lithuanian (with small minorities of Russians and Poles) and about 80% of the population is Roman Catholic. Like its Baltic neighbours Latvia and Estonia, Lithuania is a parliamentary democracy. The capital is **Vilnius**, which was founded in 1323 when the Lithuanian prince Gediminas built a castle there.

Lithuania joined the European Union in 2004 and adopted the euro as its official currency on January 1, 2015.

Vilnius's historic quarter

POLAND

The collapse of the Berlin Wall began on Polish soil, in a shipyard in Gdansk. It started in 1980 when workers defied the communist government by forming an illegal trade union called Solidarity. Their leader, Lech Walesa, was arrested several times but found strength in the words of a powerful ally – Pope John Paul II, who told Walesa "not to be afraid" as he threw the support of the Roman Catholic Church behind Solidarity. Born in Poland in 1920, the future pontiff had himself escaped arrest, at the hands of the Gestapo, by hiding in his uncle's basement in Krakow in the wake of the 1944 Warsaw Uprising.

Lech Walesa, an electrician by trade, was awarded the Nobel Peace Prize in 1983 and became President of Poland when he and his Solidarity party were swept into office in 1990. This peaceful overthrow of the communist regime in Poland was credited in large part to Pope John Paul II, about whom the Soviet leader Mikhail Gorbachev would later say, "The collapse of the Iron Curtain would have been impossible without John Paul II." U.S. President Ronald Reagan is also credited with helping to topple communism, and a bronze statue honouring the Polish-born pope and American president was unveiled in 2012 in a Gdansk park named in honour of Ronald Reagan.

Poland at a Glance

Poland, with a population of 38 million, is a homogenous country, its ethnic makeup being 97% Polish and predominantly Roman Catholic. The government is a republic and the capital is Warsaw. Poland joined the European Union in 2004. Unit of **currency** is the zloty (PLN); $1 USD = 3.5 PLN; £1 = 5.5 PLN.

Gdansk's historic waterfront

Poland's History

Slavic groups originally occupied the area of present-day Poland, its mostly flat terrain presenting few natural barriers to invasion. Ruled by the Jagiello dynasty during its 16th-century golden age, the Kingdom of Poland eventually united with the Grand Duchy of Lithuania to create an empire stretching from the Baltic to the Black Sea. However, by 1795 the nation of Poland had disappeared from the map of Europe, partitioned between Prussia, Austria and Russia.

Not until the end of the First World War did Poland re-emerge as an independent state, only to be invaded two decades later by German forces at the start of World War II. Within weeks Germany and the Soviet Union had divided and annexed the whole of Poland. War brought decimation to Poland. Six million Poles, including three million Jews, were killed in mas-

sacres, by starvation or at the Auschwitz death camp. Another 2.5 million were sent to Germany for forced labour. The Red Army drove German forces from Poland near the end of World War II and the country became a Soviet satellite state. Civil unrest eventually resulted in the labour movement of the 1970s and 80s, and Poland in the 1990s became a democratic market-oriented country.

Gdansk

The city of Gdansk is a major Baltic seaport with some of the world's largest shipyards. A medieval capital and member of the Hanseatic League, Gdansk was later ruled by Poland, then by Prussia – when the city was known by its German name of Danzig. In 1919 Gdansk was designated a free city by the League of Nations and Poland was granted special utilization rights to its port. When Poland refused to surrender Gdansk to Nazi Germany, Hitler used this as an excuse to invade Poland on September 1, 1939. The Port of Gdansk's Military Transit Depot, located on the Westerplatte Peninsula and manned by less than 200 Poles, held out for seven days against a major German assault before surrendering. In the city proper, trained civilians with a cache of weapons defended the Polish Post Office before fire drove them from the burning building to face

(Left) A Nazi poster of Gdansk. (Opposite) Shops are housed in the Great Mill.

arrest, torture and execution at the hands of the German SS. Fierce fighting in the course of the war reduced Gdansk to rubble, but the historic quarter has been rebuilt, brick by brick.

Getting Around 🏃

Gdansk lies at the mouth of the Motlawa River and is the major cruise port of the Trojmiasto (Three City) metropolitan area, which includes Sopot (a beach resort) and the port of Gdynia, located about 10 miles (16 km) northwest of Gdansk.

There are two cruise quays servicing Gdansk, both of which are located in the outer harbour about 3.5 miles (6 km) from the city centre. The large ships dock at Oliwskie Quay, from which you can travel to the city centre by tram, train, taxi or ship's shuttle (if provided). The tram stop is a short walk from the cruise dock and the train station is about half a mile (1 km) away. Taxis are also available. The other Gdansk cruise quay – Westerplatte Ferry Terminal – has fewer facilities but taxis are available.

The cruise port at Gdynia is a 45-minute drive to Gdansk's historic centre. The one-way taxi fare is about $40. Train service is also available.

Gdansk's attractions are concentrated in Glowne Miasto (Main Town) – the city's historic quarter of pedestrian cobblestone streets. **Malbork**, home to a 14th-century castle, is a two-hour drive from Gdansk and can be reached by train or on a ship-organized excursion.

Shore Excursions

Gdansk

The historic attractions in Gdansk are the focus of most ship excursions. These include a variety of walking tours of the Main Town's core attractions, some combined with other area attractions such as the Gdansk suburb of Oliwa to view its historic cathedral or the resort town of Sopot, which boasts the Baltic's longest promenade pier. The story of Gdansk's peaceful revolution can be retraced on a tour to Solidarity Square and the nearby Roads to Freedom exhibit. A popular, out-of-town excursion is the one to Malbork Castle – the world's largest brick castle – built by the Teutonic Knights and the seat of their grand master in the 14th century. Rebuilt in the 19th century, the castle is one of the finest examples of German secular medieval architecture.

Shopping & Dining

Gdansk is best known for its amber jewellery, sold in local shops such as those concentrated on Mariacka Street. A collection of shops and boutiques is housed in the Great Mill – a 14th-century brick building located on a small island in the canal running past St. Catherine's Church.

Good lunch spots in Gdansk can be found among the many cafés near St. Mary's Church, includ-

ing Cafe Kamienica on Mariacka Street and, for the city's best pierogies, Pierogarnia u Dzika on Piwna.

Gdansk Attractions

Several Renaissance gates mark the entrances into Glowne Miasto (Main Town). Visitors entering from the west along the historical Royal Road (a royal processional route) will pass through **High Gate 1** (also called Upland Gate), past the **Amber Museum** (which is housed in a medieval torture chamber), then through **Golden Gate 2** before proceeding along Ulica Dlugi (Long Street). This main pedestrian street leads to the city's central square, which is overlooked by Ratusz Glowny **(Old Town Hall) 3**. This rebuilt 14th-century building houses the Gdansk History Museum and its tall spire is crowned with a gilded statue of Sigismund II, the last king of the Jagiello dynasty. Dwor Artusa **(Artus Mansion) 4**, an elegant mansion named for the mythical King Arthur, was a meeting place of the Gdansk city nobles and is now a museum containing Renaissance furniture and artwork. Standing in the centre of the square is Fontanna Neptuna **(Neptune Fountain) 5**, its rococo sculptures symbolizing Gdansk's bond with the sea.

Green Gate 6, one of the eastern entrances to the old town, was built in the mid-1500s as the official residence of Polish monarchs, its design inspired by Antwerp City Hall and reflecting Flemish mannerism. Mariacka Gate **(Gate**

of St. Mary) **7** marks the riverside entrance to **Mariacka Street**, one of the old town's most beautiful streets, which features stone porches and dragonhead gutter spouts. This cobblestoned street is lined with shops selling amber jewellery and leads to the **Church of St. Mary 8**, one of the largest Brick Gothic churches ever built. Completed in 1343, the church initially held 22 altars. The climb to the top of its tower, which features a 15th-century astronomical clock, provides panoramic views.

The **Harbour Crane 9**, built in the 14th century to unload cargo, is part of the **Maritime Museum 10** – located on the far side of the river where the *Soldeck*, a museum ship, is permanently moored. The **Memorial to the Defenders of Post Office Square 11** is a stainless steel monument, unveiled in 1979, standing opposite the post office, which was rebuilt after World War II and now contains a small museum about the Polish civilians who bravely battled the German SS.

St. Catherine's Church 12 is the oldest church in Gdansk, begun in the 1220s, its tower constructed in the 1480s. The **13 Great Mill**, situated on a small island in the nearby canal, is a 14th-century brick building constructed by the Teutonic Knights and now housing shops.

The famous **Gdansk Shipyard** is on the north side of the old town, its entrance marked by the **Monument to Fallen Shipyard Workers 14**, commemorating those killed by security forces during a 1970 strike. The new European Solidarity Center opened in 2014 with expanded space for the **Roads to Freedom Exhibition 15**. This multi-media exhibit about the Solidarity movement was originally housed inside the shipyard in the building where the Accords were signed, then moved to the basement of the Solidarity Union's offices on Waly Piastowskie before finding a permanent home in the new center.

The **National Museum 16** is housed in a former Franciscan monastery located several blocks south of the old town.

(Opposite) Old Town Hall houses the Gdansk History Museum. (Below) Green Gate. (Bottom) The Harbour Crane.

GERMANY

Twice in the 20th century Germany rose to prominence as a formidable nation, and twice it came crashing down, destroyed in part by its own hubris. German intellectuals have helped shape Western philosophy since the Middle Ages, but the road to democracy has been a tortuous one for the German people.

The first German Empire, which lasted 47 years, was founded in 1871 under the leadership of Prussian chancellor Otto von Bismarck. Prior to this, centralized authority had eluded Germany since the dismantling of the medieval Carolingian Empire and the subsequent emergence of powerful German duchies. For centuries Germany remained a patchwork of free cities and principalities ruled by merchant princes.

Prussia eventually became the most powerful German state, ruled by William I and Bismarck. After Prussia defeated Austria in 1866 and France in 1871, William I was proclaimed Kaiser (emperor) of all Germany.

The newly formed German Empire quickly became one of the world's most powerful industrial economies and a commercial rival of Britain. Germany also expanded its navy to challenge British supremacy at sea. But the incompetent leadership of Kaiser Wilhelm II brought humiliating defeat to Germany in World War I and he was forced into exile, leaving a vanquished Germany struggling to recover under the Weimar Republic.

In 1933, Adolf Hitler seized power in Germany as leader of

Brandenburg Gate

the Nazi party. A dictator whose name has become synonymous with evil, Hitler perverted the superman teachings of the Prussian philosopher Nietzsche to justify Germany's "will to power" that would set it apart from the masses of inferior humanity and create an Aryan master race. The Third Reich plotted a course for European domination that was doomed to fail and its aftermath is still keenly felt, especially in the capital of Berlin. As the city rebuilds following its post-Cold War reunification, Berliners are also coming to terms with the past. Historic sites associated with Nazi atrocities and Soviet oppression are being turned into powerful memorials to the victims of totalitarian regimes, and Berlin today is filled with youthful energy and social tolerance.

Hitler saluting his Nazi troops at Nuremberg in 1935.

Germany at a Glance

Germany is a mostly land-locked country with the exception of its north coast, which borders both the North Sea and Baltic Sea. Here lie the country's major ports as well as numerous small ports and islands visited by small cruise ships. These include the Pomeranian port of Stralsund and Ruegen Island in the Baltic, and the port of Cuxhaven and Sylt Island along the North Sea coast.

Germany's population of 80 million is the second highest in Europe after Russia. The German economy is Europe's largest, and considerable funds have been spent since 1990 in an attempt to raise productivity and wages in the former East Germany to the same level as the rest of Germany.

German is the official language, with English widely spoken by the younger generations. One-third of the population is Protestant, another third is Catholic, and the remainder is either unaffiliated or belongs to other religions.

Germany (called Deutschland in German) is a federal republic with a chancellor serving as head of government. The current German chancellor, Angela Merkel, was elected in 2005 and grew up in East Germany. Unity Day – October 3 – is a national holiday and celebrates Germany's 1990 reunification. Berlin (pop. 3.5 million) is the capital of a united Germany. During the Cold War, East Berlin was the capital of East Germany and Bonn was the de facto capital of West Germany. Today, the capital is Berlin. Germany's **currency** is the euro.

The colours of the German flag (black, red and gold) can be traced to the medieval banner of the Holy Roman Emperor (the elected king of Germany), which displayed a black eagle with red claws and beak on a gold field.

Traditional German cuisine is known for its heavy use of *bratwurst* (pork sausage) and *liverwurst* (liver sausage), usually served with rye bread and washed down with a schooner of wheat beer. Classic German dishes include *spaetzle* (egg noodles or dumplings) and *wiener schnitzel* (breaded veal cutlets). Popular desserts include *stollen* (fruit cake), apple strudel and *baumkuchen*, meaning 'tree cake' in German for this round cake's layers of batter are added one by one on a spit and resemble the growth rings of a cut tree when the cake is sliced. Modern German cuisine is lighter than traditional German cooking, and in northern Germany fish is often featured on the menu.

Ports of Call

Rostock-Warnemünde

The seaside resort of Warnemünde lies at the mouth of the River Warnow and marks the entrance to Rostock's seaport, which is a major terminus for cargo ships and car ferries. This is a major Baltic port of call providing access to Berlin and other area attractions such as Lübeck city and the bucolic Mecklenburg countryside. Rostock was an important member of the Hanseatic League and is worth exploring for its medieval architecture and pedestrian streets lined with gabled buildings.

Shore Excursions

Germany

Shoreside options in Rostock-Warnemünde include full-day tours to **Berlin** or shorter tours of the immediate area. The selection of Berlin excursions is extensive and usually includes one that focuses on World War II sites and another that focuses on Museum Island's cultural treasures. One tour combines a morning of guided sightseeing with an afternoon of independent exploring. The trip to Berlin is by coach or train, depending on the excursion. For passengers wanting to explore Berlin on their own, a coach shuttle is usually available or you can take the early train from Warnemünde (see Getting Around).

Rostock's attractions are featured on several excursions, including one that incorporates a guided walking tour of the historic quarter. Also offered is a guided walking tour of Warnemünde combined with a miniature train ride, as well as a cycling tour of the town and surrounding countryside.

Visitors can enjoy views of the Mecklenburg countryside while on the Molli Steam Train, on a coach tour to Lubeck and Wismar, or on a coach ride to Schwerin, which includes a scenic lake cruise and visit to Schwerin Castle, the former home of the grand dukes of Mecklenburg.

Check your cruise line's website for more details on shore excursions.

Warnemünde's train station.

Getting Around

Most cruise ships dock at the Warnemünde Cruise Centre, which is a five-minute walk to the town centre and local train station. The train trip to Rostock is 20 minutes and a single-trip ticket costs about 2 euros. Rostock Cards are sold in the Warnemünde Cruise Terminal and cost 12 euros each. This non-transferable card entitles you to free public transport in the Rostock area, including the train and ferry between Warnemünde and Rostock as well as the metro, trams and buses in Rostock, and free entrance to some of the city's attractions.

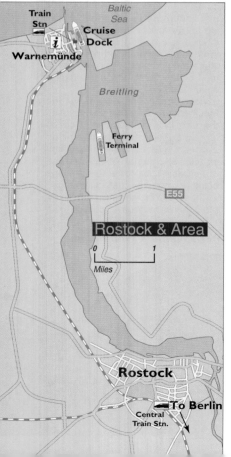

The Warnemünde-to-Rostock train makes eight stops before arriving at Rostock Hauptbahnhof (Central Station). To reach Berlin by train, you must change trains at Rostock. A single traveller ticket from Rostock to Berlin is about 80 euros (round-trip, 2nd class) and the train ride is about 2.5 hours. You arrive at Berlin's Hauptbahnhof, close to the Reichstag. Assuming you caught the early-morning train, you will have three or four hours to spend in Berlin before catching a train back to Rostock, and from there to Warnemünde.

Warnemünde Attractions

The seaside resort of Warnemünde (pop. 8,500) began as a fishing village before it became a seaport for the merchant city of Rostock in 1323. The village's beautiful beaches – stretching for two miles – began attracting holidaymakers in the 19th century, making Warnemünde one of the first German seaside resorts. The wicker beach chair was invented here when a woman asked a basket maker to make her a beach chair with a waterproof hood that also served as a sunshade.

Warnemünde's attractions are clustered around Alter Strom (old channel) which is lined with traditional fishermen's houses on one side and a fishing quay on the other. Am Stam stretches along the harbourfront and is lined with shops and cafes, as is the street directly behind it. Both lead to the lighthouse, built in 1898, which has panoramic views at the top. Beside it is the Teepott – an example of East German architecture

from the 1960s – which houses a restaurant and ground-floor seafaring exhibit. The local casino is in the Kurhaus, a Bauhaus-style building near the beachside promenade. Other attractions in Warnemünde include the neo-Gothic church completed in 1872, its original altar dating from 1475.

Rostock Attractions

Warnemünde's harbourfront. (Below) Steintor city gate in Rostock.

Rostock (pop. 200,000) was originally a Slavic fortress called Roztoc ('broadening of a river'). Torched in 1161 by the Danish king Valdemar I and afterwards settled by German traders, Rostock became a prosperous member of the Hanseatic League and founded a university in 1419. Rostock was part of Swedish Pomerania (a dominion under the Swedish crown) from the mid-1600s until the end of the Napoleonic Wars when it was transferred by treaty to Prussia.

During the Second World War, Rostock was heavily bombed by Allied planes that were targeting the city's aircraft factories. Many of Rostock's medieval monuments have been rebuilt, and a visit to the historic centre is an opportunity to view numerous examples of Gothic brick architecture.

Compact enough for walking, Rostock's historic centre is about a 15-minute walk from the main train station. Trams also depart regularly from the train station (Trams #5 and #6 stop at centrally located Neuer Markt) and taxis are available outside the train station. **Neuer Markt (New Market)** is a bustling square lined with gabled buildings and

filled with open-air markets and outdoor cafes. **City Hall (Rathaus)** ■ overlooks the square and has been the seat of Rostock's city administration for more than 700 years. Its rooftop consists of Gothic turrets and its baroque façade was added in the early 18th century. **Marienkirche (St. Mary's Church)** ■ stands at one corner of the square, its construction dating to the 13th century. It contains numerous late Gothic artifacts, including an astronomical clock and bronze baptismal font.

Kropeliner Strasse is a pedestrian street lined with shops and restaurants that leads from Neuer Markt to **Universitatsplatz** ■ where the University's main building (a neo-Renaissance structure completed in 1867) overlooks the bustling square. A statue of the Rostock-born

(Above left) Rostock's City Hall. (Left) Rostock University. (Opposite) St. Peter's Church and Kropeliner Strasse.

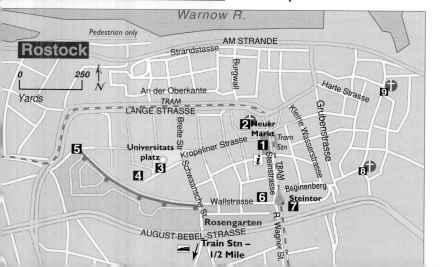

Prussian Field Marshall Blucher, a hero of the Napoleonic Wars, stands in one corner of the square, beyond which is Rostock's **Cultural History Museum** **4** housed in the Holy Cross Convent where Cistercian nuns once lived and worshipped.

Kropeliner Tor (Kropeliner Gate) **5** is one of the original 22 gates that once stood along the walls encircling Rostock, remnants of which run alongside Wallaniagen Park to Rosengarten (Rose Garden). Overlooking Rose Garden is the red-brick **Standehaus (Guild Hall)** **6** built in 1893 and now serving as a local courthouse. Nearby, on the site of the town's original main southern gate, is **Steintor** **7** – a city gate built in the Dutch Renaissance style. Richard Wagner Street leads south from Steintor back to the train station, while Beginenberg Street leads east toward **Nicholas Church** **8**, a 13th-century Gothic church now serving as a concert hall with apartments built into the roof.

Petrikirche (St. Peter's Church) **9** is perched on a hill overlooking the harbour, its site marking the town's original settlement. Built in the mid-14th century to replace an earlier church, Petrikirche was badly damaged by World War II bombings and its steeple was reconstructed in the 1990s. An elevator (2 euros per person) can be taken to a viewing platform at the top of the church's steeple overlooking the harbour.

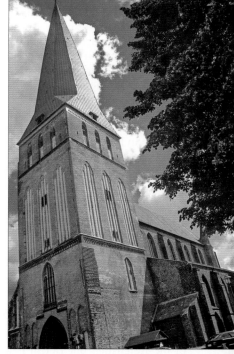

Berlin

Berlin has become a hot destination since the end of the Cold War. Following reunification in 1989, Berlin's affordability attracted aspiring young artists and the city became one of Europe's most vibrant cultural scenes with its modernist architecture and trendsetting design studios. The words "übercool" and "edgy" are still used to describe Berlin these days, although some say the rapid gentrification of East Berlin is turning it into a collection of bourgeois neighbourhoods. Nonetheless, Berlin's legendary music halls and nightclubs provide some of the most exciting nightlife in Europe.

Getting Around

The train from Warnemünde pulls into Berlin's central station (Hauptbahnhof), which is located a short walk to the Government Quarter lying just across the River Spree. Here you will find several of Berlin's best-known attractions, namely the Reichstag, Brandenburg Gate and Holocaust Memorial. Several other attractions are within walking distance of the Reichstag, but Berlin is a sprawling city and the City Circle

hop on/hop off buses (painted yellow) are a good way to get from one attraction to another. Their stops are located throughout the city (from Alexander Platz on the east side to Charlottenburg Palace on the west side), and one of the 14 stops on the circular route is located outside Hauptbahnhof. The cost for a one-day pass is 15.50 euros (a two-hour river cruise can be included for a total cost of 28 euros) and an illustrated map is provided. Berlin's public buses #100 or #200 also drive past many of the tourist sights. For more information, visit Berlin Tourism's website at: visitberlin. de/english/sightseeing.

Shopping

West Berlin's main shopping streets are Kurfurstendamn and Tauentzienstraffe, which connect at Breitscheidplatz – location of the Europa-Center. The hop-on hop-off bus stops nearby and at the famous KaDeWe department store on Tauentzienstraffe. The store's full name is Kaufhaus des Westens (Department Store of the West) and is Europe's second-largest department store after Harrods in London. KaDeWe has seven floors, with a food hall on the sixth and a winter garden restaurant on the top floor. East Berlin's main shopping street is Friedrichstrasse, which is lined with boutiques.

Lunching in Berlin

Numerous cafes are located near Museum Island, along the riverside promenades and nearby streets, such as those leading to

Nikolaikirche. The **Hause der 100 Biere** at Potsdamer Platz serves a large selection of local beers on tap and great goulash soup. An elegant lunch of modern German cuisine can be enjoyed at **Refugium** in Gendarmenmarkt or at the Hotel Adlon's summer terrace restaurant. Coffee houses include **Cafe Einstein**, a Berlin favourite at Kurfurstenstrasse 58. A second location is on Unter den Linden. **Hopfingerbra**, at the train station, is a good place to have a quick cup of coffee and dish of apple strudel.

Berlin Attractions

The **Reichstag** (German for 'imperial parliament') **1** was built to house the parliament of the German Empire and first opened in 1894. When an arsonist set fire to the building in 1933, just weeks after Hitler had been sworn in as Chancellor of Germany, the Nazis capitalized on the crime by suspending civil liberties and conducting mass arrests of communists, including

(Right) Cafes on a street near Nikolaikirche. (Below) The imposing Reichstag. (Opposite) Berlin's Hauptbahnhof.

opposition members of parliament. Bombed badly during World War II, the Reichstag was reconstructed by British architect Norman Foster following Germany's reunification. The interior was completely gutted and a huge glass dome replaced the building's original cupola. Admission is free to the dome, with its panoramic view of Berlin, but lineups can be long in summer. Germany's modern parliament – the Bundestag – has sat in the Reichstag since 1999.

The Reichstag stands at the eastern end of **Tiergarten** (German for 'animal garden'). This former royal hunting ground was transformed in 1830 into an urban park containing lakes, bridal paths and numerous monuments, including the Victory Column at its centre, from which

The British Embassy and Hotel Adlon on Unter den Linden.

tree-lined avenues radiate. A memorial to the Sinti and Roma murdered under Hitler's regime – a circular dark pool – stands near the eastern edge of Tiergarten, between the Reichstag and Brandenburg Gate.

Brandenburg Gate 2 was erected in 1791 by the Prussian king Frederick Wilhelm as a monumental entry to Berlin, its design based on the gateway to the Acropolis in Athens. The only one remaining from the original series of city gates, the Brandenburg Gate was restored in 2002, its 12 Doric columns supporting a chariot drawn by four horses and driven by the Roman goddess of victory. The gate stood in isolation during the Cold War, when the Berlin Wall separated it from West Berlin and the 'baby wall' on the other side made it off-limits to East Berliners. In 1987 US President Reagan delivered a speech before the Brandenburg Gate in which he famously declared, "Mr. Gorbachev, tear down this wall!" On November 20, 2009, German chancellor Angela Merkel marked the 20th anniversary of the fall of the Berlin Wall by walking through the Brandenburg Gate with former Soviet premier Mikhail Gorbachev.

Unter den Linden ('under the linden trees') **3** is a grand boulevard that leads from Brandenburg Gate to Museum Island and was

once a carriage-way leading from a Prussian palace to the royal hunting grounds in Tiergarten. **Hotel Adlon,** standing at the western end of Unter den Linden, welcomed the rich and famous in the 1920s and was the venue for the annual Presseball, a glittering social event at which Marlene Dietrich caused a stir when she arrived one year dressed in tails and pants. The hotel was badly damaged in a fire started by Russian soldiers in 1945 and the new Hotel Adlon Kempinski was built on this site in the 1990s. The original Hotel Adlon was the inspiration for the 1932 film *Grand Hotel*, starring Greta Garbo, and the new Adlon Kempinski made headlines in 2002 when Michael Jackson dangled his infant son from an upper-floor window.

The **Holocaust Memorial** (officially called Memorial to the Murdered Jews of Europe) **4** is located one block south of Brandenburg Gate on the site of a former SS barracks. Designed by the deconstructivist architect Peter Eisenman of New Jersey, the memorial consists of 2,711 concrete slabs laid in a grid pattern across several acres of sloping ground. A Memorial to Homosexuals Persecuted Under Nazism – a concrete cuboid –

stands on the edge of Tiergarten opposite the Holocaust Memorial. Nearby and marked with a plaque is the location of **Hitler's bunker**, dug 15 metres underground.

Bebel Platz 5 is an 18th-century square bounded by the State Opera, Humboldt University and St. Hedwig's Cathedral (Berlin's oldest Roman Catholic church), all of which were restored following their destruction in WWII. Named for the 19th-century Socialist leader August Bebel, the square was the site of a Nazi book-burning ceremony that took place on May 10, 1933, under the instigation of Propaganda Minister Joseph Goebbels. Members of the SA ('brownshirts') and Nazi youth groups tossed some 20,000 banned books onto a huge bonfire, including works by Thomas Mann, Karl Marx and the 19th-century German romantic poet Heinrich Heine, whose writings were critical of rising German nationalism. This infamous event is marked by a glass plate embedded in the middle of the square that provides a view into an underground chamber containing empty bookcases. Students at Humboldt University hold an annual book sale in the square on May 10.

Bebel Platz

Gendarmenmarkt 6 is a lovely square bounded by two 18th-century cathedrals and a 19th-century concert hall. Named for a regiment of cavalry soldiers, Gendarmenmarkt is the site of a popular Christmas market and in its centre stands a statue of Friedrich von Schiller, an 18th-century poet. The square's French cathedral was built by Huguenots and is today a museum with the church vaults now housing an upscale restaurant called Refugium. The German cathedral standing opposite was rebuilt after WWII, opening in 1996 as a museum. The Konzerthaus was reconstructed in the 1980s and is home to the Konzerthausorchester Berlin, a symphony orchestra

founded in East Berlin during the Soviet era.

Museum Island 7, which lies in a bend of the Spree River at the eastern end of Unter den Linden, has been recognized by UNESCO as a World Heritage Site for its ensemble of five museums built between 1830 and 1930. The **Alte Museum** (Old Museum), built in 1830 to house the Prussian royal family's art collection, was restored in 1966, its design based on the Stoa in Athens. The **Neues Museum** (New Museum) was completed in 1859 and contains treasures of Ancient Egypt, such as the iconic bust of Queen Nefertiti. The **Old National Gallery**, which reopened in 2009 after being rebuilt under the direction of English architect David Chipperfield, contains an impressive collection of 19th-century art. **Bode Museum** houses a collection of sculptures and Byzantine art, and **Pergamon Museum** houses the ancient Pergamon Altar (closed to visitors until 2019) and Ishtar Gate of Babylon. Also located on Museum Island is **Berliner Dom** (Berlin Cathedral), completed in 1905 and rebuilt following World War II.

Opposite Museum Island, on the east bank of the river, stands **Nikolaikirche** – Berlin's oldest church. Built in 1230 and heavily damaged in WWII, the stone church was restored in 1987 and is now a museum. About two

(Above left) Berliners along the River Spree. (Left) The German cathedral at Gendarmenmarkt.

miles east of Nikolaikirche, along the river's edge, is the **East Side Gallery** – a remaining section of the notorious Berlin Wall that's adorned with murals by international artists. Another restored medieval church, Marienkirche, stands a few blocks from Nikolaikirche near **Alexanderplatz** 🎱. Towering over the square is Fernsehturm, a television tower crowned with a spherical observation deck. Leading east from the square is Karl Marx-Allee, a street lined with Soviet architecture.

In the opposite direction lies **Hackesche Hofe** 🎱, a neighbourhood of pedestrian passages that open onto hidden courtyards (called *hofe*), their Art Nouveau architecture housing theatres, offices, shops and galleries. The surrounding area is one of Berlin's most talked-about nightlife districts with its many bars, restaurants and clubs.

Checkpoint Charlie 🔟, a symbol of the Cold War, is one of Berlin's prime tourist attractions. When post-war Germany was divided by the joint Allied military government into four zones – American, British, French and Russian – the Russian zone eventually became East Germany and the others West Germany. The status of Berlin, situated in the heart of East Germany, became

(Top to bottom) Berlin Cathedral, Old National Gallery, Bode Museum.

(Top) Checkpoint Charlie
(Above) Potsdamer Platz

a major Cold War issue. The Western powers were unwilling to relinquish control of West Berlin to the Soviet Union, and the United States defied a Soviet blockade in 1948 by airlifting food and supplies into West Berlin. In 1961, to stem the flow of East Germans fleeing to the West, the Soviets constructed a concrete fence around West Berlin and issued shoot-to-kill orders to their border guards. The guard house that once stood at Checkpoint 'C' is now displayed at the Allied Museum in the Berlin neighbourhood of Dahlem and a replica of the first guard house and sign now stand at the original site where

actors dressed in military police uniforms pose for photographs.

The **Jewish Museum** 🔟, designed by the Polish-born American architect Daniel Libeskind, is located a half mile south of Checkpoint Charlie.

Potsdamer Platz (Potsdam Square) 🔢 lies about a mile west of Checkpoint Charlie. Destroyed in WWII, this square is where Berlin's four zones converged. Later bisected by the Berlin Wall, Potsdamer Platz is once again a major city square where massive redevelopment has been taking place since the fall of the Berlin Wall. The Sony Tower is one of several high-rise office buildings now overlooking the square, and the Berlinale Palast is the principal venue for the Berlin Film Festival. Other attractions include a casino and an arcade lined with shops, bars and restaurants.

Immediately west of Potsdamer Platz is **Kulturforum** 🔢 – an ensemble of modernist architecture built in the 1950s and '60s, which includes the Berlin Philharmonic's concert hall and the Neue Nationalgalerie, which houses modern art.

About a half mile west of Kulturforum, on Stauffenberg Street, is a Ministry of Defence building called **Bendlerblock** 🔢. It was here in the fall of 1943 that a group of German officers developed a plan – called **Valkyrie** – to assassinate Hitler and overthrow the Nazi regime. Colonel Claus von Stauffenberg set the fuse on a bomb at the Wolf's Lair (Hitler's eastern headquarters) on July 20, 1944. The bomb exploded but did not kill Hitler, who subsequently ordered the arrest of Stauffenberg and his fellow conspirators back in Berlin. They were all executed by firing squad in the courtyard of the Bendlerblock.

Not far from Bendlerblock is **Bauhaus-Archiv Museum** 🔢 , which displays works from all Bauhaus stages and the trend-setting School of Design.

Charlottenburg Palace 🔢, a 17th-century baroque palace, lies to the west of Tiergarten and can be reached on the City Circle Hop-On Hop-Off bus.

Kiel

A shipbuilding and industrial port, Kiel (pop. 250,000) is situated on the Baltic Sea at the entrance to the Kiel Canal. Kiel's cruise terminal at Ostseekai is located in the city centre where attractions include a civic square bordered by a lake and a 13th-century church. Founded by a German count in 1233, Kiel was a member of the Hanseatic League until it was expelled for harbouring pirates.

Most large cruise ships cannot transit the Kiel Canal due to clearance limits under bridges. The Kiel Canal (originally called Kaiser Wilhelm Kanal) was constructed in the late 1800s to facilitate movement of the German fleet, then widened between 1907 and 1914 to accommodate Dreadnought-sized battleships. Kiel was heavily bombed by Allied air attacks in World War II and the rebuilt city is mostly modern. A popular maritime centre, Kiel hosted the sailing competitions of the 1972 Olympic Summer Games and holds an annual sailing regatta.

Hamburg

Located 70 miles up the Elbe River on the North Sea, Germany's second-largest city of Hamburg (pop. 1.8 million) has thrived since the fall of the Iron Curtain, with young Germans moving here in large numbers. Rebuilt following WWII, modern Hamburg is an elegant city centred around two lakes. Lake Alster is where the city's two landmark hotels – Hotel Vier Jahreszeiten and Hotel Atlantic opened in 1897 and 1909 on opposite sides of the lake, upon which Kaiser Wilhelm used to celebrate his birthday with a boat parade. As the birthplace of Felix Mendelssohn and Johannes Brahms, Hamburg is considered a cultural centre, and The Beatles got their start in the early 1960s playing at clubs in the St. Pauli entertainment district.

Cruise ships dock at St. Pauli Landungsbrucken (landing bridges) where a variety of harbour and/or canal boat tours are located. The city, which is Germany's busiest cargo port, is redeveloping its waterfront to include a new concert hall, Westin hotel and luxury apartments. Historic sights in Hamburg, which was a member of the prosperous Hanseatic League, include the 14th-century Church of St. Jacobi, the baroque St. Michael's Church (rebuilt after a fire) and the neo-Renaissance city hall. The warehouse district's canal-lined streets include Deichstrasse (Dyke Street) which is lined with buildings from the 17th to 19th centuries.

Azamara Journey (2007)
866 passengers, 30,000 tons

Eclipse (2010)
2,850 passengers,
122,000 tons

Costa Mediterranea (2003)
2,114 passengers, 86,000 tons

Crystal Symphony (1995)
960 passengers, 51,000 tons

AZAMARA CLUB CRUISES: This upscale brand (founded by Celebrity Cruises in 2007) operates mid-sized boutique ships offering a country-club ambiance and all-inclusive cruise fares. These finely-appointed ships are ideal for seasoned cruisers seeking out-of-the-ordinary destinations and frequent overnight stays at ports of call, often with customized evening tours. (azamaracruises.com)

CELEBRITY CRUISES: Founded in 1990 by the Greek cruise line Chandris Inc., Celebrity Cruises is now owned by Royal Caribbean Cruises Ltd. and is a premium brand offering gourmet cuisine, sophisticated service and trendsetting ships appointed with modern art. Celebrity's large-ship amenities include an extensive range of staterooms and programs for children. Celebrity's European base ports include Amsterdam, Stockholm and Southampton. City stays can be added to some itineraries. Officers are Greek; service staff are international. (celebritycruises.com)

COSTA CRUISES: Founded by a Genoa shipping family in the 1800s, Costa introduced their first passenger ship in 1948. Costa's style is upbeat, with an international ambiance and authentic Italian cuisine. Costa's Northern Europe cruises visit the Baltic and Norwegian fjords from the base ports of Copenhagen and Hamburg. Officers and service staff are international. (costacruises.com)

CRYSTAL CRUISES: This all-inclusive, luxury cruise line operates mid-sized ships which are spacious, beautifully appointed and offer an easygoing elegance. Crystal's Europe itineraries range from five- to 24-nights duration and feature signature shore excursions. Turn-around ports include London, Stockholm and Copenhagen. Officers are Scandinavian; service staff is international. (crystalcruises.com)

CUNARD: This prestigious British line began operations in 1840 when Sir Samuel Cunard, a Canadian pioneer of regular transatlantic navigation, formed a fleet of four ships to deliver mail between Liverpool and Boston. Now owned by Carnival Corporation, Cunard currently operates three classic liners offering traditional elegance and British ambiance. Southampton is Cunard's main base port for a variety of Northern Europe itineraries covering the Baltic, fjords of Norway and British Isles. Round-trip cruises are also offered from Hamburg. Officers are Norwegian and British; service staff is international. (cunard.com)

Queen Mary 2 (2004)
2,620 passengers, 150,000 tons

DISNEY CRUISE LINE: This family-oriented cruise line debuted in Europe in 2007. Disney's premium ships combine traditional ocean liner opulence with elements of fun associated with their storybook characters. Shore excursions are customized to appeal to children and adults. Copenhagen and Dover are turnaround ports for cruises to the Baltic, Norwegian fjords, Iceland and British Isles. Officers are European. (disneycruise.com)

Disney Magic (1998)
1,750 passengers, 83,500 tons

HOLLAND AMERICA LINE: This Seattle-based premium cruise line commands a loyal following, its spacious ships offering traditional features such as teak promenade decks and public areas decorated with Dutch paintings and antiques. HAL's mid-sized ships offer amenities and activities for all age groups, including children, and are popular with multi-generational family groups. In business since 1873, HAL operated transatlantic service between Rotterdam and New York for decades before turning to cruises in the late 1960s. HAL offers an extensive range of itineraries from the base ports of Harwich, Amsterdam, Rotterdam, Copenhagen and Stockholm. Pre-cruise land tours are also available. Officers are Dutch; service staff is Indonesian and Filipino. (hollandamerica.com)

Zuiderdam (2002)
1,848 passengers, 82,000 tons

Midnatsol (2003)
1,100 passengers, 16,140 tons

MSC Musica (2006)
2,550 passengers, 89,000 tons

Norwegian Star (2001)
2,240 passengers, 91,000 tons

Regatta (1998)
684 passengers, 30,000 tons

HURTIGRUTEN: This company was once southern Norway's only link to the remote fjords and coastal communities of western and northern Norway. Known as Hurtigruten ("the express route") because its steamship service was much faster than travelling overland, the company began launching larger and more luxurious ships in the 1980s to cater to the growing tourist market. Today, Hurtigruten's fleet of ships offers year-round cruises of the entire Norwegian coastline north of Bergen. Expedition cruises to Antarctica are also offered, as are cruises of Greenland and Iceland. (hurtigruten.com)

MSC CRUISES: An Italian line, MSC's mid-sized ships appeal to experienced travellers who prefer traditional cruise liners. The MSC Yacht Club is an exclusive suite enclave within the ship. Cruises depart from a variety of ports – Copenhagen, Hamburg, Kiel and Warnemunde. The mix of passengers is international. Officers and service staff are Italian. (msccruises.com)

NORWEGIAN CRUISE LINE: One of the first lines to invent modern cruising in the mid-1960s, Miami-based NCL remains innovative with its fleet of contemporary ships offering unstructured dining, a casual atmosphere, good youth facilities and excellent entertainment. From the base ports of Copenhagen and Southampton, NCL's itineraries cover the Baltic, Norwegian fjords and British Isles. Officers are Norwegian; service staff is international. (ncl.com)

OCEANIA CRUISES: This upscale line's mid-sized ships offer gourmet cuisine and attentive service in a country-club casual atmosphere. A variety of one-way and roundtrip cruises are offered from various base ports, including Southampton (London), Amsterdam, Oslo, Copenhagen and Stockholm. Officers and service staff are international. (oceaniacruises.com)

P&O CRUISES: P&O appeals to the British holidaymaker with its family-friendly and adults-only ships. Formerly a division of the Peninsular & Oriental Steam Navigation Company, P&O has been operating passenger ships since the early 1800s and is now owned by Carnival Corporation. Based in Southampton, P&O's fleet offers a variety of roundtrip cruises to the Baltic and fjords of Norway. (pocruises.com)

Ventura (2008))
3,090 passengers, 113,000 tons

PRINCESS CRUISES: This premium cruise line, based in Greater Los Angeles, appeals to a broad range of passengers with ships featuring elegant decor, excellent childrens facilities and flexible dining options. Northern Europe cruises depart from Copenhagen and the British base ports of Dover and Southampton. Princess also offers several land tours in combination with a cruise, covering such areas as Paris and the French countryside, and southern Ireland's famous Ring of Kerry. Officers are British and Italian; service staff is international. (princess.com)

Emerald Princess (2007)
3,110 passengers, 113,000 tons

REGENT SEVEN SEAS: This all-inclusive luxury line (formerly Radisson Seven Seas) offers small-ship intimacy and gourmet cuisine. Northern European itineraries are baseported in Copenhagen, Stockholm and Southampton (London). Officers are Scandinavian; service staff is European. (rssc.com)

Seven Seas Voyager (2003)
708 passengers, 42,000 tons

ROYAL CARIBBEAN INT'L: This contemporary line, based in Miami, operates handsome megaships with a relaxed, upbeat atmosphere and excellent childrens facilities. The funnel of each ship features a rock-climbing wall on its aft side, which has become the company's trademark. RCI offers a variety of itineraries from the base ports of Harwich, Southampton, Copenhagen and Stockholm. Extended land tours of London and Paris are also offered. Officers are Scandinavian; service staff is international. (royalcaribbean.com)

Serenade of the Seas (2003)
2,100 passengers, 90,090 tons

Seabourn Quest specs (2010)
450 passengers, 32,000 tons

Silver Whisper, (2001)
382 passengers, 28,250 tons

Wind Surf (1998)
310 passengers, 14,750 tons

SEABOURN CRUISE LINE: This luxury line of small ships offers gourmet cuisine, spacious all-suite accommodations and personalized service. Northern Europe itineraries include calls at less-visited ports and customized shore excursions. Base ports include Dover, Stockholm and Copenhagen. Officers and service staff are Norwegian, European and American. (seabourn.com)

SILVERSEA: This highly-rated luxury line offers a handful of unique Northern Europe itineraries that call at less-visited ports. Officers are Italian; service staff is European. (silversea.com)

WINDSTAR: A premium line of high-tech sailing ships which appeal to clients seeking both relaxed luxury and the romance of sail, Seattle-based Windstar has also acquired three small luxury ships formerly operated by Seabourn Cruises. Windstar itineraries include small, less-visited ports of call and utilize the base ports of Edinburgh, Dublin, Copenhagen, Stockholm and Reykjavik. Officers are British and service staff is international. (windstarcruises.com)

NICHE CRUISE LINES based in Britain include **Voyages of Discovery** and **Swan Hellenic**, both offering cultural/historical itineraries aboard refurbished ships carrying 350 to 700 passengers. **Hebridean Island Cruises** offers small-ship luxury cruises around the British Isles. (Queen Elizabeth chartered the *Hebridean Princess* in 2006 for a family cruise to celebrate her 80th birthday.)Family-owned **Fred.Olsen Cruise Lines** offers a British country house atmosphere and traditional cruising on its small- to mid-sized ships.

Viking Cruises, well known for its river cruises, has entered ocean cruising with the launch of several new small ships featuring Baltic itineraries that are destination focused.

INDEX

Ian Douglas, 74, 143, 152, 157, 176b, 176c, 177b, 183 (all), 186b, 187b, 191, 196, 201

Fred Jensen, 85b, 224c, 227b, 229b, 230

Reid Kelly, 86b,323a

Duart Snow, 95c, 103a, 103b, 106a, 109a, 115a, 115b, 127

Gordon Persson, 99, 100, 101

Steve Blake, 147, 149a, 155, 163, 164b, 209, 232, 233 (all), 258, 262a, 297, 299, 308, 316

Wikimedia Commons, 17, 18, 18b, 40 (Arni Frioriksson), 42, 56, 62, 64, 66, 68, 69, 73 (Petr Merkl), 81 (Andrew Horne), 82, 88-89 (David Iliff), 123, 129a, 131a, 132,135, 136a, 136b, 137a, 137b, 138c, 139, 140, 141, 149b, 151, 153a, 153b, 161, 162 (all), 165b, 166 (all) 167, 178a, 185a, 185b, 187a, 194, 195b, 207b, 208a, 244, 248c,280a, 280b, 281, 295, 296, 298, 325a, 334, 335, 336, 337, 339, 341, 342, 343a, 343b, 355

Additional Photography: 6, Royal Caribbean International
11, Terry Toohey
26, Holland America Line
54, Thomas Cook Archives
58b German Federal Archive
58c, Library of Congress
63, Library of Congress
134, Princess Cruises
172, Library of Congress
192, Belgium Tourism
210 / 211 RCI
235 Seabourn Cruises
259a, Mel-Lynda Andersen
275b, Library of Congress
346, Charles Russell Collection, NARA

With the exception of archival photos, all other images are by Anne Vipond.